S0-ECM-574

The Book Of Acts

Now And Then

Alvin Jennings,

Editor

PART ONE: **NOW**
True stories of conversions
in the present generation

PART TWO: **THEN**
The *original* Book of Acts of Apostles
gives the inspired account of
conversions to Christ
in the first century

The inspired Book of Acts from the Holy Bible, **Easy-To-Read Version**, Copyright 1987, 1989, 1992, 1994, 1995, 1996, 1997. The New Testament Copyrighted 1978, 1981, 1982, 1987, 1990, 1993 by World Bible Translation Center, Inc., Fort Worth, Texas 76182. Used by permission.

Copyright 1999 by Alvin Jennings

ISBN 1-56794-178-8

Star Catalog Number C-2522

Published by
Star Bible Publications, Inc., P. O. Box 821220,
Fort Worth, Texas 76182. 800 433 7507.

THE HIGH COST OF A FREE GIFT

Whosoever will may come and drink *freely* of the waters of life offered graciously by our Lord and Savior. He left the portals of heaven and the glory of being on an equality with the Father, emptying Himself to be found in form as a servant so that He might die for the redemption of all mankind. What unspeakable love ... purchasing salvation for the vilest sinners, for whosoever will receive the gift! Jesus paid the price. None other can purchase it or earn it.

The gospel is God's power unto salvation to everyone who believes (Romans 1:16). The faith that saves comes from hearing the word of Christ and entails obedience leading to a change of life, openly confessing Jesus as Lord, dying to sin and burying the old man in the grave of baptism. Thus is accomplished what is called in the scriptures "obeying the gospel," "obeying the truth," or "heartily obeying the form of teaching" (Romans 6:17; 2 Thessalonians 1:8; Galatians 3:1; I Peter 3:1; 4:17), sometimes referred to as rendering *primary* obedience to the gospel in that this is the first response that characterizes all conversions to Christ whenever the good news of salvation is preached. This is true in the first century and in all time that shall follow, inasmuch as the same seed of the gospel, the word of God (Luke 8:11), when planted in honest and good hearts will always produce the same results. The seed, though planted in different environments, germinates then begins growth, maturing throughout life into the likeness of Christ, producing a new creation known as *a Christian* (Acts 11:26). This new creature never ceases "obeying the truth," but this book focuses on the process of sinners first hearing the gospel and accepting the gift of salvation through faith and obedience.

The narratives in these twenty-eight chapters will focus on (1) the preaching to alien sinners and (2) the acceptance of the gospel upon the part of those who heard. Preachers and teachers in some cases sacrificed much in carrying the message of good news to the lost. In other cases, conversions involved a more natural process like when mothers and fathers who are believers pass on the faith by diligently teaching and training their own children.

In the culture in which we live here in America, it is rare that either the preacher or the new Christian experiences open hostility in the form of physical persecution. We do hear of alienation between members of a family, breaking of relationships that rend the heart and soul, confirming Jesus' word that following Him will bring division between close friends and relatives. This is *real persecution* and it is painful. Yet it should not surprise or discourage either the teacher or his new convert. See such passages as Hebrews 12:3; 4:4; 11:29; 12:7; 2 Timothy 3:12; 1 Corinthians 4:12; 1 Peter 4:12.

In other nations even in our own time, persecution has been more severe and open. It is challenging, for example, when a Christian thinks of entering a nation where teaching the Bible is illegal and imprisonment is the punishment. We have just been informed of two in Laos, a teenage girl and a farmer, who have just been released after 10 months in prison for the *crime* of teaching the Bible. This makes it extremely difficult not only for the proclaimer but also for the person who is contemplating obedience. To him it may result in immediate termination of employment, rejection by friends, alienation and/or disinheritance by family, etc. The price by comparison is much greater than in a friendly Christian environment. Very few of us have been privileged to suffer physical abuse or to shed blood because we preached Christ or because we were baptized into Him, although we assume we would be *willing* to pay such a price if necessary (cf Luke 14:25-35).

Let us remember the worthy servants of God in the Bible record. Noah was alone in his world, preaching righteousness for a hundred years to scoffers among whom there was *not one convert outside his own family*. Many of the prophets suffered grievously, but they did not recant or quit. They admitted they were strangers and aliens on the earth and of them the divine record says the "world was not worthy." They quenched the fury of flames, were tortured and refused to be released, suffered jeers and flogging, were chained and put in prison, were stoned and sawed in two, were put to death by the sword, wandered in deserts, mountains, caves and holes of the ground (cf Hebrews 11:32-38). Threats and imprisonments are in the history of the church's earliest existence (Acts 4 and 5) followed by the stoning of Stephen, marking the beginning of martyrdom (Acts 7). Later, Paul suffered greatly (I Corinthians 11:23-33), even longing to die like Jesus (Philippians 3:10).

John Foxe, church historian, first published his **Acts And Monuments**, later known as **Foxe's Book of Martyrs,** in 1554, followed by editions in 1563, 1570, 1576 and 1583 before his death in 1587. Many printings have followed since then, relating scenes of unimaginable horror, suffering and death of those who refused to deny their faith in Jesus Christ. Polycarp is one who "unmoved as if he had suffered nothing, went on cheerfully, under the conduct of his guards, to the Stadium. The proconsul counselled him to deny Christ, saying, 'Consider thyself and have pity on thy own great age.' Then Polycarp, with grave respect, beholding all the multitude, answered, *'Eighty and six years have I served him, and he never once wronged me; how then shall I blaspheme my King, who hath saved me? Hear me frankly what I am--I am a Christian.'* Hereupon the proconsul said, 'I have wild beasts; I will expose you to them unless you repent...I will tame thee with fire.'" The crowd shouted to burn him alive with fire. And so they did, after which the disciples gathered his bones from the pile, "more precious than gold and silver," and put them in a proper place.

Yes, the cost has been high, yet joyful, to many who have been faithful to the point of death. They shall receive the promised "crown of life" from the King of Glory! (Revelation 2:10).   -Editor
12/7/1998

4

CONTENTS

PART ONE
THE *NOW* BOOK OF ACTS
Conversions To Christ In our Times

PART TWO

THE *THEN* BOOK OF ACTS

PART ONE

THE *NOW* BOOK OF ACTS

True stories of conversions
in the present generation

The *Now*
Book of Acts

Introduction:

This book is a collection of narratives of conversions to Jesus Christ, the Son of God, in our own times. It is a record of responses to the same gospel that was first preached in Jerusalem in AD 33 when Peter spoke by the inspiration of the Holy Spirit to the multitudes gathered from every nation under heaven.

Although the writers of these 28 chapters make no claim to being miraculously guided by the Holy Spirit such as was the case with the first century record which we call **"The *Then* Book of Acts,"** nevertheless we believe you will be inspired and uplifted as you read about the faith and commitment of those who turned to Christ, who were translated out of the kingdom of darkness into the kingdom of God's dear Son (Colossians 1:13). You will also be challenged and will thank God for the diligence and faithfulness of those who preached both privately and publicly (cf. Acts 20:20). They make no claim to the apostleship, hence it is not another book of the apostles' acts. They are merely men and women who believe in Jesus, and therefore who have spoken of their faith to others. It is therefore a book of acts of *disciples,* not another book of acts of *apostles.*

Jesus promised to be with us as we go into all the world in response to His great and last commission, even to the end of the age. Wherever we go, Jesus is already there to comfort and to strengthen us in His work. His words are ever in our hearts:

> **"All authority in heaven and on earth has been given to me. Therefore go and make disciples of all nations, baptizing them in the name of the Father and of the Son and of the Holy Spirit, and teaching them to obey everything I have commanded you. And surely I am with you always, to the very end of the age."**
>
> (Matthew 28:18-20)

The author's name will be given in the text of each chapter or in a footnote. Following the format of the original **Book of Acts,** we shall limit our *Now* **Book of Acts** to 28 chapters. If the interest warrants such, and if God wills, another 28 chapters may follow in another volume in due time. Every conversion is a *divine act* whose story should be told, and yet rarely is one written down so larger numbers of people can be blessed. We are so thankful to each writer who has been willing to share his story with us for publication. It has taken over twenty years to gather the chapters and to publish the book since it was first announced.

Our only regret is that there are so many other stories of conversions that are exciting and need to be told, too, that could not be included in this volume. Perhaps they could be put in a volume #2, if the Lord wills.

Because "not many wise, not many mighty" are chosen and called by the gospel, most of those in our stories are just common ordinary people. You may find a few names of prominence. To God, every soul is of equal importance.

To authenticate these testimonies of faith, and to strengthen your faith, we are printing the original Book of Acts from the Bible in the second section of the book. Be sure to read and study it carefully, even if you do not read the first section!

And now, dear "Theophilus," wherever and whoever you are, we pray that God will bless you as you read. The *"Now* Book of Acts" is our fervent *un*inspired story of what happened when that same first-century gospel is told to men and women of our own generation. To God be the glory through Jesus Christ. Amen.

Alvin Jennings

October 12, 1998

CHAPTER 1

DAHMER DIES...

1 We sing, "There is power in the blood..." And there is! The grace of God is great; His mercy is unfathomable, *"higher than the heavens, deeper than the sea."*

2 "Jesus Christ came into the world to save sinners." Concerning himself as a sinner Paul stated, "I am chief" (I Timothy 1:14-15).

3 What about Jeffrey L. Dahmer, a man who abused, killed, mutilated and cannibalized 17 people over a period of 13 years, from 1978 to 1991?

4 Dahmer's murderous career began in 1978 with the killing of **Steven Hicks**, a young hitch-hiker who was picked up by Dahmer. Dahmer admitted killing, mutilating and attempting to preserve parts of the young boy's body. "I wanted total control," said the murderer, "and I wanted to keep them as long as I wanted."

5 Apparently for six years Dahmer refrained from killing. However in 1984 he yielded to what he called an *uncontrolled obsession* and began killing again. According to his own statement, he "sought out the best looking guys I could find...race made no difference to me." One after another of his victims were not only murdered, but their bodies abused and dismembered.

6 As Dahmer's sinful behavior progressed with more and more "deviant behavior," he engaged in cannibalism, eating parts of human bodies, saying that by so doing they "became part of me."

7 By 1990 his behavior had resulted in the deaths of nine men and boys. When he was finally arrested and jailed in 1991, the number of his victims had increased to 17. When asked on NBC's **Dateline** about his thoughts *when* he was committing such crimes, he said:

8 "I felt that I didn't have to be accountable to anyone...since man came from slime, he was accountable to no one." It is hard to imagine conduct more corrupt than that committed by him.

9 If Saul of Tarsus, who called himself "the chief of sinners" in the first century, were compared to Dahmer of the 20th century, perhaps the title "Chiefest of Sinners" would be handed over to this cannibalistic serial killer named Jeffrey L. Dahmer.

10 But there is more to the story. After he was imprisoned and while serving time in Columbia Correctional Instituion in Portage, Wisconsin, Dahmer was sent a Bible correspondence course first by Curtis Booth of Crescent, Oklahoma, to whom Jeffrey made a phone call. He also received a course from Madison, Wisconsin sent by **Mary Mott**, a representative of *World Bible School* in Alexandria, Virginia. Jeffrey Dahmer studied the Bible course and as a result he requested baptism.

11 Special arrangements were made and on May 10, 1994, a gospel preacher named **Roy Ratcliff**, preacher for the Mandrake Road Church of Christ in Madison baptized Dahmer into Christ for the remission of his sins. At first when Ratcliff met Dahmer, he thought from listening to televangelists that baptism was optional, but had later concluded from his Bible study that it was an essential part of his being saved.

After his immersion, Dahmer continued weekly Bible studies with preacher Ratcliff.

12 On Wednesday before Thanksgiving Day, brother Ratcliff and brother Dahmer studied together for the last time from the book of Revelation. Dahmer "led a prayer and gave me a Thanksgiving card, expressing gratitude for studying the Bible with him."

13 Preacher Ratcliff said that Jeffrey enjoyed Bible study and looked forward to the weekly studies, adding that "often Jeffrey would save up questions to ask when we were together." Ratcliff said he was "totally convinced of his sincerity by his words, his eyes, his body language, the tone of his voice and his mannerisms."

14 Studies have been stopped permanently, for Jeffrey Dahmer is dead. The convicted killer has himself been killed. An Associated Press report said in the Jackson, Mississippi, *Clarion Ledger* (11/30/94) that Dahmer's body was found lying in a pool of blood in a prison restroom. His killer had not yet been identified.

15 In a news report on CBN, telecast on Tuesday, 11/29/94, it was stated that Jeffrey Dahmer's father said that he believed his son had "gone to be with God forever." When asked "Why?" his father replied, "Because he had been baptized into Christ."

16 Preacher Roy Ratcliff said Jeffrey's father, who lives in Akron, Ohio, is presently a faithful member of the church of Christ there. His younger brother is also a faithful member of the body of Christ, having been converted while in college.

17 Dennis Gulledge listed lessons we can learn from Dahmer's obedience to the gospel of Christ. He wrote:

18 "If this story teaches us anything it teaches us the power of the gospel (Romans 1:16), and that God is no respector of persons (Acts 10:34-35). It shows that Christ can save even the chiefest of sinners (I Timothy 1:15). It teaches us that we should never doubt the effect that the gospel might have in any person's life, no matter who they are or what they have done (I John 1:7-10)."

19 Editor Basil Overton of the **World Evangelist** commented that Dahmer or any man can be forgiven by the Lord, though he must still suffer earthly consequences for his sins by being in prison or by being put to death. He can nevertheless have assurance and hope of eternal life because he has become obedient to Christ in baptism and is saved by the grace of God (Galatians 3:27; Romans:3-4; Ephesians 1:7).

INDIA INK

20 She sat in the crowd, just one of about 20 souls crammed together on the other side of the world in a village near Markapur, India. She kept her head covered more securely than most women do during worship services.

21 During my sermon, she paid good attention, but I noticed that she was keeping her *pallu* (the end of the saree brought over the head as a covering) in her hand and holding it up to her face. I thought that perhaps she was extremely shy as many village women are, especially around strangers.

22 It seemed to me that she was cowering, but after I had been speaking for a few minutes, I noticed her bare arm and I knew

why she had been keeping herself veiled so much. She had been terribly burned. She bore the horrible scars of flesh that had melted in extreme heat, almost like a candle drips over the side and then cools. She had healed in that same way. It was a hideous sight.

23 I assumed she had been burned in a cooking accident or perhaps was a victim of a dowry dispute with her husband and in-laws...a *bride burning* that occurs when an amoral bridegroom thinks he did not get enuogh cash and gold as gifts from the bride's family when he took this woman as his mate.

24 When her *pallu* fell away from her face, I was shocked...one of the most pathetic sights I had ever seen in my life. We see all kinds of illnesses, deformities and handicaps, malformed bodies and gruesome sights that are pitiful, sickening, abhorrent and heart-rending.

25 This was the worst I have ever seen.

26 At the end of the service, I asked if any wanted to obey the Lord in baptism. Three raised their hands--one was this woman. I have to tell you I was emotionally torn: here is a horribly deformed, ugly body about to be transformed into a thing of beauty and holiness by the blood of the Lamb of God.

27 She was immersed the next day and began her new life in Jesus. Becoming a Christian would not change her physical appearance but would give her the power to cope with this nightmare she has to live with every day. I later discovered what had really happened: she had been attacked by 3 men who had thrown acid in her face. These reprobates then threatened to kill her if she informed the police.

28 I was sickened and consumed with a righteous indignation. We are praying for her that something can be done so her face will not make her look like a sideshow freak, and also are checking on what can be done medically to help her.

29 I thought about "all things working together for good to those who love God and are called by His purpose" (Romans 8:28), and wondered if she may not have sought the Lord if this had not happened to her. Will you pray for her, too?

30 Will you pray for all those in India who live in similar hardships with no one to plead their cases? This is the essence of Christianity, that we practice the Golden Rule (Luke 6:31).

The amazing conversion story in verses 1-19 is based on an editorial by A. L. Franks in **Magnolia Messenger**, published in Kosiusko, Mississippi, and from a story by Roy Ratcliff, a graduate of York College and Oklahoma Christian College. The latter was published in **Christian Woman**, March/April, 1995.

Ron Clayton wrote in verses 20-30 this heart-rending account in a newsletter from the church in Hamilton Alabama. He has completed 20 years in the work in India, a work that he calls "a winner" because of God's having given marvellous growth. There have been 750,000 souls baptized into Christ, 6,200 of them denominational preachers, the key to this phenomenal growth. Over 33,000 congregations have been planted, bringing to around 45,000 congregations in India now. It is impossible to take a count because much of the work is indiginous. Joshua Gootam said he believed there are 1 million members; Clayton believes it is 2!!

CHAPTER 2

MARIA
Story of Coincidence or the Hand of God?

1 It was June, 1961, when 13 North American families arrived in the 3 million populated city of Sao Paulo, Brazil, to establish churches for their Lord, Jesus. Not knowing the city, with no good information as to the best part of that huge city where they might locate themselves, they chose the district called *Brooklin,* perhaps because it sounded like "home."

2 Renting houses, buying furniture and settling in took some time. However, language was the priority. A committee of three was chosen to locate language teachers.

3 **Maria Luiza Toledo** lived in Brooklin district. She was one of the language teachers that would be selected to teach the missonaries. Of the committee of three of the missionaries chosen to find language teachers, two of the three rented houses just one block from Maria Toledo's home. *Coincidence or God's hand?*

4 One way to select a language teacher would be to select a language school from the yellow pages of the telephone book. The three committee members discovered there were many language schools and not knowing any of them, they selected one at random. When they arrived at this school to hire a teacher, they met the director, Miss Maria Toledo. *Coincidence or God's hand?*

5 Maria sent them a teacher, but after a few weeks she suffered an accident, breaking her leg. The owner of the language school where Maria was a director asked her to substitute for this teacher because he had no other to send. Maria agreed and began teaching the missionaries and their families.

6 When the other teacher was ready to resume the classes, the missionaries knew Maria was the best they could ever find and requested that she not leave them. An agreement was made with the owner of the language schools, so Maria continued as their teacher along with the two who had been hired earlier.

7 Six months passed and the 14th member of the Sao Paulo mission team arrived. He was a Texan named Allen Dutton, the only single member of the team. He began language study with the three teachers. Maria told him that because he was six months behind, she could help with extra language classes. Maria told Allen that if he had any questions about the Portuguese language he could come to her home for extra assistance.

8 Yes, Allen had *many* questions. Soon Maria's sister said, "Maria, I think that young man has too many questions for you. Why does he come so often?" It was not long before Maria and Allen knew there was more to their interests than merely the Portuguese language. *Coincidence or the hand of God?*

9 Language studies continued, along with dinners together, movies and long talks. The missionaries began a chapel every day to which they invited their language teachers so their Portuguese language could be improved. Correcting their sermons and classes during chapel caused the language teacher to become interested in what the Bible said. Discussions followed concerning Biblical subjects as well

as over the correct use of their new language.

10 Suddenly, Maria disappeared. She stopped all language classes and stopped seeing Allen. Dot Stewart went to visit Maria to find out what was wrong. Maria told her she was a Catholic and Allen a Protestant and that she would never change...that it would never work out. She had become confused because of what the missionaries taught as compared to what she had always been taught and believed.

11 Dot said, "I know Allen. He is very sincere and if you could convince him that he is wrong and you are right, I know he would change. In fact, Maria, if you are right and I am wrong, I want to change, too. I want the will of God in my life; I want to do what is right.

12 Then Dot said something that opened Maria's heart when she asked, "Maria, would you teach me your religion?"

13 Maria responded by saying that she really did not know her own religion well enough to teach it, but that there was a class in the Catholic Church where she attends and where Dot would be welcome. Dot agreed and they went to class together to study Roman Catholicism. After the study, Dot said, "Now, Maria, you can go and teach Allen."

14 Maria set a time for her and Allen to study Catholicism; they studied three times each week. Allen would always answer her Catholic teaching with verses from the Bible. This confused Maria even more. One day she asked if Allen would go with her to study with a Catholic bishop who could speak English, as Allen had only been in Brazil a few months and Portuguese was still too difficult for him to engage in such an important subject as God's Word.

15 From classes with the bishop, Maria began to realize she was losing because the bishop would only answer Allen's Biblical questions by referring him to certain Catholic books to read. He never gave a direct answer himself. Maria requested they not study with him any more. For the following months, Maria and Allen studied the Bible alone three times each week for two or three hours at a time.

16 Dot's husband, Ted Stewart, was helpful as he and Allen studied together preparing lessons for Maria. The subject that opened Maria's mind was on church history, especially such topics as the worship of Mary, the mother of Jesus. Allen was very careful with his words concerning Mary.

17 Maria had been born into a traditional Brazillian Catholic family. Her family name, Todedo, is highly respected in Brazil as her father's family had been in Brazil for 300 years. They had come from Toledo, Spain. Her mother's family, the Fluery family, had come to Brazil almost 400 years earlier from France.

18 Family members on both sides have been active in Brazilian history and politics. Lauro de Toledo, Maria's father, was owner of a large coffee plantation with 300 families living on his farm. Maria always enjoyed languages, graduating from the Catholic University in Sao Paulo with a Master's degree in German, Latin, French and English. She had received a Fulbright Scholarship to the University of Michigan to advance her language skills.

19 Many times during the Bible studies with Allen, Maria would become confused so she would go away for weeks at a time, usually to the family's mountain cabin where she could pray and think. She would return, call Allen and they would resume their Bible studies. This study and retreat , study and retreat continued for 5 months until one day Maria called Allen to her home with a request.

20 She said, "This morning I made a fire in my back yard and burned all my images. I have some made of metal that will not burn. I want you to take me to the lake so I can throw them in the lake because I want to be baptized today."

21 It was on October 14, 1962, that Maria Luize Toledo was baptized into Christ by Ted Stewart. When Maria told her father of her plans to follow Jesus in a way that he did not approve, and of her plans to marry Allen, he said,

22 "You do not know this man well enough. How do you know he is not after the money he thinks you have? How do you know he does not have a wife in the United States? We have been Catholics for 400 years and not one time has our blood line been broken. I do not approve of you marrying a foreigner. If you go against my will, I will disown you."

23 From that time when Maria took a firm stand with Jesus, her father never spoke to her again. They lived in the same house but he never spoke to her. He said that she had died as far as he was concerned. He had Maria taken out of the inheritance.

24 On November 20, 1962, Maria and Allen were married at the School of the Bible with the 13 American missionary families present plus Maria's sister and brother. Don Vinzant, one of the mission team members, officiated at the marriage ceremony. Maria's father never talked with her, never visited in the home of Maria and never saw his three grandchildren with which God had so graciously blessed the lives of Maria and Allen Dutton.

25 Four years passed. One day Maria received a letter from her brother saying that their father had observed her marriage relationship and had heard good things about Allen. He requested that she sign the papers he had enclosed, papers that would put her back into his will and testament. *Coincidence or God's hand?*

26 What a glorious day when four years after her marriage, Maria's father received her and Allen in his home and kissed his grandchildren for the first time! Lauro Toledo never understood the gospel of Jesus, but he did understand the beautiful life his daughter, Maria, had chosen.

27 In the language of the inspired apostle Paul, we close our story: "And now these three remain: faith, hope and love. But the greatest of these is love."

28 The conversion story of Maria Toledo *was indeed* the hand of God's wonderful love.

Written by Ted Stewart and Allen Dutton, 1998. The Duttons are still serving as missionaries 37 years after his arrival in Brazil.

Studying the Scriptures together.   Maria before her marriage.

Left to right: Ted & Dot Stewart with **Allen & Maria Dutton (1997)**

CHAPTER 3

SEED PLANTED IN NIGERIA GROWS AN ABUNDANT HARVEST

1 You are about to read one of the most exciting stories in the history of Christianity, a story of how the Nigerian restoration was begun in West Africa by C. A. O. Essien, a member of the Efik Tribe in Eastern Nigeria. He was born in the village of Ikot Usen in 1915.

2 I first learned of Coolidge Essien when I was asked by the Lawrence Avenue church of Christ in Nashville, Tennessee, to accompany Boyd Reese to Nigeria in 1950 to investigate rumors of a Nigerian restoration. Both Reese and I were serving as missionaries in southern Africa at that time.

3 We flew to Lagos, the capital of Nigeria, then took a small plane on to Port Harcourt in eastern Nigeria where we were met by brother Essien who had come from the village of Ikot Usen. He came in a rented car to take us back to his home village.

4 When we arrived at Ikot Usen we were introduced to five other evangelists who with Essien had baptized *ten thousand people* in their area. Small church buildings displaying prominent **Church of Christ** signs had been erected in all of the nearby villages and they even had started their own preachers' training school.

5 We were astonished and asked Essien how it all came about. This is his story:

6 "I served in the British West African police from 1938 till 1940 and was stationed in British Cameroon. At that time I was Presbyterian, but diligent study of the New Testament convinced me that I could not stay with that group, so I joined the Pentecostals.

7 "However, further study of the scriptures showed me that they also were in error. No other religious group in Nigeria seemed any closer to the truth, so I concluded that the church of the New Testament no longer existed on earth.

8 "I wished to gain a better command of the English language so I replied to an ad in a magazine and was enrolled in an English course from International Correspondence Schools in Munich, Germany. The tutor assigned to me was a Miss Braun.

9 "One day when I was about to mail a completed lesson to Miss Braun, purely on impulse I wrote at the bottom of the lesson, *Do you know of anybody who has a correspondence course on the Bible?* The marked lesson came back with the note, 'Try the Lawrence Avenue Church of Christ in Nashville, Tennessee.'"

10 When I heard that, I asked brother Essien in amazement, "But how would a woman in Munich, Germany, know about the Lawrence Avenue church?" Brother Essien shrugged, "I have no idea." These Bible lessons convinced Essien that he had found the church of the Bible and he and five friends began preaching.

11 Boyd Reese and I returned to South Africa and sent written reports of our trip to Lawrence Avenue. Before leaving Nigeria, brother Essien had exacted a promise from me to return in 1951 to spend some time with them teaching in the preachers' training school.

12 Since the Lawrence Avenue brethren were enthusiastic about sponsoring such an undertaking, I spent five months in Nigeria in 1951 working closely with Essien and the other five pioneer evangelists. During that time, I got to know them really well.

13 One day they came to my house (the church guest house) and asked if they could speak to me privately on a very delicate matter. Their matter of concern was that not one of them had been immersed, although they had immersed ten thousand others. As they explained it, they had nobody to immerse them at the beginning and later were afraid that it would cause too much consternation in the churches if it became known that they were unimmersed when they were immersing others.

14 I told them, "It is no great problem. During the lunch hour today, the six of you go to an unfrequented stretch of the river and baptize each other. They did that and it never was known to the brethren.

15 The church in Nashville asked me to come there and give them a current report. I did that in November, 1951, and told the same story I have told here,

emphasizing the puzzling story of the message on the English lesson from Miss Braun.

16 At the conclusion of the service, Gordon Turner, a former minister to the congregation and the author of the Bible correspondence course, came to meet me and exclaimed, "I never knew your part of the story, but I can tell you the part that's missing."

17 It seems that after the initial work in Germany was started in Frankfurt just after World War II, a number of workers went to Germany to establish the church in other cities. One group planned an evangelistic campaign in Munich (around 1947-48) and had teams of workers inviting the public to a forthcoming meeting. Two young men went into the offices of the International Correspondence School to invite the personnel there and met a certain Miss Braun (Anne Marie).

18 Simply as a ploy to establish rapport with her, they mentioned that their church also sent out correspondence lessons, but the course was on the Bible. She inquired where the lessons came from and they replied, "The Lawrence Avenue church of Christ in Nashville, Tennessee."

19 By remarkable coincidence (?) this happened just at the time an English lesson paper arrived from Essien in Ikot Usen.

20 And so, in a most unlikely way, a chain was linked that began a movement that was to result in the largest known membership of

churches of Christ outside the United States.

This story was written by Eldred Echols in June of 1988. Echols served Jesus in spreading the gospel in Africa for over forty years, being with Boyd Reese the first white men to witness this phenomenal planting of New Testament Christianity in the nation of Nigeria. Another account of these events was written by Eugene Peden.

African Christian Schools has also published a booklet of 64 pages, THE GREAT NIGERIAN MISSION, giving the same information from their perspective, published in October, 1964. They estimated by that time there were 475 congregations with approximately 40,000 Christians. African Christian Schools may be contacted at P O Box 41120, Nashville, TN 37204; Henry Huffard, Jr., President. Further confirmations and up-dating may be obtained by addressing Etim Asuquo, P O Box 290, Surulere, Lagos State, Nigeria, W. Africa. Some suppose there are over 100,000 members of the church in Nigeria now. Some reports indicate there are more members in India where there has been remarkable growth also.

C. A. O. Essien and native preachers who began vast restoration movement in Nigeria. Essien is shown seated at left.

Gordon H. Turner, former minister and elder of the Lawrence Avenue Church of Christ, who originated the world-famous Bible Correspondence Course in 1944.

Home of the Lawrence Avenue

Church of Christ

CHAPTER 4

NOT ALL HAVE A LOVE FOR THE TRUTH

1 Some do not receive a love for the truth, whether it be in Jerusalem, Judea, Samaria or some of the uttermost parts of the world like in America where this writer lives (cf. Acts 1:8; 2 Timothy 3:1-5; 4:3-4). A remarkable trait of the Bible is that it records the truth about men and women, the good qualities of bad people as well as the weaknesses in some of the best of God's own people.

2 In the *NOW* **BOOK OF ACTS** we shall have our main focus on those who loved the truth when they heard it, but we shall give some attention like in the *THEN* **BOOK OF ACTS** of the first century to those who "judged themselves unworthy of eternal life" by turning away from the gospel.

3 There is a sad part of the story because not all men believed, and in some instances though they believed they were not willing to pay the price to be a disciple, to leave all to follow Jesus (see Luke 14:25-33). Most of those who reject the gospel were religious people who were unwilling to leave the religion of their family; they loved the acceptance and praise of men more than acceptance by God (John 12:42b).

4 Because it is hard to change, especially among the prominent people, only a few will be saved. Jesus had said that is harder for a camel to go through the eye of a needle than for a rich man to enter into the kingdom of God (Luke 18:25). Even though some hear Jesus gladly at first and they know he loves them, still they love the things of this life more and the turn away sadly like the rich young ruler (Mark chapter 10).

5 Among the cases of *non-conversion* in Luke's second book commonly called **The Book of Acts**, there were the thousands in chapter 2 who did not believe and obey. In chapter 4, the temple guard captain and the Sadducees were "greatly disturbed" because of the apostles' preaching so effectively that the number of disciples came to about 5,000. So they seized Peter and John and threw them in jail.

6 "The number of disciples in Jerusalem increased rapidly," and when a large number of the priests "became obedient to the faith" a host of non-converts seized Stephen and stoned him to death (chapter 7). Unbelievers sometimes not only reject the gospel for themselves, but also hinder others from hearing...sometimes even turning against the preacher as though he were a dangerous enemy. In Luke's second book he tells of persecutions against the church in chapter 8 and elsewhere. Men like Saul of Tarsus were zealous in punishing any of "The Way." He saw that many of the early Christians were not only willing to suffer, but were willing even to die for their Lord.

7 The Lord struck down Herod who did not accept the message, after he made a great speech and gave himself the glory instead of God (chapter 12). On the island of Paphos, a man named Bar-Jesus rejected the gospel and opposed Paul, as did Elymas, a child of the devil whom Paul struck blind for a time (see chapter 13).

8 Crowds were filled with jealousy in Antioch of Pisidia, when they saw nearly the whole city turned out to hear the word of the Lord. Paul said the Jews who rejected the good news did "not consider themselves worthy of eternal life," so he turned to the non-Jews (Gentiles). He travelled on to Iconium where he found many other non-converts who "refused to believe" and "poisoned the minds" of the people against the brothers (14:1-2).

9 Most prominent among those who heard but were not converted were King Agrippa (who "liked to hear" Paul preach and was "almost persuaded to become a Christian," 25:22 and 26:28) and governor Felix (chapter 24).

10 Felix was acquainted with the Way, but when hearing about righteousness, self-control and the judgment, became toubled and said "That's enough for now; leave and when I find a convenient time I will call for you." That time never came. Whether a person is sympathetic and *nearly willing* to take a stand with the disciples, or on the other hand *openly rebellious and hostile,* the result is the same.

11 As we turn the pages of time to the NOW GENERATION some 2,000 years later, we see some are willing to pay the price and become followers so they can be just like the *New Testament Christians* and who wear *only* the name of *Christian.* In this book of conversions in modern times, our main purpose in the following 27 chapters is to focus on them.

12 We feel a compulsion, though not a happy one, to give a few examples of non-conversions as a means of warning and admonition to all who read. We take no more pleasure in relating these than Doctor Luke did in telling of those who did not obey in the first century. To give a true narrative and to give balance, our story includes both the good and the bad, the strengths and the weaknesses, in human nature.

13 In my early days of preaching in Canada, I knew a wonderful little lady named sister Stinson. In body she was fragile and aged, but sweeter than nearly any saint I have ever known. She had no car, so we gave her rides regularly to the assemblies of Christians and she always expressed sincere gratitude for these favors, whether it was forty degrees below zero in the cold winter or in the mild summertime.

14 Just as sweet and congenial was her husband, Roy. He was always friendly and cooperative in helping his wife and encouraging her to attend. He even spoke strongly at his job in favor of the church, but he never obeyed or participated himself. He would always say, "Don't worry about me; I will be OK." But time went by, though he knew the gospel and talked the gospel, he never repented of his neglect. Sad to say, though we all loved him so much, he went to his grave outside of Christ.

15 And there is Bill who has been our neighbor for over thirty years. He will do anything for us, loan us anything or give us anything. He takes care of our mail when we are away and looks after the yard and house just like his very own. Ellen and I have talked with him many times about his soul and have urged him countless times to worship with us.

16 But Bill always has an excuse ready. He is too busy with his yard work, he has company coming, has a bridge party scheduled, doesn't feel like it or *something.* We conclude that if he does not *want* to change his lifestyle, one excuse is as good as another. He is retired now, is 75 years of age, losing his eyesight

and knows his time on this earth is limited. We love him and his wife, Wanda, and shall never cease to love them or to pray for them. We hate to think of them as we see them from day to day that on the Last Day, they will be on the left side. We have done all we can in speaking for Jesus and in living the Christian life before him, and feel that we have cleansed our hands of his blood.

17 Looking at another area of our life, we turn to the office of Star Bible Publications. We began this business in 1965 "to publish the word of the Lord throughout the region" (Acts 13:49) and God has been with us in preparing gospel papers, books, Bibles, correspondence courses, tracts, etc., to the point it is difficult to count them all. A few years ago, the number was over fifty million pieces of literature. They have gone all over the world and we get appeals from practically every nation and language on a daily basis for more; we are sorry there are not funds to send all they beg to receive.

18 In our office we communicate daily by letter, by phone, fax and E-mail with preachers, missionaries and other church leaders who order these materials. We consider these to be like the "books and parchments" that Paul called for to use in his ministry. In the words from one newly-formed church in Africa, they wrote "Your books are our preacher." All our co-workers are devoted Christians, baptized members of the body of Christ, *all except one.* Some have been working with us for as much as 25 years up to the time of their retirement.

19 But that *one* who is not a member of the body of Christ is Lucy. She has been with us 17 years. She speaks with courtesy and respect to all who call in person or on the phone. She drops whatever she is doing to come at my call and is willing to perform any kind of task no matter how trivial or unpleasant. There is nothing in the office or warehouse she is not willing to tackle with all her might. I trust her more than I trust myself to work honestly and diligently in all ways. Ellen and I love her with all our heart and soul.

20 However, when it comes to hearing, reading or discussing the gospel so far as her own life is concerned, I am so very sorry to have to say, she consistently yet politely refuses. She kindly declines when earnest invitations are extended to attend Bible classes or worship services. Her opportunities have been so numerous.

21 Yet she has never been buried with her Lord in baptism and has not been added to the body of Christ, the church of the New Testament. Unless she changes soon, time will run out and one of the saddest realizations of our life will be that Lucy has not been "born of the water and the spirit" and thus will not be eligible to "enter the eternal kingdom of God" (John 3:3-5; Acts 2:47).

22 But now we turn to happier thoughts as we see how the hearts of so many good and honest people have been opened to the truth of the gospel.

It has been in our heart to publish this book for nearly twenty years. Some of the stories have been awaiting publication since that time when the book was first announced. Editor.

CHAPTER 5

HOW A CHAIN REFERENCE BIBLE HELPED

1 One Monday afternoon a young insurance salesman knocked on my front door. He was asking for only five minutes of my time. I reluctantly agreed and gave him my time and attention.

2 As he was giving me his "sales pitch," somehow it came up in the conversation that I was a preacher. He then began to share an experience with me of how he had repented one night in a hotel room.

3 He told me that he did not know at that point whether or not he was saved but he sure *felt better*. The door was opened.

4 I began to talk with him about the gospel. I told him of the death, burial and resurrection of Jesus Christ. I then took him to Acts chapter 2 and showed him the proper response after a person has heard the truth about Jesus as the Son of God. I was able to show him that Peter preached Jesus Christ to the people and they asked,

5 "What shall we do?" (Acts 2:37). I then showed him Peter's reply in the following verse: "Repent," and then I paused. I said to him, "This is what you did, isn't it?"

6 "Yes," he answered. I then pointed out to him that there was more. Peter goes on to say, "And let every one of you be baptized in the name of Jesus Christ for the remission of your sins and you shall receive the gift of the Holy Spirit."

7 We then turned over to Acts chapter 8 (the conversion of the Ethiopian eunuch), chapter 9 (about Saul's conversion), chapter 10 (the conversion of Cornelius) and then chapter 16 (the conversion of the Philippian jailer). We then read I Peter 3:21 and Mark 16:16. At this point he said to me, "I need to be baptized, don't I?"

8 The scriptures made it obvious to him what he must do. I told him if he believed that Jesus Christ was the Son of the living God, then he could...and should. He was still somewhat unsure, so I gave him a copy of the Bible which I had purchased, a New King James Version New Testament with chain references, used by Larry West's seminars called the *We Care Ministries*.

9 I told him to begin by carefully considering the question on the front cover (**What if the Lord were to come right now! Would you know for sure, nothing doubting, that you would go to heaven?**), then to follow the questions and answers as instructed and let me know what he thought.

10 I did not know if I would ever hear from that young man again, but I did know that the seed had been planted.

11 One week later, I received a phone call from him. he said he had gone through the references in the Bible with the questions relating to them and that now he wanted to be born again of the water and the spirit, to be baptized into Christ.

12 I thank God that I was able to give him *more* than five minutes of my time, just a little time for me but it will make an eternity of difference for him if he continues faithfully following Jesus to the end.

13 If someone comes to you thinking they have something *you* need, remember you have something *they* may need, the message of salvation through the gospel. Let us strive to recognize

and to sieze every opportunity God gives to us.

14 Just one chance may be all we have.

We are indebted to David L. Lynch for writing and sharing this experience he had while working with the Swallowfield church at 13813 Owenton Road, Swallowfield, Kentucky 40601.

We have taken it from **World Radio News,** May-June issue, 1993. Readers may want to contact the church there and hear *the rest of the story.* The chain-reference testament is called **The Soul Winners' Checkbook Edition** arranged by Larry West with a helps section in the back edited by Alvin Jennings. Published by Star Bible, Fort Worth, Texas 76182 (800 433 7507).

"This is our chain reference on the gospel presentation, and we are excited about publishing it with the NKJV. We are concerned about our need to take the students to the **gospel.***"*

Larry West

HOLY BIBLE
The New Testament

What if the Lord were to come right now? Would you know for sure, nothing doubting, that you would go to heaven? Please to turn to page **362**

Chain Reference New Testament

Edwin Myers baptizes in Odessa, Texas, *We Care Campaign.*

CHAPTER 6

GOD CAN PENETRATE CONCRETE HEARTS

By W. Neil Gallagher, Ph.D.

1 If I ever see Don eye-to-eye, I am going to tell him that because of him I know Jesus Christ.

2 Don does not know that. He was a missionary in Northern Thailand where I was a Peace Corps teacher and medic in leper colonies. For my Peace Corps service, I recieved Thailand's *Foreign Service Award* and *Outstanding Young Man of America Award*. Don is the one deserving awards.

3 I want to hug Don and to shout at him, "Don, don't ever, ever, ever give up! Don, the Word of God you carry really does burn into concrete hearts like mine." Right now I want to see Don because he might be discouraged, assaulted with thoughts common to a Christian: "No one listens. What's the use? I'm a failure. Maybe God never wanted me to teach the Bible."

4 Forget all that, Don, because God (through *His* Word and *your* teaching) changed me -- and probably a lot of others. You just don't know how all of us turned out. Although it happened many years ago, I hope and pray that somehow you can hear my story.

5 Don, his wife and I met in a small, fly-filled cafe, opposite Chiengmai's railroad station. After exchanges of small talk, he invited me to look through the Bible with him. I said okay. I was curious, so we arranged to meet.

6 Our second meeting in a matchbox apartment on a steamy Thai afternoon turned me off. At first it was going smooth...at least I thought so. After each of Don's remarks, I would jab with remarks like, "The church is full of hypocrites...Look at all the good Budddhists and Moslems in the world, they're doing all right without Christ." Or, "The Bible is nice, but it's myth and symbolism." Don was polite; I was imperious.

7 Stunned at my attitude, Don stopped talking, knelt beside me and prayed -- OUT LOUD -- for me. No one had ever done that before. I thought: This guy is a religious fruit!

8 His prayers, however, were what I needed. I later found out that a tiny church in New Bedford, Massachusetts, had been praying for me -- 12,000 miles away. Other missionaries in Thailand, Lefty and Jean Reed, had requested the prayers in my behalf.

9 The third meeting was in Don's leaf-roofed shack-on-stilts in a village outside Chiengmai. This went on deep into the night. I listened more but remained unconvinced.

10 In the morning, sitting cross-legged on bamboo-sheathed floor and breakfasting on peanut butter, crackers and warm tea, we talked more. I remained self-satisfied. I reassured myself that I, of course, was the master of my life. I know what was best for me. I left Don before noon, never guessing where his Bible messages would lead me, nor that one day I would desperately want to locate him.

11 There is so much I want to tell him. I want to tell him that during the year following our last meeting, I daily read Bible chapters. I considered myself

"well educated." I considered myself open-minded. "If the Bible were true," I reasoned, "I wanted to know *why* it was true; if false, *why* was it false?"

12 I want to tell Don that I began to ask God (if there were a God) to direct me in the pursuit of truth, wherever that pursuit would lead. I want to tell him that God responded to my cautious, inquisitive prayers. As I prayed and read the Bible, He gradually imparted Himself to me -- quite apart from my expectations.

13 One day He overwhelmed me. I know it sounds crazy. I did not know things like that happened to people. Especially people from Northern metropolises, Eastern schools and Ivy League cultures. But it happened to me, and I came to understand the meaning of the phrase, "**Jesus is Lord.**" I knew what it meant to be born again, relieved of insecurity and fear, melted with the Maker of the universe.

14 I knew what it was to enjoy with Paul, "For me to live is Christ, to die is gain." I knew what it was to "be saved," even though I had never realized that I or anyone needed "saving." I learned this truth: "When a person is saved he lives for the Lord. He gives the Lord credit for everything; he talks about the Lord and he loves to read the Bible and to go to church. It's just way different from what it was before."

15 I want to tell Don that because God gave me His will in place of my jealous and frightened will, I now am at peace with myself and others. I want to tell him that I now see **what I am doing here, where I came from and where I'm going.** I want to tell him that I kept studying, searching, praying.

16 Eventually I met Bob Davidson and Bill Beck, then missionaries in Thailand (Bob is now Campus Minister at Texas A&M in College Station; Bill later preached and taught at International Bible College in Florence, Alabama.) They "taught me the way of the Lord more perfectly," showing me verses on baptism. I dramatized my choice of Christ by identifying with His death, burial and resurrection in the watery grave of baptism.

17 I want to tell Don that I no longer feel compelled to prove that *I am somebody.* I want to tell him that I now see and share the truth that the greatest force of love in the world, Love Himself, (I John 4:8,16), accepts me, loves me and sacrifced for me. Just as I was, just as I am.

18 More than "just somebody," He thinks I am everything! He thinks so much of me that He came to make His home in me...I am the home, He is the resident. I no longer have to prove that I'm anybody anymore. I claim His confidence and His kindness in my life.

19 God, through His dynamic Word, exploded the prejudices and cliches in my mind.

20 He changed me, the chiefest of sinners!

21 I was a smug, cynical, promiscuous and beer-guzzling tough...and He changed me.

22 From the status of an "Eastern intellectual elite," I learned and came to *enjoy* the truth of the meaning of life that is summarized in ten words: *"For me to live is Christ, to die is gain"* (Philippians 1:21).

Gallagher has published 60 articles and 4 books. This article is adapted from **Don't Go Overseas Until You've Read This Book**, published by Bethany Fellowship, Minneapolis, MN 55438. For many years Gallagher preached the gospel and led aggressive warfare against the evils of pornography, conducting campaigns across the nation in stores, university campuses and churches. He has debated ACLU attorneys, professors and entertainers on numerous talk-shows and public forums on the subjects of truth and morality. He holds four earned degrees in education, history, Biblical studies and philosophy (Ph.D., Brown University).

He now has his own financial consulting company and is heard regularly on a Dallas-Fort Worth radio station. He and his wife Gail are active members of the church of Christ in Southlake, Texas. They have three children: Mitch, Beth and Matthew. He can be contacted at **817-281-7589** or **817-485-1825**

Neil "Doc" Gallagher

CHAPTER 7

SNATCHED FROM DEATH AT BIRTH AND DESTINED TO SAVE MULTITUDES IN AFRICA
By Jacob Sianungu

1 I, Jacob, was born in southern Zambia 46 years ago. I was orphaned at age two days when my mother died from internal bleeding.

2 The custom of my village was to bury me with my dead mother, but my uncle had some knowledge about the civilized world, so he intervened.

3 Then my uncle, poor as he was, took me to a Church of Christ Mission for orphans where out of 162 children, only 80 survived. My uncle was convinced that more knowledge of the civilized world would help me and maybe someday, his people.

4 I was brought up in the Christian environment of the orphanage. We were taught more about God's Word and I decided to follow Christ at age 12 years and was baptized by Orville Brittell.

5 Even as early as 7 or 8 years old, I would go to the villages on missionary and evangelism trips. This is where I first saw the great need for God's work. I went to my father's village and lived with my uncle, the same man that pulled me from the grave. He died 4 years after my return.

6 Jacob was featured in a book written by Augusta Brittell, entitled *The Mother of Eighty*, published by J. C. Choate.

7 Academically, Jacob attended the Sinde Mission Primary School in Namwianga, Christian Schools and Linda Secondary School. At the completion of High School, Jacob decided to serve full time in the ministry of the Lord. While at High School he saw the need for his fellow students to study God's Word and he influenced many of his schoolmates. Also some of the teachers were attracted.

8 Moreover, he managed to encourage church leaders at Livingstone Central Church of Christ in organising church meetings and Bible study at High School which led to him forming a Christian chorus and a Christian Club at two secondary schools which are still functioning. The clubs are known as **Timothy Christian Movement.** This group visits hospitals, old folks homes, homes for the blind, opening up a venue to non-members to understand what it is all about. This led many to accept Jesus Christ as their Savior.

9 An annual Gospel Meeting was held whilst he reached his final in 1980 by two American missionaries, namely by Alvin Hobby, C. R. Polk and a Canadian, Eugene Perry. All these

men have now left Zambia, but native leaders such as S. Chikuni and J. Keenga helped...they are all dead by now and their wives help in teaching the girls. So far we had 96 souls added to the family of God. I had a direct hand in this and many are still faithful.

10   Out of the eighty orphans, Jacob felt the drastic situation which overshadowed his childhood and brutal murder in cold-blood of one of the pioneer missionaries to Zambia, his foster mother the late Elaine Brittell. Due to no missionaries returning to Zambia, this motivated him to be more prayerful and to accept the challenge of seeing the gospel propagated throughout the Republic of Zambia, his home country. The missionaries of the 1960s have left, so Jacob decided to continue with the missionary activities which they left in Zambia.

11   I believe this was the same that was expressed by the apostle Paul in writing to Timothy, "*And the things that thou hast heard of me among many witnesses, the same commit thou to faithful men, who shall be able to teach others also*" (2 Tim. 2:2).

12   Furthermore this led me to pursue my Biblical studies in Swaziland for a period of two years and brother Eldred Echols who was a missionary to Africa for 40 years (now retired and a member of the Richland Hills church in Fort Worth, Texas), issued me a Diploma. I studied in Swaziland at the Manzini Bible School from 1982 to 1984 and then taught in the school for 7 months during 1996. Then I was accepted to Southern Africa Bible School where I spent 3 years and studied Greek and Hebrew from 1985 to 1987.

13   Brother Echols' influence has been great on my life. He was one of the founders of these great institutions which I benefited from, so may our living God bless him for that. We did meet each other on several occasions when he came out from the USA on his trips. However, the one in 1997 was exceptional when he came out with the deacons from Richland Hills Church of Christ on a great campaign in Botswana where many souls were brought to Cherist.

14   While in Swaziland, I converted 22 souls and when I returned home in 1995, I was appointed to teach at Kabanga secondary grades 8 and 9. While at that school, 322 people were baptized by me, that includes areas like Chiiki, Siamafumba, Moka, Kalichi and Katumbi village.

15   In Choma camp meeting in November 1994, 42 souls were baptized over a three day meeting. In Namwianga, Kalomo, 48 people were brought to the Lord in waters of baptism and at Tomango,

12 souls were added to the family of God.

16　In December 1997 on my outreach program at Mwata Church of Cherist, I baptized 16 people. In Livingstone area the number baptized since 1988 to 1998 is 762 and the latest of last week's service we baptized 29 more (you will see photographs of some of the recent converts).

17　I have other conversions by God's grace at the Livingstone Central Prisons. Numerically since 1990 the prisoners converted were 410 besides 2 members of staff.

18　With the help of Richland Hills Church, World Bible School country-wide indirectly with the help of others in different areas, about 3600 people have obeyed Christ since 1988 to date. This number would have risen had it not been that a lot of contacts were to be taught and many came up with unnecessary excuses that they are not ready for baptism but still need teaching -- while in their response to their teacher they had indicated they would like to be baptized. Usually you find there isn't anyone in the area and one has to wait for maybe two days.

19　Moving in public transport is not a reliable means to travel. The work would have been very effective if transport was made available specifically for the work I am doing. This has been my cry since that time I came overseas in 1989, my cry to the Lord that one day my prayer will be heard to boost the ministry I am doing. Everything is possible through Him. Brothers and sisters, could you kindly help, that I may bring more glory and honour to reach out farther for the Lord with even greater impact?

20　*Peace be to the brethren and love with faith from God the Father and the Lord Jesus Christ. Grace be with all those who love our Lord Jesus Christ with a love incorruptable* (Ephesians 6:23-24).

Written by Jacob Alvin Brittell Sianungu. P. O. Box 60132, Livingstone, Zambia, Central Africa. Serving Christ as a preacher of the gospel supported by Richland Hills Church of Christ. EMail contact: rhcc@flash.net.

**Jacob Sianungu and
Eldred Echols**

CHAPTER 8

THREE CONVERSIONS REACH THREE NATIONS IN AFRICA

1 This story will resemble the story of the Ethiopian who became a disciple of Christ as recorded in Acts chapter 8. It is reported that after this man's baptism, he went back to his native African nation of Ethiopia and established the church of Jesus Christ there.

2 So far as is known, the three African men about whom we shall now learn also returned to their three respective homeland nations and planted the cause of Christ among their own people. Unfortunately, the details of the actual occasions of their baptisms are not available to us, but the fruit of their labors is so abundant that their story needs to be included here.

3 For the beginning of this enthralling account, we go back to a man who was born October 23, 1864, on the other side of the world in New Zealand. His name was John Sherriff, the son of a monumental stone mason. After learning his father's trade, he went to Melbourne, Australia, where he was converted to Christ. He surrendered his life to God and was faithful to death, June 30, 1935.

4 Through a series of tragedies in his life, he was thrust out to a great and needy mission field, landing at Cape Town, South Africa, on February 28, 1896, where he immediately advertised in the newspaper for "believers in Christ to meet for the breaking of bread."

5 Following his trade to Pretoria, he worked on the Law Courts and Kruger's Church. Here he led two of his fellow-workmen to Christ, baptizing them in the Public Baths, and started a little Sunday School for theDutch children. One knew some English and did some interpreting for him.

6 He was from the instrumental brethren in New Zealand who, like some Christian Churches in the United States, wore the name "church of Christ." After he visited congregations in America in 1924 (during which time he raised financial support from them), he undertook, out of respect for our fellowship's position on instrumental music in worship, never to use it in the churches he established in Africa, although he had no personal convictions against its use.

7 After his death, his widow, Emma, continued with the mission school at Forest Vale. She never allowed instrumental music in the worship there, explaining that "that was brother Sherriff's policy."

8 In July, 1897, he left by mule coach for Bulawayo, Rhodesia, arriving there on August 2, three months ahead of the railroad. On January 2, he began breaking bread with three other disciples.

9 So far, he had only sought to reach white people but one night, returning very late from the bedside of his sick business partner, brother Sherriff peeped through the cracks of a tin shanty occupied by his workers in the stone-yard and saw them gathered around the stub of a candle stuck on the floor, trying to learn to read.

10 The scene moved his heart and he resolved at once that he would teach them to read and also teach them the gospel of Christ. He opened a night school in his own room and soon drew around him a number of African men eager to learn.

11 Always keeping "Christ and

him crucified" in the foreground, Sherriff led his students to a clear understanding of the gospel and many of them were destined to become powerful preachers and leaders of the church -- not only around Bulawayo, but also in other cities and states hundreds of miles distant.

12 GEORGE KHOSA, whom brother Sherriff called his *mustard seed*, became a self-supporting preacher in Johannesburg, even supporting others who served with him in the gospel His native country was Mozambique, of the Shangaan tribe.

13 When he was six years old, there was a rebellion against Portuguese rule in Mozambique and his family was caught up in it. George escaped with a white family to South Africa where he grew up and worked in the gold mines for a time.

14 As a young man he left the mines and migrated to Bulawayo where he found work in John Sherriff's stone work business. Eldred Echols met him in 1950 in Johannesburg and described him as "small, dignified and highly intelligent."

15 He, like his mentor, Sherriff, regarded the instrumental music issue as irrelevant, zealously preaching and teaching, dividing his time between the Shangaan migrant workers in the gold mines and in the southern part of his native Mozambique. He even supported others who worked with him in the gospel.

16 Then there was **PETER MASIYA** who established the first church in Northern Rhodesia, living for a time at the site of what would later become known as the Sinde Mission. At one time he spent three weeks under a tree with nothing to eat but roots and a little wild fruit while he waited for his chief to give him permission to teach his people.

17 Brother Echols writes that he never had the pleasure of meeting Peter Masiya, although he lived for a time at Sinde Mission. He tells about the time when he and Jon Jones visited Lloyd Hinson's preacher training school outside Livingstone in about 1990 when they were introduced to one of the teachers who was named *Peter Masiya!*

18 Echols said to him, "You wear a very illustrious name. Are you related to the Peter Masiya?" He replied, "I am his great-grandson."

19 The third convert whom we shall note in this chapter was a man who became a highly successful evangelist by the name of **JACK MZIRWA**. John Sherriff started a mission school east of Salisbury, Rhodesia, in 1930 that became known as Huyuyo Mission. This was a follow-up of the effective preaching of Jack Mzirwa.

20 Others who followed in this early work at Huyuyo were Dewitt Garrett and W. N. Short (Short had established Sinde Mission in Northern Rhodesia).

21 After the stock market crash of 1929, brother Short lost his support and moved to a farm a few miles from Huyuyo near the site on which Nhowe Mission was later established by W. L. Brown (1941). Brother Short supported himself by farming and building and selling "Skotch carts," large two-wheeled farm wagons.

22 Jack Mzirwa continued to preach in the Huyuyo area where he baptized hundreds of people. He was a very impressive fellow, large with a big black beard and a booming bass voice, highly respected throughout his region.

23   Eldred Echols tells about visiting the white congregation in Bulawayo in the 1940's and describes their having a nice little building on Colenbrander Avenue. In 1949 this church invited Foy Short, W. N. Short's son, to become their pulpit minister, an offer he accepted.

24   At this time there was agitation led by F. L. Hadfield (who had been sent by the Christian churches in New Zealand to help brother Sherriff), to introduce a piano into the worship.

25 Foy Short steadfastly opposed and when a piano was purchased, he resigned and started another congregation and located it in Queen's Park, a Bulawayo suburb. The new (non-instrument) congregation very soon surpassed the Colenbrander Avenue assembly.

26   Men like John Sherriff are the real heroes in missions, in Echols' estimation.   Twenty-five years after his death the Bulawayo Chronicle ran a full page spread of pictures Sherriff had taken of the town and the monuments he had erected. The write-up begins: "Ah, there was a man among men...John Sherriff, the most monumental mason of them all...he came to Bulawayo with a Bible in the 90's, bound to be a missionary."

27 He built things to endure, not for time, but for eternity. He taught and prepared the way for those who learned from him. On Sunday, June 30, 1935, he "broke bread" for the last time and his last words were: *"Eager eyes are watching, waiting, for the lights along the shore."*

28 His body lies under a granite slab at Forest Vale with this simple inscription:
   "TILL HE COME."

Gratitude is expressed to DeWitt Garrett for valuable information contributing to the writing of this chapter. His biographical account of John Sherriff was printed in Missionary Pictorial, edited by Barney Morehead, 3rd edition, 1968. Also to Eldred Echols, forty-year veteran of African evangelism, we give our thanks for personal interviews and for an historical document hand- written to the editor, November 29, 1996.

John and Emma Sherriff, 1930

CHAPTER 9

COULD THEY FORGIVE THEIR SON'S KILLER?
[Reprinted from the
Reader's Digest, May 1986]

1 The call came at 10:40 p.m. on Thursday, December 23, 1982. Elizabeth Morris, then 37, and her husband, Frank, 41, were at home in Pee Dee, Ky. Their only child, 18-year-old Ted, was due in soon from his vacation job at a music store. He was home for the holidays after a semester at college.

2 "This is the Jennie Stuart Medical Center," a woman told Elizabeth. "We need permission to treat your son. He's been in an accident."

3 The 15-minute drive to the hospital seemed endless. Then they were leaning over Ted who lay deep in a coma. The doctors, having done all they could, had him taken by ambulance to a Nashville hospital just across the state line. Perhaps neurosurgeons there could help. But on Christmas Eve, he was pronounced dead.

4 Police later told the Morrises that Ted had had no chance of averting the crash. A car driven by Tommy Pigage, 24, had veered over the center line and hit Ted's car head-on. Pegage, who suffered a gash on his forehead, had reeked of liquor. Blood analysis showed a .28 alcohol level, nearly three times the presumed level for intoxication. Pigage was charged with murder and released on a $10,000 bond.

5 Hungry for details of their son's killer, the Morrises looked up his picture in a high school yearbook. While Ted had been a tall, clean-cut, sunny youth, Pigage

looked to them like a street tough. "A punk" was Frank's disgusted comment.

6 At a court appearance on January 21, 1983, the Morrises learned that Pigage had drunk himself into a stupor the night of the accident after leaving his job as a laborer at a tobacco warehouse.

7 Of the crash itself, he remembered nothing. When he had been told that he killed a man, he buried his head in his mother's lap an sobbed, "God, why couldn't it have been me?" But in court his instinct was to absolve himself. He pleaded not guilty to the murder charge.

8 Elizabeth reeled as if slapped. *Not guilty? Is he saying Ted is to blame? Tommy Pegage should be the one in the grave. It was his fault.* Outside, she turned fiercely to Frank. "If ever I see Tommy Pigage on the sidewalk, I'll run over him with my car."

9 "That won't solve anything," replied Frank, who wanted the man tried, found guilty and executed by the law. The thought of Pigage in the electric chair pleased Elizabeth. "I'd gladly throw the switch myself," she said solemnly.

The Despised

10 As the weeks went by, hatred and grief devastated Elizabeth. Normally vivacious, she became withdrawn. For hours at a time, she lay in her son's bedroom, crying into his pillow.

11 Both she and Frank, Christians, managed a stoicism in front of fellow members of the Little River Church of Christ where Frank was a leader. Some praised their staunchness in accepting Ted's death as God's will.

12 "It is *not* God's will!" Frank

said angrily when he and Elizabeth were alone. "God doesn't kill eighteen-year-olds like Ted. It was the *devil's* work."

13 At her lowest ebb, Elizabeth considered suicide. "God, I know this is a sin of which I cannot repent, but I cannot bear this life. Please, God, if I do this, let me be with Ted." She put a loaded .22 pistol to her head; then she let it fall away and wept with shame.

14 Pigage's parents persuaded him to enter a 30-day rehabilitation program for alcoholics, and for two weeks afterward, he stayed sober, grappling with remorse. Then hoping to ease the pain, he tried one beer, and another. Soon he was drinking himself into a wretched sleep each night. Walking to work, he cast his eyes down not wanting to see or be seen, certain everyone despised him, as he despised himself.

15 In February, a grand jury reduced the murder charge to second-degree manslaughter. Then came a series of delays in the trial.

16 The longer the wait, the more Elizabeth was tormented by her death wish for Pigage. Her only respite was in a letter-writing campaign she and other concerned parents waged against the lenient treatment of drunk drivers in Kentucky courts, where punishment was at the discretion of judges.

17 The Morrises were now members of a tri-county chapter of Mothers Against Drunk Driving (MADD) which had been fighting for tough, uniform laws. Several new statutes took effect in July, 1984, one mandating a jail term when a drunk driver injured anyone.

Startling Words

18 It was not until September, 1984, 21 months after the accident, that the case against Pigage moved toward resolution. The plea was now guilty, which relieved Elizabeth, and the prosecution was urging a ten-year prison sentence. In the event of probation, which Circuit Judge Edwin White was bound to consider, it was stipulated that Pigage spend two days in the county jail every other week-end for two years.

19 Immediately the Morrises and other members of MADD met with the judge to add more conditions to probation. They argued that Pigage should pass a breathalizer test every time he came to jail and should participate in MADD-sponsored programs in high schools.

20 Judge White fixed the maximum ten-year sentence and then suspended it in favor of every one of MADD's recommendations. Any violation, he ruled, would result in Pigage's imprisonment.

21 Elizabeth's friend Rose Jeffcoat Wyatt, vice president of the local chapter of MADD, had loved Ted Morris like a son and shared Elizabeth's disappointment that Pigage was not sent to the state Penitentiary. But Wyatt conceived a way to punish him herself. His first high school appearance was on December 5 would be at Ted's alma mater in Cadiz, Ky.

22 Elizabeth went, expecting to see Pigage squirm. A smiling picture of Ted appeared on the projection screen as Wyatt recounted the terrible events of the night nearly two years before. Then Pigage rose awkwardly and spoke to the 1,000 students in a slow, halting voice. His first words startled Elizabeth.

23 "I killed Ted Morris,"

Pigage began. "It's something I'm never going to overcome. I blacked out because I was drunk. And I was driving a car. It was my fault. The next morning he was dead. I didn't know what to do. I mean, this is their only child, and he's dead because I was drinking and driving."

24 Elizabeth had expected excuses, not a confession. After reading aloud the conditions of his probation, Pigage went on: "That's a very light sentence. I should be locked up. I was lucky. But there's nothing that's ever going to change the way my life is from now on."

25 When he finished speaking and the students had filed quietly from the gymnasium, Elizabeth approached Pigage. He recognized her and was clearly apprehensive. "Don't worry, Tommy," she said. "I'm not going to slap you. I really appreciate what you said. You accept the blame, and that helps me."

26 Elizabeth could see that Tommy was crying. She reached out to touch him and was momentarily stunned. His breath smelled strongly of liquor. At her accusation, he protested that he had been taking medicine, but Elizabeth summoned a state trooper from the foyer and demanded a breathalizer test for Tommy. The trooper refused, saying that he had no cause.

Not Enough Punishment

27 The following evening, Elizabeth confronted Tommy outside his apartment. "Why did you lie to me?" she asked.

28 "I didn't want to go to prison," he replied frankly. Though his breath was again sour with liquor, Elizabeth felt compelled to stay and talk. Under gently questioning, Tommy unburdened himself. He had been addicted to alcohol since age 16 and the grief he had brought on his family and frriends had made him drink all the more. Sober, he could not endure his guilt and shame.

29 As he spoke, Tommy brightened. *She actually cares,* he thought. Readily he promised to call Rose Wyatt and apologize for drinking prior to the high school program. He also agreed to work on Bible courses with Frank.

30 Two days later, Tommy checked into jail for the weekend and blew into the breathalizer bag. The alcohol reading was .12. Judge White ordered Tommy held behind bars until a hearing was arranged.

31 That Monday, probation officer Steve Tribble phoned the Morrises. "The guy felt he wasn't being punished enough," he speculated. "He wanted to be caught. We're going to get his probation revoked."

32 "He's been in since Saturday?" Elizabeth asked. "Who's been to see him?"

33 "Nobody." Abandoned like this, Elizabeth thought, Tommy would continue to drink--and perhaps kill again. Ted's death would be in vain. Tommy needed help dessperately; just as badly, she realized now, as she needed someone to mother. "I want to visit Tommy in jail," she told Tribble.

34 It was scary for her to enter the jail. But she saw that Tommy, too, was frightened and it established an empathy. "Tommy," she began hesitantly, "you know that when someone asks

forgiveness it must be given."

35 "You will *forgive* me?" he asked incredulously.

36 "Yes, but you must forgive yourself and you must forgive the hate I had in my heart."

37 "I do," said Tommy.

38 Later, Elizabeth recounted the meeting to Frank, hoping he, too, would offer forgiveness. He refused. The anger walled inside him would not permit it.

39 A month later, the Morrises were diriving Tommy back to jail after one of his MADD speaking engagements. He talked of the Bible tracts he had been studying and how he felt strengthened by them. He said he was now committed to living his life for the Lord.

40 "Have you been baptized?" Frank asked.

41 "No, but I would like to be," Tommy replied. Baptism by *lay members* of the congregation was customary in the Morrises' church and so, when the road took them past the Little River Church of Christ, Frank pulled in. "Let's do it now," he said.

42 Draping himself with white garments, Tommy entered the frigid waters of the baptistry. Frank immersed him completely. Emerging from the water, Tommy put his arms around Frank and begged his forgiveness. "Yes," said Frank tearfully, "I forgive you."

At Peace

43 After serving three months in prison, Tommy was returned to the conditions of his original probation. Today his once dissolute life is crowded with MADD duties, Bible study classes and church services with the Morrises. At the tobacco warehoue, he is training to be a superintendent. He calls Elizabeth daily and visits often. "I'm happy with myself because I'm doing the Lord's work," he says.

44 For Frank Morris the ordeal is not over, nor will it ever be. "We forgave our son's killer because it was right, but we do not forget," he says. "We still believe that the stiffer the penalties, the fewer drunk drivers there will be on our roads."

45 Elizabeth remembers a talent Ted had for helping friends in need by offering words of advice. In the pit of her hatred, she had heard his voice saying, "Mom, you have to forgive him." When finally she did, Elizabeth Morris was at peace with herself--and with her son.

The ravages of alcohol are no respecter of persons. This story was reprinted in the **Christian Woman Magazine,** November-December, 1986, by special permission of the Reader's Digest, and is reproduced here with permission of The Gospel Advocate Company, publishers of **Chrisian Woman.** The story was told in various newspaper, magazines and tabloids as well as on television programs around the nation.

Elizabeth Morris commented on the story and its far-reaching appeal in these words: "We view ourselves as private, downhome people. Tommy was converted to Christ in January 1985 and it was not until June that the media began to spread the story. No one has put the facts completely as they really were, but the important points of the story have usually been correct. Many people have called to say how touched they were. Ted was our only child, a typical boy growing up. He had high moral standards and to our knowledge never smoked or drank or used abusive language. He made us proud. Every night after we'd have prayer together, Ted would kiss us good night and tell us he loved us--6 feet 3 1/2 inches tall and 18 years old, but not too big to kiss us good night and tell us he loved us. If we allowed our thoughts to stay on the accident, we could hate Tommy all over again. But we try to focus on the present and look to the future. Only by the influence of God in our lives have we been able to progress this far and to continue on. There were times when we thought we could not forgive. But one needs to remember what Jesus said in Matthew 6:15, 'If you do not forgive men, then your Father will not forgive your transgressions.' Drunkenness is a sin for which one needs forgiveness. Alcoholics can know that there is hope for changing their life. Tommy is an alcoholic, but

has stopped drinking by obeying the gospel of Christ. He is a faithful member of the Lord's church and has gained strength through association with Christian people. There is a God who is able to take tragedy and turn it around for good. God did not say everything that happens to us will be good. Losing our son was the worst thing that ever could happen. But God did promise in Romans 8:28 that all things work together for good to them that love God. He fulfilled that promise in our lives."

A full-length book was written by Bob Stewart about this marvellous story. It is entitled, **REVENGE REDEEMED,** published by Fleming Revell Company. Bob Stewart lost a 25-year-old brother to a drunken driver.

PHOTOGRAPH COURTESY OF GUIDEPOSTS MAGAZINE/WILL McINTYRE

Ted's High School graduation

Frank & Elizabeth Morris with Tommy Pigage, their new son in the gospel of Christ.

ILLUSTRATION BY NICOLE DUNAY

Elizabeth Morris with Rommy Pigage (at microphone) and Ted in background.

CHAPTER 10

IF PERSONAL REASONS COUNTED, I WOULD NEVER HAVE LEFT THE BAPTIST CHURCH
By Grover Stevens

1   I would like to say in the beginning that I have no animosity whatsoever against Baptists. Personally, I have no reason for leaving the Baptist Church, because personality is in their favor, especcially is this true of the congregation of which I was a member.

2   I believe the Baptists are for the most part splendid people, honest and sincere. I believe that most Baptists who read this want to know what the truth is, and that they will consider what is said honestly and open-mindedly.

3   I beg you to hear what I have to say, study it carefully with an open Bible in hand, then out of honesty to your own soul and to God Almighty, to embrace all that you find to be in harmony with the Bible. The Baptists hold the Bible up and say, "We preach the Bible." If the Baptists stand on the Bible and nothing else, I never would have left them.

4   When I came into this world, I found it divided religiously. When I was old enough to notice things, I found a church on every hand, and they all claimed to preach the Bible yet wore different names and taught different doctrines. This sentiment seemed to prevail: "It doesn't make any difference what church you are a member of, or what you believe, just so long as you are honest and sincere about it. Everyone ought to go to church and be a member of some church of his own choosing."

5   Since this was the general feeling in religious circles, there was resentment toward the churches of Christ, because they did not believe and did not teach that way. My purpose is to explain these two different ways of thinking and to show clearly what the Bible teaches concerning them.

Baptists Teach Much Truth

6   I do not believe that eveything they say is false; they preach much that is true and I am glad to accept it. But the things they preach which are not the truth made me leave them. They preach strongly against immorality which is good, but what they preach that is untrue *perverts* the true gospel of Jesus Christ.

7   When a person attends the Baptist Church, he hears preaching against sin, and recognizes the fact that he is a sinner, that he is lost. Then being convicted of sin, and desiring to be saved and do what is right, he joins the Baptist Church or some other church. A person convicted of sin is ready to do anything he is told to do.

8   For example, when I first became associated with the church of Christ, I wished that the Lord had left baptism out of the Bible. I said to myself, "Everything that the church of Christ teaches is fine and I believe that most of the people in denominations believe exactly what this church teaches, but when they come to baptism, they all seem to resent that part. If the Lord had just left baptism out, then everything would be all right."

9   I have learned since then that was not the truth, for I learned that people do not mind being baptized when they are convicted of sin and when they want to obey God's will. They will not mind *anything God commands when they*

surrender whole-heartedly their own will to God's will. This is the reason I joined the Baptist Church.

10 When I was a little fellow I attended Sunday School at the Baptist Church in Caddo, Oklahoma. After we moved to Texas, I did not go much at all until my mother started attending the church of Christ in Borger. So I began attending Bible study there and continued for several months and was impressed with the way they studied the Bible. But I got sick and dropped out and lost interest. Later some friends encouraged me to go to Sunday School at the Baptist Church, so I did and became regular and made 100 in Sunday School right along. Our class won the Banner.

11 Those of you who know Baptist grading system know that I had to stay for church to make 100. It was not long until I began to realize that I was lost and in sin and needed to be saved. I wanted to be saved so one Sunday night when the preacher invited any who knew that they were lost "and desired the prayers of the church" to hold up their hand. So I did; it was difficult at first. As I held up my hand my face burned and my heart came up to my throat.

12 When the preacher said, "God bless you, my son," my face burned more and I was very self-conscious. Afterwards, several came to me and told me how proud they were of me and I was also proud of myself. My Sunday School teacher and a few others encouraged me to join the Church. I talked to my mother about it and was persuaded to wait awhile; she felt I was being persuaded and may not realize what I was doing. After some time I began to visit the Methodist Sunday School and church with a friend. Finally, I quit attending at all.

13 About a year later I made a speech at the Annual Boy Scout Father and Son Banquet, and after it the Methodist preacher and also the Baptist preacher approached me and urged me to come to Sunday School. After some delay I began attending the Baptist Church and soon was under conviction again. Late one afternoon I went to the church building to see the preacher and asked him if he would baptize me.

14 He asked me, "Are you saved, Grover?" I said, "Well, I don't know; I guess I am." After we talked quite a while, he told me I had been saved back when I had an experience. I accepted that for I remembered how I had felt after they had prayed for me. That night I confessed that "God for Christ's sake has saved me from my sins, and I want to join the Baptist Church." Upon hearing that confession, they voted to receive me and I was baptized into the Baptist Church that night. It was April 24, 1938.

Zeal In The Baptist Church

15 I took a personal interest in the work. I was diligent in leading several people and they joined the Baptist Church. I was given a Sunday School class, was made the assistant director of the BTU and was licensed to preach.

16 Then one day my brother and my mother told me how the Bible was being preached in the church of Christ, and urged me to attend a series of gospel meetings that was to start in a few days. What I had been told about the church of Christ was with contempt, so I had begun to feel that way toward them. However, I made up my mind to attend and listen to what was said and accept all I could. I wanted to learn what

was taught whether I believed it or not.

17 A. G. Hobbs was doing the preaching. He is a very plain preacher, kind but he never leaves a doubt as to what he is talking about. I went home and looked up some of the scriptures. On many points I would say, "I believe he is right about that," but on others, "Now he just missed it there. If I could show him a few things in that connection, he'd see differently." I learned that when I offered my objections to his position, it was even more evident that he was right.

My Attention Challenged

18 The first thing that challenged my attention as I listened to A. G. Hobbs was that there was just one church. I suppose there is nothing in the bible more plainly taught, yet more disavowed. The church "is the body of Christ" (Eph. 1:22-23) . "There is one body" (Eph. 4:4). The church is the body; there is one body; therefore there is only one church. I saw that there was just one church, but *which one*? So I began to study.

19 I wondered about God calling all preachers to preach, then causing them to preach conflicting doctrines? Does He call Baptist preachers to preach immersion as the only kind of baptism and ordain them and give them authority to baptize, and at the same time call a Methodist preacher to preach that sprinkling is baptism? And does God authorize them to teach different about such things as falling from grace? Does God call both of them to preach these contradictory doctrines? John 17:20-23 and I Cor. 1:10-13 teach that He does not.

20 Why become a member of a church? Because of parents, friends, relatives, a nice building conveniently located, because they do a lot of good works? These are reasons we give. The large majority of people in the denominations join them without knowing what they teach or what they stand for...perhaps 85% or 90% do not know what their church teaches. Some say, "I know that they teach such and such a thing, but I don't believe it."

21 Many Baptists and others are members of something that they do not know what it teaches, and second many support doctrines they do not believe. If I were supporting doctrines I did not believe, you would call me a hypocrite.

Why Not Join All Churches?

22 I want to know why you do not join all the churches in town? You have friends in all of them; they all teach some truth from the Bible. They all do many good works in helping he poor and needy. There are good people in all of them. The reasons for belonging to *one church* could be given as resons for belonging to *all churches*. If you are a Baptist, you could go join the Methodist Church next Sunday and then the following Sunday join the Presbyterian. Folks will begin to say that you are not sincere or that you "are not all there." I know a family that did just that, but they got the reputation of being hypocrites or insane.

23 But why? We are told it is good to stand up for Baptist doctrine, and another person is told it is good to stand up for Methodist doctrine, but that it is NOT all right to stand for both at the same time. *Is Jesus Christ a member of all churches?* Is He? Is He the head of the Baptist Church, the Methodist, the Presbyterian, the

Episcopal, the Aventist, the Mormons, the Pentecostals and all of the hundreds of different churches?

24 There is a good question in the Bible along this line in I Cor. 1:13: "**Is Christ divided**?" Just three words, "Is Christ divided?" The apostle Paul asked the question in condemning religious division. What is the answer? What is *your* answer?

25 One day one of the Baptist Deacons came to me in the store and we went into a back room where we could be alone. He said, "Grover, I heard you are about to join that _____ church (he used a term of contempt and made it sound like it was the worst thing in the world). I stammered a little and said, "No, I have been attending their meeting, but I am not about to join. They really know and preach the Bible, though." He said it was "the most narow-minded and bigoted bunch of people in the world and that that they thought everybody was going to hell that didn't belong to their church." When he finished he left such a stigma I concluded, "Surely a fellow would be insane who would go with that group."

26 That helped for a while and eased my conscience. However on the day the meeting closed, the preacher Hobbs came to see me. He took my Bible, sat down beside me and as I asked questions, he turned in the Bible and had me read the answers. When I did not ask a question he had plenty of things to show me. He offered to talk to me in the presence of the Baptist preacher, or to talk to the Baptist preacher in my presence. I did not want to ask him, because I knew he would not do it. He took my church manual and showed me where Baptist doctrine contradicts the Bible. I saw the truth plainly.

27 Brother Hobbs insisted that I come hear him; I made every excuse but he wouldn't hear them. I told him I had a part on the BTU program and could not get to Borger in time. The real reason I could not go was was that I hated to face the Baptists and explain my absence from the church which they would surely notice. He preached on church history that night, showing the origin of denominations and how the church of Christ stands for New Testament Christianity free from all denominations. When he was finished, I wanted to accept the invitation but thought on what I should do and what my Baptist friends would say. My head just whirled. I managed to stay in my seat, however.

Personal Study

28 The meeting ended and I settled down to a long, hard study of things all by myself. I read the New Testament through and underlined the passages on baptism, the Holy Spirit, the plan of salvation, apostasy, etc. I copied each verse into a notebook, using a separate sheet for each subject.

29 The more I studied, the more I realized the Baptists were wrong, and the more it bothered me. I couldn't keep my mind on my work. I couldn't sleep, but would lie there sometimes till daylight, thinking, praying, studying and wishing that something would happen.

30 I struggled on until time for the Southern Baptist Convention which met that year in Oklahoma City. Then I decided to go to the convention and forget about the church of Christ. I went with the local preacher and registered as a delegate. I returned, feeling much better ... but not for long. Every

time I read my Bible I noticed those passages which I had marked. And I still had my notebook, too, and it was not long till I found myself spending sleepless nights again. I prayed, "Thy will be done." This continued for three months.

31 Then one Sunday afternoon as I was studying and thinking, it suddenly dawned on me that the Bible is God's way of revealing His will to us. I had been praying for God's will to be done, but subconsciously I had been holding out on the Lord in my desire to remain a Baptist. *My whole struggle was rebellion to what God was telling me to do.* The Lord was trying to guide me through the light of His word, but it didn't shine in the direction I wanted it to. Most of our struggles between right and wrong is not what is right and what is wrong, but surrendering our desires for what we want, to what we know is right.

32 After considerable study and prayer that afternoon, I gathered up my clothes and went to services at the church of Christ. When they offered the invitation, I went forward, confessed my faith in Jesus Christ and was baptized into Him the same hour of the night.

33 The *truth* is what made me leave the Baptist Church. I now invite your attention to some of those truths.

34 The Baptist Church is not the church you read about in the Bible. Out of the 112 times the word "church" is used in the New Testament, not one time does it refer to the Baptist Church or to any other denomination.

35 The church is "the called out," a body of people called out of the world, out of sin, into Christ. You can be saved without being a member of any denomination, but if you are saved God will add you to the one church, the body of Christ.

36 There are two different processes of salvation between that taught by the Baptist Church and that taught in the New Testament. You had to confess that you were saved *before* you could join the Baptist Church, *before* you could be baptized. But in the New Testament, confession is made of Jesus as the Christ and baptism follows immediately *in order that forgiveness of sins and salvation might result.* This is a vast difference. It is enough to cause every honest person to see why he cannot afford to be a Baptist or remain a Baptist.

37 The Baptist Church is unscriptural in name, it is unscriptural in its teaching of salvation, and it is also unscriptural in worship. It refers to Sunday as the Sabbath, whereas the Sabbath is now and always has been the seventh day, known as Saturday. In Acts 20:7 we learn that the disciples came together to break bread on the first day of the week. Baptists teach that people ought to keep the ten commandments, including the Sabbath command, yet they will meet on *Sunday*, the Lord's Day (Rev. 1:10) and teach that Sunday is the Sabbath day. This confuses people; it confused me when I was a Baptist.

38 Baptists use mechanical instruments of music in their worship, but the New Testament church did not use mechanical instruments of music. Neither Jesus nor His disciples used them. They had it to use, but did not use it.

39 Baptists set aside the Lord's Supper and say it makes it too common to take it every Lord's Day as was done in the first

century (Acts 20:7). They do not consider taking up a collection every Sunday makes it too common, nor preaching every Sunday. Remembering the Sabbath Day in the Old Testament meant to remember and observe it as often as it came and that was every week.

40 The Baptist Church has a minister whom they call *Pastor*. They also have deacons, but have no elders. This is not the way the congregations were organized in the Bible, when there were always a plurality of elders (also called pastors or shepherds). I left that denomination in part because of the unscriptural organiz-ational system. They also refer to their preacher as *Reverend*, a term that is only applied to God in the Bible (Psalm 111:9). We cannot read about *Reverend Peter, Reverend Paul* or *Reverend* Timothy.

41 Indeed, the real issue is: *Who is King? Who is Head? Who has all authority?* I decided to follow Jesus as the only Lord and Master. I could not do that and follow the Baptist Church's teachings at the same time. I plead with all to renounce all denominational affiliations and authorities and to humbly submit to Christ as Lord of Lords and King of kings.

Grover Stevens was born in Caddo, Oklahoma in 1921. He joined the Baptist Church and became a Sunday School teacher, assistant Director of the Baptist Training Union and a delegate to the Southern Baptist Convention (1939). On July 25, 1938, he "surrendered to preach" for them, beginning his ministry at Sanford, Texas. After coming into the church of Christ, he preached regularly for five years at Fritch, Texas, and later for many years for churches in many

cities. He attended Freed-Hardeman University. He has conducted two public debates (with Church of God and Baptists), and always welcomed discussions with anyone who wanted to serve God more perfectly. The chapter above was edited from his chapter in the book, **Why I Left**, transcriptions from discourses delivered in Fort Worth, Texas in 1940. His discourse was more lengthy than this chapter, hundreds of thousands of which have been printed in a small booklet entitled **Why I Left The Baptist Church**.

GROVER STEVENS

CHAPTER 11

MY WHOLE WORLD
FELL APART

1 Let me start by giving you some background. My name is Doug McKnight. As 1982 began, I was a 32-year-old CPA and vice-president of finance for a medium-sized, publicly owned oil and gas exploration and production company in Midland, Texas.

2 I was highly paid, in good health, had been married to Pam since my second year of college, had twin daughters, two expensive cars, a brand new 3,000 sq.ft. house with a three-car garage and money in the bank.

3 In other words, I was a full participant in the *American Dream*. Then my world suddenly fell apart, or so I thought at the time.

4 After a skiing trip to Ruidoso, New Mexico, in January, 1982, I began getting numbness in my hands and feet. After seeing several doctors, three hospital stays and a rapid advance of symptoms, I was diagnosed as having multiple sclerosis ("MS"). This is an incurable disease of the central nervous system (spinal cord and brain).

5 I had developed crushing fatigue which prevented all but the most sedentary and short-lived activities. There were several other bothersome and frustrating effects of MS and by April I could not walk. After four more months I was no longer able to do my job, was retired on partial income from disability insurance and became a *house husband* while Pam took a full-time job.

6 In case you or someone you know ever receives such a diagnosis, MS does not usually come on so quickly and very often does not result in needing a wheelchair.

7 My whole world had turned upside down and most of the things in which I had previously taken pride and trusted had vanished -- my career and the income and status it provided, my physical strength and other aspects of my manhood.

8 My ego and confidence in the future were shattered. Like most people in such a situation, I attributed my disaster to God and could not understand why He was *supposedly* punishing me so harshly when I had been a relatively good man.

9 Although I had been a Christian since age ten, it had been a very superficial aspect of my life, at least in terms of spirituality. Yes, I had always been a church-goer, as little as possible to still "save face" with my peer group. I was honest and faithful to Pam.

10 But my personal spiritual life was a virtual zero. I never prayed or studied the Bible except at church. I was hypocritical in the sense that I had the outer appearance of being a Christian, but lacked the inner relationship with God and commitment to Him.

11 I was just too busy working my way up the corporate ladder and too distracted with the everyday events of life in general to think about spiritual matters. I did not recognize a need for God until MS knocked out from under me everything else that had taken priority in my life.

12 It took over two years of depression before I came to terms with my new situation and came to understand that God may not have directly caused my predicament ...

although He was at least allowing it to continue. I began to believe that He would help me adapt to it and hopefully become closer to Him as a result of the struggle.

13 For several years now, personal prayer and Bible study on a regular basis have been an integral part of my life. I now have a sense of inner peace and joy that I never had before.

14 I do not mean to imply that I think I am now some kind of a *super-Christian* nor that I never get depressed. However, I have come to realize that God is the source of whatever strength I have and I am now at least heading toward rather than away from Him. **15** After moving to Fort Worth in 1985, I have had opportunities to give talks and write essays that have been published on what I have learned about suffering.

16 There are many things in my life for which I am thankful and about which I often talk with people. But the *best news* in my life is something I have been reluctant to bring up in conversation with others, I regret to say. That news is simply this: that God exists, He has provided a way for our souls to spend eternity with Him and we can also have a more fulfilling and peaceful way of life while still on earth as a result of choosing to accept that gift.

17 I have resolved to begin sharing my faith more boldly and openly with those around me. Please read on with an open mind and heart.

18 My purpose is not to try to convert you to any specific Christian denomination. I am just a *non-denominational Christian* and I just want to share some basic principles with you (and with everyone) about what the Bible teaches on how one becomes a Christian and what being a Christian means for your life now and eternally.

19 The bottom line is to ask that you study with me concerning non-denominational Christianity based on the Bible *only* and not on additional man-made creeds. I am offering to study with you face-to-face, or I could give you a simple Bible correspondence course to study at your own pace by mail.

20 You may be thinking, "Well, this does not pertain to me because I am already a Christian. I go to church often enough. I am satisfied and don't have a need for more than that." I hope you sense enough about me to realize that "putting you on the spot" is not my intent.

21 I do not know where you are in your feelings about God and religion, but wherever you are, that is where our discussions would start. For example, if you question the existence of a Supreme Being, I would show you some very convincing *objective evidence* separate from the Bible itself that can lead you or any honest seeker of truth to a belief in God.

22 There is logical evidence that supports a belief that the Bible is God's inspired communication to man. It is not my intent to argue on obscure and meaningless theological points.

23 A few years ago I read: "If God *does* exist, nothing else matters; if God *does not* exist, nothing matters at all." The entire conduct of our life hangs on the one all-encompassing question of God's existence. If He exists, we need to know what He expects of us and what we can expect of Him as we live our lives in relation to Him.

24   On the other hand, if God does not exist, then we are miserable creatures with no way to know where we came from nor why we are here, living a life of utter futility with no hope of anything beyond the grave.

25   If you do not believe in God and you are **correct**, what do you have to lose by discussing Christianity just once? Maybe just a little of your time. But if you do not believe in God and you are **mistaken**, you may have everything to lose, in the spiritual sense. Is it really worth the risk?

26   Are you thinking, "It's not that I believe God does not exist, but it's just that I have not decided yet." Surely you can see that the *failure to make* a decision has the same practical effect as an outright denial of God.

27   Whatever your response to this invitation, *please* do not wait like I did for a crisis of some kind to force you into a real study of this vital subject. *Your* crisis might be a fatal car wreck, heart attack or some other situation from which there can be no recovery and that offers you no second chance.

Doug McKnight maintained a strong and growing faith in God through sixteen years of gradual deterioration of health. He continued to attend worship assemblies with the untiring assistance of his faithful wife and continued until death to study the Bible with anyone who would come to his home or who was willing to correspond with him by mail. His highest joy was to share the gospel of Christ with the lost. He initiated World Bible School at his congregation in 1985, resulting in over 89,000 lessons being sent out and in 1,748 requesting to be baptized. He wrote several articles that were published...also his personal testimony which he circulated as widely as possible to encourage others and also because it carried his offer to study with anyone who read it. Just a few days before his death, he was contacted by another CPA by the name of Mr. Randall Arnhart who had kept this unique testimony over six years before contacting Doug and asking for an opportunity to study the Bible with him. Doug's excitement was immeasurable as he phoned to tell me it was one of his testimony sheets I had delivered door to door tht prompted the call after all these years. This was just a few days before he passed away, so others are following up in his behalf. He resided with Pam at 7813 Owen Drive, North Richland Hills, TX 76180 until the Lord released him from the prison of MS on Monday, September 21, 1998. He was faithful to the end of his earthly pilgrimage -- a model in generosity, in speaking the gospel to all he met, in marriage and in worship. I write this on the day a huge crowd assembled at his funeral, when we all praised God for the way he lived and the way he died. In the service, many incidents were told which illustrated Doug's faith, such as his increasing his weekly contribution to make up for several years of his neglect in tithing. --Editor.

In   1997

The American Dream Family, 1982.

CHAPTER 12

DISCOVERING GOD THROUGH BIBLICAL TRUTHS

1 *"This book will tell you who you are, where you are going, and the road you will need to take to get there."* The preacher who spoke these words had placed a Bible on the desk between us.

2 These words reached a mammoth cavity in my soul which had never before been exposed, even when I was a deeply religious Roman Catholic nun.

3 The impact of this statement changed the direction in my life on earth and my focus for eternity. At no other time in my religious upbringing and in the fulfillment of my "divine vocation" as a nun had anyone pointed me to the Bible as the source for spiritual therapy and deliverance from my past sinful life.

4 The challenge of these words resonating in my heart prompted me to respond to the scripture which reads: *"And you shall seek me and find me, when you shall search for me with all of your heart"* (Jeremiah 29:13).

5 As theologically fortified as I was in Canon Law, the Laws of the Roman Catholic Church, Apologetics and the teachings in the Baltimore Catechism, I had very limited knowledge of God's plan for my salvation as outlined in His Word.

6 So began my quest for this revelation. Admittedly, at first I searched the scriptures to find inner peace and happiness for a life that had become fragmented since my departure from convent life in 1968. As I delved into God's revealed and inspired Word, I also began to question the total commitment I had made as a young child to the doctrines and tradition of Roman Catholicism.

7 In daily studies for six months, I learned five major life-changing facts regarding my self worth: (1) God made me and made me into His own image and likeness, Genesis 1:26. (2) God loves me, John 3:16. (3) God planned for me. Psalm 139:16 states that God recorded every day of the psalmist's life before he was born. I reasoned: Doesn't that apply to me also?

8 (4) God gifted me, Ephesians 4:7. (5) Christ died for me and gave me value, 2 Cor. 5:15,21. These points were recorded in my book, **A Change of Habit**, page 91. In the depths of my soul, I knew God valued me highly.

9 I knew also that I was a sinner and needed forgiveness and restoration before Him. Lamenting my deeds and longing for God's healing, I plunged into an intense study of His Word.

10 Time after time, I tried desperately to reconcile the teachings of my faith in Roman Catholicism with scriptural doctrines that I believed are without error and God-breathed. Time after time, I was astounded, bewildered and confused that doctrines I had taught and believed as a Roman Catholic nun were without scriptural basis. Among these are:

11 Peter as the first Pope and the uninterrupted Apostolic heritage of popes since then; the concept of celibacy; the mass as the pinnacle of worship; the division of sin; the various forms of grace; baptism; the institution of the sacraments and all other beloved traditions and teachings involving worship and sacrifice.

12 Consequently I began attending early morning mass at the local Catholic Church and then would drive to the Church of Chrit to participate in their 10:00 A.M. worship service. This practice proved to be an avenue of further confusion and frustration as I experienced the friendliness of the congregation and witnessed their closeness to God through their prayers, participation in remembering the Lord's Supper and the congregational singing.

13 I listened carefully to the preaching of the Word of God, writing down the chapter and verse of each and every scriptural quotation that related to the subject discussed. Like someone under a spell, I was drawn to the power of God's word influencing my thinking and the decision I would make that would determine the remainder of my life.

14 This process took a new and unexpected turn. After many months of inner conflicts between scriptural truths and long-held doctrinal beliefs of Roman Catholicism, fears of family exclusion and God's eternal judgment, I chose to surrender my will to His. At the invitational call I heard the words:

15 *There is a fountain filled with blood, Drawn from Emmanuel's veins, And sinners plunged beneath that flood, Lose all their guilty stains!*

16 I stepped out in faith into a new life in Christ (Galatians 3:27) in full assurance of the promises of God.

17 Today, many years later, through my writings, traveling and speaking, I have impacted the lives of many others seeking answers to the same questions I had years before: **Who am I? Where am I going? What road do I need to take to get there?"** I have taken seriously my role as an ambassador for Christ in fulfilling the Great Commission as given by Jesus in Matthew 28:18-20:

18 *"Full authority has been given to me both in heven and on earth; Go therefore, and make disciples of all the nations, baptizing them in the name of the Father, and of the Son and of the Holy Spirit. Teach them to carry out everything I have commanded you. And know that I am with you always, until the end of the world."*

19 In 1986, I published my autobiography which was entitled **A Change of Habit.** In 1995, I compiled informtion in a book entitled **From Nun To Priest**. This was a comparison of the teachings of Roman Catholicism with those of biblical truths. Both books were followed by a video entitled **"The Journey of Spiritual Discovery With Joanne A.**

Howe."

20 Little did I know or relaize that the publication of this material would open many doors for the cause of Christ. I am humbled particularly by the numerous letters and phone calls I have received with the most important question I asked as I began my own search for God's direction: "What Must I Do To Be Saved?"

21 I continually stand amazed at the numnber of individuals who have been influenced by my personal testimony and have commited their own lives to obedience to the gospel. Upon completing the reading of my first book, my dear mother was appalled at the mental and religious cruelty I had experienced as a nun under the disguise of spiritual discipline. Her own soul-searching questions have led her to put on he Lord in baptism at the age of 78. She is convinced that it is imperative that others should learn of my life-long search and final discovery in God's Word.

22 Wherever I travel, either by plane or car, to hold seminars, retreats, ladies' days or lectureships, I find myself speaking about spiritual matters to whomever I meet along the way. Fifteen women have responded to obeying the gospel immediately following my personal testimony given at retreats and seminars. How often the simple action of reading from my Bible has been the impetus for the start of a conversation on God's plan for our life.

23 As I look back at the spiritual fork in the road I faced and the decision I made, I believe, like the poet Robert Frost, that I chose the *different road*. This road has made all the difference for me and I hope and pray for the kingdom of God.

24 To **know** the will of God has been the greatest knowledge for me to acquire; to **discover** the will of God has been my greatest triumph; to **obey** the will of God in the waters of baptism has been my greatest achievement; to **experience** the love of God is my greatest joy; to **anticipate** the joys of heaven is my greatest hope.

25 But to miss being with God for all eternity would have been my greatest **disappointment.**

26 To Him alone belongs any glory I have received because of this testimony.

Joanne A. Howe

Joanne A. Howe now resides at Hendersonville, Tennessee (Box 872, zip 37077; phone 615 826 4791). For information on her books and videos, contact her or Star Bible Publications. We are indebted to her for writing this testimony of conversion especially for this book.

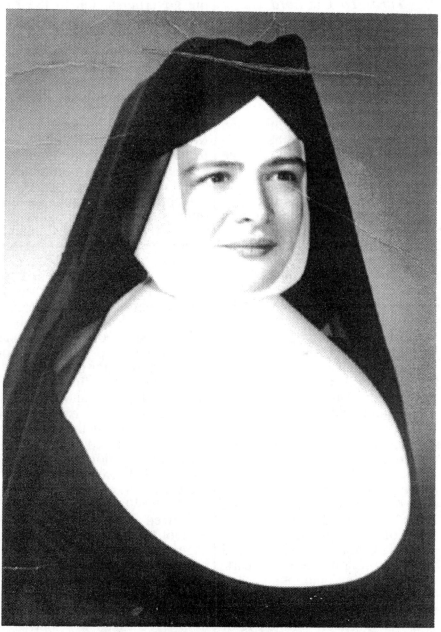

JOANNE A. HOWE
Before She Was Transformed From A Nun To A Priest

CHAPTER 13

UNG POCHENG
SUM C. MCDONALD,
A Brave Woman
Turns To The Lord

1 "What's going on here?"

2 Ung Pocheng Sum C. McDonald shook her cane at a policeman standing nearby. Although small in stature, she is a bold woman.

3 From her vantage point as she crossed a bridge near the Thai-Cambodian border, she could see several children hanging from poles. Their hands were tied and their hair was shaved on one side as a mark of shame. The date was April 1993 and the blistering tropical sun added its rebuke to the childrens' heads.

4 The children, the officer explained, were orphans caught stealing food and clothing in the open-air market.

5 "I will pay their debt if you will release them," she bargained. "Yes, I will release them if you will keep them from coming back," he countered. The Association for Cambodian Children was born. The day also marked a new beginning for McDonald, 68, who has devoted the rest of her life to helping childen in war-torn northwestern Cambodia.

6 A widow with crippling arthritis, McDonald travels the dirt roads of Sisophon, Banteay Meanchey, Cambodia, with the aid of a cane or in a horse-drawn cart. The surrounding mountains and lush fields are imbrued with tropical rains and the blood of civil war, a war that claimed the life of her first husband and left her a political refugee.

7 Her first husband, Sum Chhum, formerly was Cambodia's minister of agriculture. He was assassinated in 1975 along with other leaders of the republic when the government fell to the Khmer Rouge Communists led by Pol Pot. As special assistant to the First Lady, McDonald's life was spared only because she was out of the country at the time, attending President Jon Nol and his wife in Bali, Indonesia.

8 Fearing for her life, McDonald sought political asylum in the United States. Even as she grieved the loss of her husband, childen, home, work and country, she used her language skills to help other Cambodian refugees. She speaks five languages: Cambodian, Vietnamese, Chinese, French and English.

9 She was remarried in 1980 to John McDonald, an American serviceman. After his death two years later, she took a job in a bakery. She soon became manager and eventually saved enough money to buy her own store.

10 Meanwhile, in Cambodia the Khmer Rouge and two non-communist groups each controlled different parts of the country. In 1982, the non-communist groups formed a coalition and in 1989, the first attempts were made to resolve the civil war.

11 When the government stabilized somewhat that year, McDonald returned to Cambodia, eager to see her aging mother before her death. Why McDonald has remained there, her sons cannot imagine. One son lives in France, the other son in Italy and both have asked her to live with them. As an American citizen, she could stay in the United States.

Yet, she chooses to remain in one of the poorest, roughest places in the world to help children.

12 "I like to help people in trouble," she explained.

13 Familiar with the ways of the government, McDonald immediately began seeking assistance for the orphans. Her appeals were rewarded. King Norodom Sihanouk gave her permission to begin the Association for Camodian Children. The governor of the Banteay Meanchey province gave her 10 acres of land in Poipet. The United Nations gave her building materials and a water pump. The chief of Mine Clearance came with a team to clear land mines and later returned with a generator, sewing machine and food.

14 Using money from her second husband's military pension and donations from friends and family, McDonald hired two carpenters to train herself and 10 children to build their first building. Other people joined the vocational training program and they soon had a building large enough for separate sleeping rooms for the boys and the girls, a dining room, a kitchen, a storage room and a small classroom.

15 One of the many people who donated food, money and school supplies to the orphans was Utan Nop, a Christian businessman. Born in Cambodia but living in Bangkok, Thailand, Nop owns an import business and makes frequent trips across the border. On one such trip, Nop brought his friend Russell Pennington, an American missionary living in Bangkok. They stopped to visit McDonald.

16 Shortly after their visit, McDonald's life changed again.

The Khmer Rouge began shelling Poipet and the Untied Nations High Commissioner for Refugees and an American ambassador persuaded her to evacuate the children. She sent 33 children to a French orphanage in Sisophon and she was evacuated to Phnom Penh.

17 "I was brokenhearted because I had wanted so much to help the poor children. It seemed all my time, energy and money and all the donations and work by so many people had been spent for nothing," she said.

18 When she returned to Poipet a week later, she found the military had taken all the supplies and had torn down the building. She salvaged what she could, took it to Sisophon and began building a school.

19 Exhausted from all that had happened and angry with Buddha for not helping her, McDonald went back to Phnom Penh for a few days of rest.

20 "While I was resting, I had a dream in which a man with a long beard told me not to worry -- that he would take care of me," she said. At first she thought it was her father, but then she concluded that perhaps it was the God of the Bible. "I decided I wanted to serve Him," she added.

21 As she prayed to God from her bed in Phnom Penh, Pennington prayed from his bed in Bangkok. He had received donations from the United States for the orphans, but did not know how to contact McDonald. Unable to sleep and fearing for everyone's safety, Pennington prayed for God to help him get in touch with her. He also sent a fax to Phnom Penh, hoping someone there would know her whereabouts. McDonald

happened to be in the city when it arrived and she arranged to meet Pennington and Nop at the border.

22 Complications forced the two men to go to the border a day earlier than the set meeting. Then, because of continued shelling by the Khmer Rouge, the border guard refused to allow the American missionary into Cambodia. Nop crossed the border alone to look for McDonald in Sisophon.

23 "He was looking for me among 200,000 people, asking if anyone knew about me or the foundation," she said. "At the same time, I went to find a phone booth to call Russell to check out what time I was to meet him the next day. All of a sudden, Nop and I saw each other. It truly seemed to be a *miracle.*"

24 She went with Nop back to the border to meet Pennington. "We talked fast because the border was closing in less than two hours and we set another time for him to bring his missionary team to meet the children in Sisophon," she said.

25 At the next meeting, the border guard again refused to let the Americans into the country. As bombs exploded nearby, the missonaries knelt outside the office and prayed. After two hours, the officials relented. Before the missionaries left Cambodia that day, McDonald was taught further and was baptized in a large earthen water pot.

26 "I am really happy in my new life as a Christian," she said. "I believe that God has been with me through all the changes, that He has brought me to this time so I can teach others how He will take care of them."

27 That is exactly what she is doing. Her school in Sisophon has grown to 215 children and goes through the fourth grade. McDonald cooks for the malnourished children, sews uniforms from donated material and teaches. She has hired additional classroom teachers who are supported by private contributions and the government. However, the school is in danger of losing government funding because McDonald has removed the idols from the buildings and now teaches the Bible. She is working through the challenge legally.

28 Despite this and other persecution, McDonald also has started a congregation that meets at the school. The church has grown to 42 members and is comprised of students and people from the community whom McDonald has taught. Bold in the Lord and in life, McDonald even uses her arthritis as an opportunity to share the gospel.

29 "She cannot travel alone because of her physical condition. So when we meet at the border, she always brings two or three people along with her for us to teach," Pennington said.

30 I have seen such a difference in her from the first time I met her," he continued. "She was helping the children but didn't seem to have much joy. Her face seemed really hard. But now every time I see her *she has such a beautiful smile.*

31 "It seems like wherever she goes, God is right there with her, helping her, encouraging her. It is just amazing all that she has lived through. I think you can see that God had a plan to use her."

Dana Robertson of St Louis wrote this wonderful story which was published in the

Christian Woman Magazine in their July/August issue, 1997. It is reprinted here with permission of the Gospel Advocate Company, Nashville, TN. Contact the publisher for current information about this work with the children and their need for donations of supplies, food, medicine, clothing, etc. You may also obtain an update on the Cambodian Church of Christ that was begun by this most compassionate and noble lady.

Mrs. McDonald and students in Sisophon, Cambodia

The Cambodian Church of Christ was begun by Mrs. McDonald (back row, left).

CHAPTER 14

HOTEL PRAYER LED ROD

1 Rod Schaefer is a young, smart, aggressive entrepreneur who provides a service to our apartment properties. He is a vendor of ours who was invited to our annual company meeting/trade show.

2 As a matter of practice, I say a prayer before we serve the meal which we provide to our entire company and vendors that choose to come and support this outing.

3 I believe that Rod's interest in the Lord was certainly there before, but this prayer, which I am told by the hotel people and caterers, is a rare thing. It opened the door for further discussion.

4 Over a period of four or five years, our conversations and friendship developed to where Rod felt very comfortable asking biblical questions and engaging me in his personal struggles and beginning walk with the Lord.

5 One day Rod called and said he had accepted the Lord into his life. He also discussed baptism, but wanted to wait for the right time.

6 God works in wonderful ways. I told Rod that I really wanted him to talk with other Christians as I was pretty much his focal source of Christianity. I told him he should go to Desert Palms to visit and study with Cliff Crumpler. He immediately said his grandmother lived in Desert Palms and that he was leaving the next day to go there for a week!

7 He and Cliff studied and talked about God for much of that week and soon after, I received a phone call asking me to come to San Diego to witness his baptism.

8 At the same time, he mentioned that his dad, mom, brother, sister-in-law and nephew all wanted to be baptized!

9 It was not hard getting me to San Diego to be a part of that experience. I was standing in Rod's swimming pool as Cliff baptized all six of them!

10 Talk about rejoicing in heaven!

BEGINNING OF THE QUEEN MARY CHURCH

11 My name is John Maples. Please come with me now as we go back several years in time to 1956 and across the ocean to South Africa as I rehearse what God did through my beloved father who since then has fallen asleep in Jesus. May his memory be blessed and his God glorified is my prayer as I write.

12 It was in 1956 that my parents, the John Maples family, moved to Durban to preach the gospel of Christ. Upon arrival and unaware of any existing Christians, they began their labor of love for the lost by meeting as many people as possible. The first man my father taught and baptized was without doubt in a way that proves God's providential involvement in giving increase when the seed is sown in honest and good hearts (Luke 8).

13 While walking down the street in an Indian section of the city, he met a man who was on his front porch reading his Bible. To my father's astonishment, the white-haired gentleman said that he and his wife knew that the Maples family was coming to Durban because Reuel Lemmons of Texas had announced his coming at the conclusion of a sermon preached on a powerful African radio station.

14 This aged man and his wife, Mr. and Mrs. Orsen, had been eagerly anticipating my father's arrival because they wanted to ask Maples if he would baptize them "into Christ." They had learned about the importance of baptism through the radio sermons and by confirming what they heard by reading the Bible references Lemmons had given. And behold, there is the man standing on his porch!

15 Sadly, however, his wife had become ill and had died the very day that our ship had entered the harbour. My father did baptize Mr. Orsen and that marked the beginning of one of the strong churches of Christ in South Africa.

Clay and Cherry Hart from America are among the workers now serving with this congregation.

16 The Queen Mary Avenue congregation among the white population grew quickly and several entire families were converted in those early days, including many who became life-long friends of mine. The Zwart family, principle members of that church, visited us and the Richland Hills church last year. They are a vital part of the family of God there that has developed many church leaders and has been a springboard for several other congregations in South Africa.

17 This story reminds me of Paul's statement in his letter to the Corinthian church, that "I planted, Apollos watered, but God gave the increase" (I Cor. 3:6).

THE *AROMA OF CHRIST* DREW ME TO HIM

18 Growing up and on into my adult life, I always knew there was a God.

19 This was knowledge from my mother speaking of God to me and telling me that we were Catholic.

20 By the time I reached the age of 29, I found myself single *again* and a man of the world. I found little joy in living and asked myself, "Is this as good as it gets?"

21 Attending church was something I had experienced only a few times in my life, but my life had reached such a low ebb, I felt a need to start praying to God. It was awkward because I was so far from Him and did not know how to pray.

22 It was at that time that something happened that changed my whole life. I met someone who had the aroma of Christ all around her. Her name was Chris.

23 When I began asking her questions about her faith and what it was about her that made her different, she answered in meekness and modesty. What made her radiate what seemed to be a *divine sweetness* was obviously that she was a child of God.

24 She, in return, asked me some questions that led me to a study of how I also could share in the same benefits that set her apart from all the worldly people I had known. Chris pointed to the passages in the Bible that led me to become a child of God as well.

25 I have changed my life and am no longer the same man of the world that I used to be. I am convinced that true happiness can come only from what can be found in Christ and in yielding one's life completely to His service and praise.

26 I feel unworthy of myself to have a place in one of the chapters of this book. Yet, because of His grace, His righteousness and His forgiveness that are now mine, I now have a confidence and peace that has lifted me to a higher plane and set my foot on the eternal rock of ages.

Pat Holder, writer of verses 1-10, is an executive with Lexford Properties in Irving, Texas. He is a graduate of Abilene Christian University and now serves as an elder of the Richland Hills Church of Christ. This manuscript was submitted by Pat in 1996.

Dr. John Maples, D.C., shared the story found in verses 11-17. He, like Dr. Luke who wrote the *original* Book of Acts and who was a frequent traveller with the apostle Paul, is fully devoted to the cause of Christ. He speaks often to his patients about the Bible which he keeps always at his side.

Tom Oxley reluctantly consented to allow his story in verses 18-26 to be used. He is a member of the same congregation as Pat Holder, John Maples, this writer and 5,000 other spirits of "just men and women made perfect in the blood of Jesus Christ." His joy was made complete when Chris consented to become his wife, now joined by their lovely little daughter, Briana. They reside at 5603 Andelusia, Arlington, Tx 76017, where they work together in winning souls ... also in what has become by God's grace a state-of-the-art T-Shirt manufacturing business.

Chris & Tom Oxley

CHAPTER 15

GEORGE PEPPERDINE SAYS
"FAITH IS MY FORTUNE"

1 "Some authors are greater than any of their works, while some men are greater than anything their biographers can say about them. Such is George Pepperdine," wrote M. Norvel Young. He said that some biographies cry out to be written, while some others should never have been written...of the former is George Pepperdine.

2 This story must be told, not because he made millions and gave them away, not because of any other such superficial pretext, but because of what he is within himself. In his benevolences, you would think he was receiving rather than bestowing. For many years he served as chairman of elders in the church where he attended and he was regularly a visitor at the university that he founded and which bears his name.

3 The spirit of humility, love and service which made his life full will be passed on through the lives of those whom he influenced and inspired from generation to generation.

4 This man who made his fortune in his thirties and forties and gave the bulk of it away during his fifties lived, by the grace of God, to see the fruit of his tremendous energies in his sixties and seventies.

5 This is not just a story of a farm boy that was blessed. It serves a more worthwhile purpose, teaching eternal principles. "I wanted," said Pepperdine of his story, "for it to give clear reasons why strong faith in God is worth more to us than all the treasures of earth; more than any fortune man can acquire. All wealth, fame and earthly glory fades out when compared to the value, the beauty, the satisfaction and comforting hope enjoyed through unwavering, unfeigned faith in God. I can say with deep emotion: **Faith Is My fortune!"**

On The Kansas Frontier

6 Our story begins with John Pepperdine as he worked in the hot sun of his cornfield, while reflecting uneasily on his one-room cabin nearby where his wife, Mary, was in childbirth labor. She was being attended by old Mrs. McGraw, the midwife and another neighbor lady, Mrs. Bowman. Both of the attending women felt John's presence would be superfluous -- and also entirely *unseemly*.

7 Land here was less expensive than in the central fertile area of Illinois from whence he had migrated, and it required unrelenting toil to wrest a living from these rolling hills in the 1880's. He was young, strong and not afraid of work.

8 Mrs. Bowman called from the door and he came quickly where he found his wife pale but all right, and there beside her was another boy. "I would like to name him George after my brother," he said. He and Mary agreed. That was June 20, 1886.

9 The Kansas frontier was "wild and woolly" with its conflicts with Indians, its wagon trains traversing the Santa Fe Trail or the Oregon Trail in the mad rush across the prairies to supposedly greener grass and richer fortunes farther west. Only four years before George was born, Jesse James was killed near the Missouri border and his band was dispersed. "Buffalo Bill" Cody was 40 years old at the time.

His job was to supply buffalo meat to the workers building the Kansas Pacific railroad across the state.

10 It had only been three years since the family had come in a covered wagon with their baby Fred. They set about at once to build their one-room cabin out of rocks from the hillside...it wasn't much, but it was their own. John was a good farmer and with the family growing, he later added two lean-to rooms on different sides of the house.

11 When little George was only five years old, he gathered up all the items he could find made of iron and piled them up under a tree where he proposed to have a sale. It had not occurred to him that some of those things, including his mother's iron skillet and a few useful small farm implements, were *not junk*. He got a spanking for this lack of discernment in what was apparently his first business venture.

A Religious Revival

12 When John and Mary came to Kansas they were not especially interested in spiritual matters. John's people were not very religious, although they had inherited a strict moral code from their Episcopalian background. Mary was not a member of any church but had a background of Baptist ancestors.

13 Eighteen miles away at Parsons there was a Church of Christ which was evangelical in spirit and sent its preacher to other communities to preach in school houses. Not long after the Pepperdines arrived, a protracted meeting was held in the Park school house a few miles away.

14 Hungry for human contacts, John and Mary attended this revival meeting. They soon fell under the eloquence and force of the preaching and found themselves captivated by a moving vision of Christianity. Convinced of their personal need for a Savior, they turned from their sins, confessed their faith in Jesus as the Christ and were baptized into Christ and into a new life.

15 Several other people were also baptized and the nucleus of a new congregation was formed. They could not support a regular preacher of their own or build a meeting house, but the Parsons church sent their preacher once a month to strengthen the new converts. John and Mary were firm in their adherence to the new cause. In this, they remained faithful the rest of their lives -- over half a century.

16 Space will not allow us tell about the rural Willow Branch School, the "chart class," the new leather boots, learning to milk cows, the prairie fire, fishing and swimming holes, sorghum molasses, corn bread, turkeys, George's first and only cigar, rabbit hunting and a thousand other things. But we will tell *one* story.

17 George's dad helped him build a rabbit trap out of a wooden box one day. This resulted in George gathering any stick of wood he could find and any wooden box to build more traps for catching cottontails that could be sold. At first his catch was only a cat, but sure enough, one morning he found a rabbit in one. This set him into what for him was a big business; he made about fifty traps in all and eventually strung them out as far as two or three miles from the house. He would saddle old Nellie on Saturdays and carry his catch to the market, adding nickel by nickel to his savings for a new saddle.

18 Some of George's schoolmates saw his success and

wanted to get in on the profits, too. They made a few attempts, but soon wearied of all the work, the trips to the markets and all the hassle, leaving only George as the sole trapper. The same drive to succeed as a boy with a chain of rabbit traps was later to stimulate Geore Pepperdine, the man, to succeed with a chain of auto supply stores.

George's Head Was An "Idea Factory"

19 The lad worked hard on all the farm chores, but his heart was not always in it. He was continuously thinking of guns, boats, motors, or some gadget that he wanted to make...thought of as a boy as full of ideas as a dog is full of fleas!

20 Among other things, he made a wind motor, a home-made boat and an intricately fashioned home-made gun. When the family moved to town, George met new friends at school and church where the family had an active interest. Public affairs were also of intense interest, especially voting on prohibition of liquor sales and farm issues that affected the welfare of the people. George was always a *teetotaller* who could never be persuaded to take the first drink.

21 He had no sympathy for the person who would waste his money, dull his reasoning power, injure his health, character and reputation by drinking alcoholic beverage which George said, "You could not force a dog or a hog in Kansas to drink."

22 In 1905 George saw his first automobile on a street in Parsons, but ironically in the light of his later activities, the contraption did not arouse much interest...even though some were predicting the machine would suspercede the horse and buggy. None in the rural districts or small towns really took the idea seriously. The appearance of this machine that had been bought by the hardware store owner did create a sensation, however, and George chased it on his bicycle but did not succeed in catching up with it before it reached the end of the gravel street at the edge of town.

23 In 1907 George persuaded Lena Rose to become his wife, and his employer gave him an immediate raise to $15 per week. He was just two days married when he was ordered to tell an untruth to creditors. George refused. "You can either do what I say or quit," he was told. After some reflection, he faced his boss and said: "I won't tell a lie for anybody." To his surprise, the employer's whole demeanor changed and overcome by shame he asked George to stay and promised that if there was any "white-lying to do" he would do it himself.

24 The story of George founding Western Auto Stores is too involved to give here, but it can be read elsewhere. Suffice it to say, from the one retail store he started in 1908, another was started and another until he had built 14 large warehouses and a chain of 256 retail stores plus 1,867 "associate" stores all across the western states. Sales totalled over $45 million the year he sold his controlling interest (in 1939); he sold out because he wanted to give his remaining years to "helping good causes." Twenty years later the number of stores had doubled, to the great satisfaction of its founder.

25 From childhood, George had seen religion in its simplest, yet most profound manifestations. His parents had accepted God as naturally as breathing, and as a boy he had seen Christ in the lives of those whom he loved most. He obeyed the gospel in his early teens and never looked back. He kept his eyes focused on Jesus, "the author and perfector of his faith," until death.

26   In his commencement speeches at the university that bears his name as well as in various other presentations both oral and in print, his faith and philosophy of true religion have been recorded. One of his booklets, **More Than Life**, was written in the early 1940's and has been circulated in the millions of copies...some sold and some distributed free of cost through his generosity.

27   On the last page of his biography, the following **Fare You Well** appears, written by George Pepperdine just a few days before his death. It reads: "And now, to all people of good will everywhere, who love and serve the Lord, I wish you hapiness in this world and the next. I hope to meet you on that Golden Shore, where friends and loved ones part no more. *'Now to Him Who is able to keep you from falling, and to present you faultless before the presence of His glory with exceeding joy. To the only wise God our Saviour, be glory and majesty, dominion and power, both now and forever. Amen.'* (Jude 24-25) Yours in Faith, Hope and Love, (signed), George Pepperdine."

Information for the above narrative is from the book, **Faith Is My Fortune**, by Richard L. Clark, Ph.D., and Jack W. Bates, Ph.D. Introductions by Wade Ruby, Chairman, Department of English, George Pepperdine College, and M. Norvel Young, President of George Pepperdine College. Date not known, cir 1959. Published by Pepperdine College Bookstore, Los Angeles, CA. 316 pp. The book, now out of print, can be seen in Christian College Libraries and in many personal libraries.

GEORGE PEPPERDINE

— at 10 —

— at 38 —

— at 73 —

First store, Kansas City

Pepperdine University,
Los Angeles, California

This photo was taken about 1921, the last time the family was together for a visit before father passed away. Above: George, Ben, Fred. Below: John and Mary.

CHAPTER 16

"AND THE ANGELS SANG"

1 It was in the year 1972 when three elders from the Sunset church of Christ in Lubbock, Texas, flew to Lagos, Nigeria, along with Truitt Adair whom we were to support in a mission venture in that city.

2 We were guests in the home of brother J. C. Thomas, an employee of the Gulf Oil Company and a former elder in the church at Baytown, Texas.

3 While brethren Abe Lincoln and Norman Gipson were busy engaging government officials in an attempt to wrest from them authorization to establish a school of preaching there, brother Truitt and I had the unexpected but pleasant privilege to study the Bible with a businessman downtown.

4 This man, Mr. Amaichi, knew the Bible surprisingly well. In fact, he would quote along with us the latter part of many of the Biblical verses we began to cite. He only lacked an understanding of the proper concept of how one becomes a child of God. After we had studied the better part of three hours he asked to be immersed.

5 When we called brother Thomas to ask where, when and how we would accommodate this brother-to-be in his strong desire to become a member of the Lord's family, he asked us to return to his home because he lived very near the river where most all of the baptisms in Lagos had been performed.

6 He told us that several times during an ordinary week a group of people would walk to that spot, the baptisms would take place, then the service would be dismissed with a prayer and a song of rejoicing.

7 It was just at the close of day when the four of us approached the spot where we left the street to walk down through tall cane-like growth to the water's edge. Just before we left the street we encountered eight or ten small children noisily playing a sort of hop-scotch game.

8 As we approached they ended their play and courteously watched as one black man and three white men turned to go to the edge of the stream where hundreds of baptisms had been performed through the years.

9 Unknown to us, the children followed us. They had probably accompanied many other groups to this place before and knew well the routine for the rest of the service. They stood quietly while Truitt lowered Mr. Amaichi into the watery grave.

10 But when he raised him up from the water I heard the most beauutiful chorus I have ever heard. Their voices blended perfectly.

11 Those children were singing words which they probably could not have defined, but words which they had heard many times before. They were not children of Christian parents. Their parents probably worshiped the heathen gods so common in Nigeria.

12 But they sang like angels! I stood chilled and transfixed as they sweetly intoned:

O happy day that fixed my choice
On Thee, my Savior and my God!
Happy day, happy day,
When Jesus washed my sins away.
He taught me how to watch and pray,
And live rejoicing every day;
Happy day, happy day,
When Jesus washed my sins away.
[Words by Edward Rimbault; music by Philip Doddridge]

GOD IS REAL

13 My name is Emma Felps. I did not grow up going to church much or knowing much about God.

14 When I was twelve I had polio. It advanced until almost all of my body was paralyzed. I could not move my head, arms or legs. After a time I regained use of my head and arms, but not my legs. I spent my time in bed and had to be carried from place to place.

15 My parents were referred to the Scottish Rite Hospital in Dallas. We had never been to Dallas, as we lived in the northern corner of the Texas Panhandle where my Dad operated a farm and ranch. We seldom went anywhere except when supplies were needed. Our family of nine were special and each one had a special way of adding to my happiness as we waited and hoped for my recovery.

16 Daddy made application for my entrance to the hospital in Dallas and I was accepted and was put on a waiting list. Two months passed until I was admitted. My first stay was for six weeks with exercises, massages. My legs were strapped in bed-splints. I was told to lie flat on my back, so the days were long. The entire ward was under a quarantine so there were no visitors.

17 There was a very special man, however, that brought joy to our hearts when he came to sweep our ward each evening. He had a big smile and filled the air with singing as he worked. Yes, Jasper Brown will always be remembered as a bright light as we struggled there in our illness.

18 After my stay there, I went back many times for check-ups. My precious mother gave me olive oil massages and exercises, and finally I regained use of one leg. The other was fitted with a full leg brace which enabled me to be out of bed and walking a part of each day. I thought the brace was to be temporary, but was crushed when I saw others who had to continue wearing a brace all their lives. I was very troubled.

19 Later when I was fourteen my parents decided it might help to take hot mineral baths at Hot Springs, New Mexico, for the summer. Mother went with me there and the first week we were there, she said a very odd thing. She said we were going to church on Sunday. I wanted to object. We were not in the habit of such, but we children did not respond to mother like that. I dreaded mainly going to a public place because people would see my leg and watch, since I could not walk like others do.

20 Sunday came and mother and I went just like she said. I heard for the first time of how God has a plan for our life, and how He wants us to be saved from our sins, and of forgiveness that had been made possible by Jesus giving His life on the cross. I had never known about these things.

21 All week I couldn't quit thinking about what the preacher said. I was anxious to hear more, even though the leg part was dreaded. The time came for mother to go home after we had heard the preaching for three Sundays. I continued to go each week after mother left and was captivated by all I was learning.

22 It had never occurred to me that people needed to respond somehow to God, but a precious widow named sister Ross took me under her wing, invited me home often and explained to me more about what the preacher had said. The visits to her home were so enjoyable, not only because of what was being taught but also because she had a daughter my age who became a very good friend.

23   The summer ended and I went home disappointed that my polio leg had not improved one bit, but with some encouragement because of what I had learned. In fact, I had a pressing desire to become a Christian. It seemed impossible that this could be as we lived twenty five miles from town and normally only went there when we needed supplies. I knew no preacher there, but soon the Lord provided a way for me to obey Him in baptism. Not only that, I even was able to attend church on a regular basis. My family started going as well.

24   As I learned more about God's Word, He gave me better and more important things to think about than about my leg. He also provided activities in which I could be involved and placed people in my path to encourage and help me at every turn. My family, as always, were very supportive in my new life of being a Christian.

25   After a time, I was again loving life and living it to the fullest. God is so good. Sometimes we never are able to see how a problem can be used for good. Now all of my six younger brothers and sisters have become followers of Jesus Christ and also my Daddy. Mother and my aunt became active Christians, also.

26   We then could not think it likely that we would see the third generation from mine living the Christian life, all traceable to polio taking me to Hot Springs where I heard God's Word.

27   I sometimes think of David's words in Psalms when he wrote, *"It was good for me that I have been afflicted so that I might learn your decrees. The law from your mouth is more precious to me than thousands of pieces of sliver and gold"* (119:71-72).

Cline Paden, writer of verses 1-12, who founded (1962) Sunset International Bible Institute in Lubbock, Texas, said that he hears stories of conversions very often. He chose this one and wrote it for publication in our book of modern day conversions because it has like many others, interesting elements that he says are unique. He explained: "When we interview incoming students we ask them to relate how they came to know the Lord. Miracle is not the word. Conversion that is scriptural is the result of compliance with law. But people use the word *miracle* to explain things that are a bit un-ordinary." Cline Paden, formerly a missionary to Italy after World War II, could write a large volume of conversion experiences from Italy alone, but we are grateful he has chosen this one for this book. A more dedicated man to world missions, a more gifted man in speech, nor a more capable man in gathering about himself a staff of extra-ordinary men of like mind, we have never met. At this writing he is in his 80th year.

Emma Felps, author of verses 13-27, has now retired as an elementary grade school teacher. She is held in the most high esteem by all who know her. Her husband, Wade, "calls her blessed." He served as an elder of the church for many years and now their children are among the most respected and competent teachers of the Bible in the congregation where they worship. The Felps reside at 6124 Abbott Avenue, Fort Worth, TX 76180. Her story was written in September, 1997. Yes, she still wears the leg brace, but her friends love her all the more because she serves so joyfully in spite of it (maybe *because of it!*). I have known her over 50 years from her days as a student at West Texas State in Canyon. Editor.

Cline Paden, Director
Sunset International School
of Evangelism, and former
missisonary to Italy.

Wedding of Emma and Wade Felps

CHAPTER 17

WHY I LEFT THE PRESBYTERIAN CHURCH
By Horace W. Busby

1 It is not the big thing in my life just to leave something. Sometimes people come in among us like they go into various churches because they became angry at somebody. They did not think they were treated right, so they wanted to leave.

2 But that is not so in my case. I did not get mad at anybody. I have just as many friends among the Presbyterians as I ever had. I know I have no enemies. They all conceded that I had a right to do as I pleased about religion, and I saw fit to obey my Lord more fully than I could and be a first-rate Presbyterian.

3 There was a great fight in England a long time ago when Presbyterianism first made its appearance through John Knox and others. It looked like it would conquer the empire, and it almost did.

4 The Presbyterian form of religion was contrary to their wishes, because they taught the rule should be in the hands of several like we have in our government, and like we have in the English government now, but did not then. So the fight began between the Episcopalian idea where a bishop ruled a whole province, and where elders would rule locally.

5 John Calvin is the author we might say, of Presbyterianism. He was an eloquent man and a very great peacher. He went from Geneva over to Scotland and from there started the Presbyterian Church in Scotland. John Knox was his disciple. We are quite familiar with the history about these men. I am familiar with it for several reasons: I was raised on it, I read a lot about it.

Not Ashamed Of The People

6 I am not ashamed of the crowd that I ran with when I was a Presbyterian as far as the people are concerned. Some of the greatest men of our country have been Presbyterian. We have had more presidents of the United States from Presbyterian families than any others.

Cannot Follow Christ And Creeds

7 The church of the Lord Jesus Christ is something that He founded on earth; and where Christ's teaching goes contrary to any human theory, if we want to love the Lord and be blessed by Him we have got to say good-bye to every earthly tie and follow where we believe Jesus is leading.

8 Jesus says, *"Unless you take up your cross daily and follow me, you cannot be my disciple"* (Matt. 16:24). Nearly all the creeds of the great reformers carried that principle very strongly in them: that we take the Bible as our rule of faith and practice. That is, among Protestant people. John Calvin did that; John Knox did that, as also did John Wesley and Martin Luther.

9 They all took the position that the Bible is a sufficient rule and the people all started for the same position where we stand today. But as time went on they grew to a great group of people; they had to form a creed to hold what they had together, they thought. That is how creeds were formed: each man wanting to hold his group together. There has got to be some leading

principle put into a written document before anybody knows what his faction is.

10 John Calvin gave the movement life and power. For good life and dignified living, he headed all the rest of the reformers. He was very strict on moral teaching; so much so that he became a burden to some people who wanted to mix up worldliness and their religion. We call them Puritans in our country.

Studies The Bible

11 I began to study my Bible early in life. My mother taught me the Scriptures before I could read. I could quote many passages from memory. In fact, many of the passages that I can quote easily today I learned before I could read. My mother taught me. She knew a great deal about the Bible. That was not foreign to Presbyterians either. They were great Bible students. Most of the works in your library as Christian men and gospel preachers were authored by Presbyterian scholars.

12 The only question that I bring up is, "Do they know how to rightly divide the scriptures; do they give the proper division of the Old Testament from the New?" That is where I became dissatisfied with my part of it.

The Name

13 I began to read and study my Bible. After I was grown I continued to study it, and to study it hard. I studied to midnight and my father who was then an elder in the Presbyterian Church would often come to my room and want me to go to bed. He said,

14 "You will go crazy reading the Bible so much. You don't need to read it so much." I became dissatisfied with a good many things. One was the name: "Why do I have to tell people that I am a Presbyterian, when I read my Bible and became a follower of Christ? Why do that?" That was the question, and I could not answer it by the Bible.

Could Not Find Infant Baptism

15 Another question that bothered me was: We believed and taught infant baptism. I began to read and search the Bible for it, but could not find anything about it.

16 I wanted to be able to answer everybody that asked me why we did so and so. But I could not find it in the Bible, even though I tried hard.

17 I went to Dallas and called on the pastor of the largest Presbyterian Church in the state. When I asked him, he just referred me to the library to read some books.

18 He did not answer my question. That threw me into greater dissatisfaction.

19 One of the greatest men among them referred me to some books of men instead of to the Bible--the book that I was anxious to learn. So I went back home and studied some more.

Sprinkle Or Pour For Baptism?

20 I had been sprinkled when I was a child. I was old enough to remember what they did. The preacher said, "Horace, arise and be baptized."

21 And so I stood up, he dipped his finger in a glass of water and placed it on my face. He said the same ceremony that I have said hundreds of times in baptizing people now. I could not find any proof for sprinkling and it made me very dissatisfied that I had to tell people that I had been sprinkled or had water poured on my face for baptism.

22 However, they did not *force* sprinkling or pouring on us. The first immersion I ever saw was performed by a Presbyterian preacher in Red Oak Creek. They made a confession of faith in Christ; they did not say, "We believe that God for Christ's sake has pardoned our sins," like some people do today. The people could see that it was done in a very fine way.

23 They were not dogmatic about sprinkling and pouring, but their doctrine was that you had a choice. They believed that baptism could be done by *pouring or sprinkling* water on the individual OR by *immersing* the whole body. And so, I began to study the question; perhaps it bothered me more than any other one thing.

About The Purpose Of Baptism

24 Another question that came into that particular study was, "What was I baptised for?" The answer they wanted me to give was: to get into the *visible* church on earth, Before, when you believed on the Lord, you then entered into the *spiritual or invisible* church, but now baptism puts you into the *visible* church.

25 When I read in my New Testament that we are "baptized into Christ" (Romans 6:3 and Galatians 3:27), I could not fix that thing and my conscience was not at ease. That question could not be answered by staying where I was and letting the Presbyterians answer for me.

26 In studying the question of what baptism is for, I noticed it was *"for the remission of sins"* in Acts 2:38. And Ananias said in Acts 22:16, "Arise and be baptized and wash away thy sins." The preacher had told me to arise and be baptized, but he did not say to me what Ananias said to Paul. I was disturbed.

27 Then I read Paul's explanation of his baptism when he said, "As many of us as were baptized into Christ, have put on Christ" (Galatians 3:27). His baptism was *into Christ*; mine was *not*. Paul also said, "We are buried with him by baptism into death and raised to walk a new life" (Romans 6:4). I thought I had the new life *before* baptism, and then as a child of God I was obeying a simple command that placed me into the *visible church here on earth*.

28 Of course I was dissatisfied. Reading my Bible made me so. I was not dissatisfied with the group I was running with. They were my kin people. They were the ones I went to school with and loved very dearly. It was really a hard fight to have to leave that group religiously over nothing but doctrinal differences, but I did.

Studies With Elderly Woman

29 I went to Oklahoma and while there I heard Henry Warlick preach a sermon. It was very much along the line that I had been studying. I was disturbed. It was out in a community where there was no church, but somebody had invited him to come there and make a talk. I listened to it and I saw that he had something that I had been craving.

30 Back home, I went out to an uncle's home whose wife was a very fine Bible student and I said, "Aunt Lizzie, I want to study the Bible, just study it. My mind craves to know more of the Book and you are an able teacher."

31 She said, "Horace, I'll let the

girls take care of the house, and we will just study." So from breakfast at six o'clock until midnight every night for ten days we just sat there and studied the Bible on these questions that were hard for me to grasp. She did not say a word about my religion, nor about the people with whom I associated, nor the church I was a member of. She just showed me in the Book what the New Testament church was.

32 That was all I cared about. I knew about the other. There was no need to waste time by telling about those other things that were wrong.

33 My uncle was not much of a Bible scholar, but was a Christian doing the best that he could. It was something like Priscilla and Aquila who taught Apollos the way of the Lord more perfectly. Priscilla was mentioned first which shows that she did the teaching while Aquila sat there like uncle did and listened. That straightened Apollos out (Acts 18:26), and that straightened me out.

34 My uncle said, "Horace, if you ever decide that you would like to be baptized and become a New Testament Christian, I'll get a preacher to do the baptizing."

35 I said, "I am ready now, Uncle Tom." So he got up early the next morning and hitched two great big grey horses to an old-fashioned Spaulding hack and drove twenty-two miles to Marie, and called for Henry E. Warlick. On Sunday the house was full and Henry preached. But my mind was made up before I heard his sermon and so I started down the aisle to make my confession.

36 I told them I wanted to be baptized into Christ for the remission of my sins; that I did not want to be anything but just a Christian nor to have any church affiliation except the New Testament church, which is called the church of Christ, the church of God or the church of the Lord (Rom 16:16; I Tim 3:15; Acts 20:28).

37 My wife went with me, and my uncle's daughter-in-law went with us, three of us. We were baptized that afternoon in Brother Weston's tank.

Begins Preaching

38 At the end of four years I was preaching. I baptized my father; my mother came into the church and my brothers and sisters heard me and my sisters were baptized.

39 We want everybody to go to heaven. We are not trying to send anybody to hell. We want everybody to be right. We cannot afford to compromise the truth even with father or mother or ourselves, because it will not do us any good. If I wanted to compromise any truth at all, I would have remained with the Presbyterians because that is as fine a body of Protestant people as can be found.

40 But I cannot do that. I want to go to heaven, but I know I cannot go to heaven weakening on the truth of the Almighty God, and preaching it some other way than is found in the New Testament.

41 I have sat down with preachers of that group and have talked about these things. I said, "Now, here, I'm not mad at you. I am not a denominationalist. I am nothing of the kind. I believe this Book, do you?"

42 "Well," one of them said, "Yes I do believe this Book." I

said, "Well, now this is what this Book says." He said, "I admit that. I think you are all right and I think you will go to heaven, but I believe I can go to heaven, too."

43 That is about as far as some of them would ever go. Just close the Book, their mouth and their heart and everything else to the truth...when I was doing the greatest thing I could possibly do for their soul. They have always treated me very fine, but they would not pay any attention when I tried to teach them God's ways.

44 The gospel came from heaven (I Peter 1:2), not through a conference of men, not through a presbytery made up of elders and preachers, and a few presbyteries making a synod that could vote and make a law equal to the pope and his cardinals.

45 I saw this thing standing out clearly in my Bible which you can read easily. The little boys can read it. It is not hard to read God's word. David says in Psalm 19, *"The law of the Lord is perfect, converting the soul."* What men make is not God's law (Matthew 15:9).

This chapter has been taken from a chapter in the book, **Why I Left**, published in 1959 by Guy V. Caskey and Thomas L. Campbell, Ft. Worth, Texas (pp 30-59). Horace Busby was born in Lawrenceburg, Tennessee. He moved to Texas when he was seven. He preached at the Vickery Boulevard church of Christ in Fort Worth for five years, his only local preaching work. The invitations became so numerous for him to preach in gospel meetings in other places that he gave up local work so he could devote full time to evangelistic meetings. He never held less than 25 in a year, and kept this up for over 30 years. An average of 28 were baptized in each of his 450 series of meetings. Over 17,000 souls obeyed the gospel under his preaching, among whom were many who became leading preachers and educators. Dr. Larry Calvin's mother was baptized by him, and many years later Larry wrote his Master's dissertation at Abilene Christian University on Horace Busby as a gospel preacher.

Horace W. Busby

CHAPTER 18

DOES GOD EXIST?

1 I accepted the traditions of my childhood, as most people do. But unfortunately, my belief system was one of **atheism**. My parents said things like, "Do you really believe there's an *Old Man* up in the sky zapping things into existence here upon the earth? Do you really believe that the church makes any difference? How can anyone believe all that *mumbo jumbo* that preachers preach?"

2 By the time I was 8 years old, I had accepted the notion that only foolish, ignorant, uneducated people believe in God. As I moved into adolescence, I became increasingly active in atheism. As my science education accelerated, I became more and more committed to the idea that science and technology held the keys to solving man's problems. By the time I was 16, I was a hard-core, aggressive atheist, attacking anything that smacked of religion.

3 Late in my high school career, I had the fortune to take a physics class under a teacher named Mr. Gross whom I had grown to respect from my contact with him in the 8th grade. This class had laboratory periods when a student could talk to the teacher and get to know him. My caustic remarks about God and the Bible were always met with a warm smile by Mr. Gross, but never a response.

4 One day after an especially biting remark from me about the "stupidity of religion and the Bible," he asked me if I had ever studied the scientific accuracy of the Bible. I had never even read the Bible, much less studied it, so I had to answer negatively.

5 He said, "You know, John, I had a terrible time trying to decide whether to become a teacher or a preacher. I finally decided that God speaks as well in His creation as He does in the Bible and the two agree exactly. I suggest that you study both. Start with Genesis..."

6 I was shocked to learn that this man whom I respected as a scientist would be a believer in God, much less that he had considered becoming a minister. I was even more appalled that he would suggest that Genesis 1 and science would agree. All my life I had heard that the biblical account was a lot of foolishness and myth that no logical person could accept. If Genesis were a myth, it could not be scientifically accurate.

7 In addition to this stimulus from Mr. Gross, I had a young lady friend who was encouraging me to read the Bible. She was a Christian who attended the services of the church regularly. We had been dating two years or so and I suspected that I was in love with her. She was a moral giant, uncompromising in her beliefs and confident about her faith.

8 When arguments came up, she always reverted to the Bible as the basis of her decisions. I decided that if I could prove the Bible wrong, I could win a lot of arguments with her as well as prove to myself that Mr. Gross was wrong. So, I decided to study the first chapter of Genesis in detail.

9 I was sure that with the knowledge of geology and evolution that I had gained by that time, I could easily destroy any credibility the Bible might have. My parents had told me that the

Genesis record gave many teachings which modern science had proven to be false. I was so sure about the ease with which I could destroy anyone's belief in the integrity of the Genesis record that I decided to take exhaustive notes and write a book which I could title *All The Stupidity Of The Bible.* Now I could add the making of money to all the motivations I had to prove the Bible wrong.

10 Armed with this truck load of prejudice, dictionaries and a dozen or so books on geology and evolution, I began my personal annihilation of the Genesis account of creation. Having never attended a Bible class and not having heard a sermon would turn out to be an advantage for me, for I had no preconceived ideas about what the Genesis record taught.

11 My first surprise came in the very first verse of Genesis. When I read, "In the beginning God created the heaven and the earth," I realized that this first verse dealt with a subject to which evolution could not address itself--creation. As an atheist, it had never occurred to me that evolution *assumed everything.* Genesis 1:1 states that matter exists and it exists in a way that could produce and sustain life. Evolution does not deal with creation. It only deals with how things may have changed once they were already created.

12 I dislike the term *creation science* when that term is applied to rebuttals of theories of evolution. The creation of the cosmos "out of nothing" is creation. Hypothetical models of how living things may have changed from one from to another is *not* creation!

13 My second surprise in Genesis 1:1 was that it was not dated. I had always been told that the biblical record taught that the earth was created in the year 4004 B.C. To maintain such a position, every verse in the Genesis record had to be dated. This first verse was not dated. It also was not stated as a summary verse, but as an historical event. The verse does not say that the next 28 verses are explaining what the first verse says. "In the beginning God created..." is an event. Something took place. It is not an introduction to duplicate statements in later verses.

14 As I continued reading through the early part of Genesis 1, I read about other conditions on the earth which I knew were essential to the development of life. The atmosphere, water, land and all the other conditions needed for life were described. I became uneasy as I saw this careful and accurate description, but was still confident that the evolution of life would ultimately expose the fallacious nature of the Bible's history.

15 At verses 10 and 11, I came in contact with the first description of life on the earth. In my studies in science, I had learned that the first living thing on the earth was a plant. It was logical that an organism which could turn sunlight into food was necessary for the origination of life.

16 In addition to this logic, I had seen plant fossils and had studied the sequence that plants follow in populating a barren area whether it be on land or in the sea. I know that simple plants like algae or lichen are followed by gymnosperms (ferns and conifers) which are followed by angiosperms (seed plants like dogwood or apple trees). Imagine my surprise when

I found Genesis giving exactly the same sequence!

17 "God said, Let the earth bring forth grass..." The Hebrew word *deshe* is used here, indicating moss or algae or lichen. The word *catshir* is not used, which is the kind of grass on which one uses a lawnmower. The second kind of plant was "the herb" from the Hebrew word *eseb.* This word is used when referring to the kind of plants science calls "gymnosperms." The most recent kind of plant, according to Genesis, was the flowering "tree yielding fruit."

18 What better description could be given of the succession I knew to be a modern concept of science? How could the ancient writers of Genesis have accurately described the logical sequence in which plants were created?

19 In verse 20, I was to receive more surprises. The biblical record identifies the first animal to appear upon the earth. The statement was clear and for the first time, I thought I had something in the Bible I could prove to be wrong. "And God said, Let the waters bring forth abundantly the moving creature that hath life..." Clearly the indication was that the first animals upon the earth were water creatures. That point could not be argued.

20 The trilobite and other marine fossils have strongly testified that animal life began in the sea. The Genesis account indicated that many forms of sea life came into existence at the same time. In my biology classes, I had been taught that life began as simple animals and gradually evolved to more complex animals. I had drawn models of how the sponges might have evolved into corals and how the various mollusks might have led to higher forms of life.

21 I had been told that backboned (*vertebrate*) animals were very recent additions to the earth's life forms compared to the trilobite and its friends.

22 I was elated at this obvious conflict between the biblical record and the facts and I rushed to the geology library to get pictures to document the facts. As I studied the listings of fossils and their ages and classifications, I found Cambrian fossils (the geologic period at the beginning of life on earth) which were extremely advanced. The graptolite was a fossil which was very abundant in the fossil record of the Cambrian period; but the graptolite was classified as a vertebrate.

23 The acorn worm and lancelot were other Cambrian fossils which were vertebrates. In no way did the fossil record verify the transitions that I had always had presented to me. I returned to Genesis 1:20 and received another blow to my confidence in evolutionary theory.

24 One of the models used in evolution is the model of the evolution of the bird. The theory has usually been that the first birds were walking birds like an ostrich. The idea is that the breast bone, wing muscles, feathers and hollow bones would have to develop gradually over long periods of time. The idea then was that flight evolved. Good flyers would be the more recent birds and the first birds would have been non-flyers or poor flyers.

25 In Genesis 1:20-21 we are told that the "winged fowl" became

abundant "in the open firmament of heaven." Once again, I was confident that this biblical assertion that the first birds were flying birds could be proven to be wrong. And once again, a visit to the geological library proved the Bible to be right. Today the earliest known bird is called "protoavis." It is a bird that could fly beautifully. All the equipment needed for flight is there, in advanced form. The archaeopteryx, a fossil of more recent age, is also capable of flight and possesses feathers and bone structures designed to use in the air.

26   As I continued to read Genesis, I found the mammals were the next living things to come into existence on the earth. The most recent thing to appear on the earth, according to Genesis, was man. Once again I could offer no criticism. The fossil record supports this sequence of life beautifully. I could not find a single statement in the Genesis account that I could prove to be in error.

27   There were many things the Bible did *not* explain, but everything it did say was correct. Amoebas, viruses, platypuses, echidnas, walking and swimming birds and a myriad of other life forms were not included in the account, but what was described was correct. Many questions about "time" remained unanswered because they were not germane to the Bible's message that God created all things.

28   All this destruction of my prejudices about the Bible led me next to question further what I had been told about the theory of evolution. It was obvious that *change* was a working agent in

creation and that this type of change could in a sense be called "evolution." New breeds of dogs, cattle, roses, cats, etc., are not alien to the Bible. Jacob used this kind of change in manipulating Laban's cattle. The fact that all races of men on the earth are descendants of Eve (whose name means "the mother of all living") further demonstrates that evolution (minor change) takes place.

29   The question, then is whether evolution can explain the existence of 20th century man in terms of "natural chance modifications of an original amoeba." My faith in evolution had been shaken by the biblical confrontations; so now I wanted real proof that the evolution of man from an original amoeba was true. By this time, I was in college. My training in science was advancing rapidly.

30 During my sophomore year at Indiana University, I enrolled in a geology course taught by a well-known atheist. He began the class by holding up a Bible and stating, "I'm going to show you that this (the Bible) is a bunch of garbage." This was my golden opportunity to get the proof of evolution that I desired and so I tore into the text and the course with enthusiasm and anticipation.

31   My joy in anticipating this newly-found hope of information was short-lived. As we studied the fossil record, we were given sheets of paper showing evolutionary sequences from one form of life to another. When we studied the evolution of mammals from the reptiles, we were shown a fossil which was obvious to me to be an alligator skeleton. Written on the specimen was the term, "therapsid-

-mammal-like reptile." For nearly an hour, I studied the fossil, unable to find anything in it that was mammalian in nature.

32 The therapsid is supposed to be "the best of the transition fossils" between major groups of living things. I finally went to the professor and told him that I could find nothing mammalian about the fossil. He pointed to a small bone in the inner ear and another small bone in the lower jaw and said, "These two bones are mammal-like." As I looked at the specimen next to mine, I saw that the bones were somewhat different from those in my specimen. When I asked about this difference, I was told that they were just variations between individuals.

33 It was obvious to me that some choosing was being done here about which variations would be considered and which should be ignored. "Is this really the best transition fossil we can see?" I asked, referring to the therapsid. I was assured that it was.

34 In the class we learned other things that I could not fit in with evolution. We learned that evolution is dependent upon the assumption that the earth has always functioned in a consistent way--that there have been no global catastrophes like the flood, which could have stopped evolution and made gradualism impossible. Even at that time, I had seen pictures of quickly frozen elephants and had seen huge meteor craters, both of which indicate that uniformitarianism in geology was a bad *assumption*.

35 In the 1980's there have been discoveries of asteroid material in stratified layers marking the mass extinctions of such animals as the dinosaurs. These discoveries have further supported catastrophism as an agent of change in the earth's history. It was becoming obvious to me that my faith in evolution as the explanation of how everything came to be was based on some bad assumptions.

36 My further study of Genesis and my experiences of life convinced me on one more biblical truth which ultimately led me to become a Christian. That was the realization that man is not just an animal, as evolution would have us to believe, but he was rather a spiritual being, uniquely and specially created in the image of God!

37 When the Bible writer tells us that we are created in God's image, it should be obvious that the Bible is not referring to our physical bodies. God is not a man, but a spirit (John 4:24). If we are all in God's image, we must all be alike, in some real sense. Obviously we are not alike physically, so it must be our spiritual nature that the Bible is referring to. Even as an atheist, when I looked at a man's creative ability in art and music, his ability to experience such emotions as guilt and sympathy and compassion, and man's desire and ability to worship, it was obvious that man was not just a "naked ape." There had to be more to man's existence than what I had experienced and learned as an atheist.

38 When I discussed these characteristics with my anthropologist friends, I found them trying to explain them in terms of intelligence or environment. In my studies in psychology, I had seen that putting

intelligent apes in human homes would not make them human. I also had seen severely retarded humans who could do all of these things.

39 To try to explain all of man's unique characteristics in terms of intelligence or environment is to ignore mountains of scientific and educational data that show that man is a special and a spiritual being. Questions of morality and love cannot be answered in the framework of reducing man to a purely physical being.

40 I became a Christian because of the evidence available to support belief. My journey arrived at faith, which although it reaches beyond a certainty, is not near the "leap of faith" which the atheistic evolutionist has to take. My experience since my conversion to Jesus Christ has brought me to see that we live in a world where many want to believe, but the saturation of our world with bad theology and bad science has made belief difficult for many.

41 Let us speak to this frustrated world with both clarity and love, to come to God the Creator by studying both His Word and His creation.

This testimony is used by permission of the author, John N. Clayton, reprinted from *Evolution and Faith,* Abilene Christian University Press, Abilene, TX, 1988. The book is now out of print, but the article (an appendix to the eleven chapters) was reprinted in the journal, **Does God Exist**, July-August, 1998, published by Donmoyer Avenue Church of Christ, South Bend, Indiana. Clayton wrote a more extensive book, **Why I Left**

Atheism, in 1971, and both are available through the Donmoyer church. John Clayton was born Febrruary 22, 1938. He is married to Phyllis and has three children. He has several university degrees in Physics, Mathematics, Chemistry, Geology, Earth Science and Psychometry and has been an instructor in these sciences in Indiana schools since 1959. His honors in the education and science fields are too numerous to mention here. He has also served as a preacher and and an elder at various times. He gives lectureships throughout the United States and several other countries, with an average of 15 to 20 apearances at colleges and universities per year in addition to an average of 20 per year in congregations of churches of Christ. He has developed special programs in the area of Christian Evidences including video tapes, audio tapes, correspondence courses, books, TV programs, etc. He may be contacted at 1555 Echo Valley Dr, Niles, MI 49120. 616-687-9426. Fx: 616-687-9431. E-mail: jncdge@aol.com.

God Made The World

CHAPTER 19

HE WAS TAUGHT
THE WAY
MORE PERFECTLY

1   Renato Natad, a young Pentecostal leader age twenty who resides in Esperanza, Philippines, near where a congregation of the Lord's church was established two years earlier through a radio program, was converted to the truth.   He was baptized at Lumbocan by Agapio Catamora on August 20, 1998, after consistently listening every Sunday morning to the radio program.

2 He also had the opportunity to attend a public debate in Butuan City in June. "Dodong," as he is fondly called by his parents and friends, was a member of the Assembly of God denomination, having been associated with them since he was only 12 years of age. His faithfulness with that sect led him to be recognized as a youth leader.

3   When this evangelist happened to meet him in the home of a Christian a year ago, he was taught *the way of the Lord more perfectly, knowing only the doctrine* of the Pentecostals. He continued attending the services at McArthur to observe how the members of the Lord's church worship God "in spirit and in truth," as Jesus had instructed in John 4:24.

4 Before his leaving that group, four major isues were tackled by this evangelist to teach this young man. They were: (1) speaking in tongues, (2) the duration and purpose of miracles, (3) tithing from the Mosaical dispensation, and (4) the use of mechanical instruments of music in Christian's worship. Other matters were also studied, but these were of primary concern.

5   When leaders of his denomination detected that Nenato was in company with those other than their own group and was attending our worship services at McArthur (where my two sons are ministers, Alrey and Oliver Catamora), they dispatched one of their preachers to try to win back the feelings of this young man.

6 On one occasion, while this evangelist was at McArthur, one of their ministers confronted this evangelist with a semi-formal discussion to tackle the issue of using instrumental music in worship. He tried to affirm that such is authorized to be used in the Christian age.

7 During the interrogation time, this evangelist asked his opponent: "You tried to define that the Greek word *psallo* means to "sing and use mechanical instruments in music, am I right?" With his positive answer, I made the follow-up question: "When you gather together to worship God, are all members of the Assembly of God singing and at the same time is each one playing on a mechanical instrument in music?"

8   When he answered in the negative, I quoted I Corinthians 14:26 where Paul states, "Whenever you come together, each of you has a psalm..." If the Greek word *psallo* includes mechanical instrument in music, it follows that each member has a mechanical instrument every time they meet together. But this case is not true in your group and the truth of the matter is that the instrument to be used was "the heart," Ephesians 5:19, like *plucking the heartstrings* in a figure of speech.

9   In the presence of many visitors, guests and members of the church of Christ, the Pentecostal preacher was unable to prove

beyond reasonable doubt that mechanical instruments in music are authorized in the New Testament to be used during worship to the Lord. It was concluded he was heeding to a wrong direction that does "not abide with the teaching" of the Lord (2 Jonn 8-9).

10 Renato Natad was present at the time of the discussion. He was enlightened to the truth, as were some others. After several more discussions and by the help of the Lord, he decided to leave this modern denomination of men, the Pentecostals; hence his baptism into Christ when he was added by the Lord to the church of Christ (Acts 2:38-47).

11 He expressed to help in preaching the gospel by the distribution of tracts, follow-up to our radio listeners, teaching the truth through the Jule Miller films and videos and the recruitments for more enrollees with our World Bible School (WBS).

12 It is hoped and prayed that he can lead others into the fold where our Lord is the Good Shepherd, where they can have hope and enjoy eternal life in Christ Jesus and the everlasting happiness in heaven.

13 To God be the glory forever and ever! Amen.

Renato Natad and Agapio Catamora

Baptism In The Ocean At Lumbocan

Agapio Catamora submitted this story, written by him in September, 1998. Agapio is an evangelist and radio minister who resides in Butuan City, Philippines 8600. He preaches at the Lumbocan Church of Christ, address P. O. Box 60. He enjoys a fine reputation as a faithful minister and his reports can frequently be read in *World Radio News*, *The World Evangelist* and the *Christian Chronicle*.

CHAPTER 20

CESAR BOWS TO
THE KING OF KINGS

1 It happened Tuesday. A call came from a man who was telling about having attended what he said was *a hundred churches, trying to find the church like the New Testament church.* He was distressed because he said he checked the yellow pages in the phone book and found over 300 different kinds of denominations.

2 After visiting many he saw they all had big bands and other traditions and practices not in the Bible. He was raised Catholic, but saw when he started reading his Bible that this was not the same at all. Somehow (and he did not say how) he came across a book called **TRADITIONS OF MEN VS. THE WORD OF GOD** in which the history is given of about twenty prominent denominations, plus a comparison of their traditions alongside what the Bible says on the same subjects.

3 He said he read not only all of it, but every passage of scripture in it. He was praising this "really outstanding book" that convinced him there is only one church, and that any other church established later than AD 33, at any place other than Jerusalem and by any man other than Jesus Christ "just has to be false!"

4 This man is Cesar Eguren, age 56, living in central Texas. He said his children are all grown now, and that he is at an age he is deeply concerned about his eternal destiny and where he will spend eternity.

5 "Can you tell me if there is a New Testament church anywhere in this area? I am seeking and God promised that if I seek I will find.

I went to one that was called *New Testament Christian Church* and had my hopes all up until I went there and found more traditions of men and not much Word of God. Also, I used to take lessons from the Jehovah's Witnesses, but by reading this book I had to give them up as just another false way governed by a council of men in New York."

6 "Just one more question, please," he continued. "When I was a baby I just had a little water sprinkled on me, and I know that is not Bible baptism. With all these churches that are around me not matching up to the Bible, who can I get to baptize me the right way and be assured that it will not be invalid?"

7 When he was told that the Bible does not say our immersion depends on the faithfulness of the one who does the baptizing, he was relieved. It is usually the one who does the teaching that does the baptizing, and that could be any other Christian (or two non-Christians who learned from reading their Bibles and not from any man, they could baptize each other if they were just starting a new church after the pattern of the Bible in their community).

8 He was also troubled about prayer, afraid that since he has not been baptized according to the Word, that he has never been forgiven of his sins and that he does not even have the Holy Spirit in his life (referring to Acts 2:38). "I am convinced now that my prayers *just go up in the air* since I don't have the Holy Spirit in my life and am not in the family where I can call on God as my Father. I am a sinful and weak man and need forgiveness every day."

9 When told about this phone call, Joe Dodd said: "Let's get in the car and go and baptize that man right away!" We were ready to do this, but felt that since there are nearly 3,000 churches of Christ in Texas, that surely one could not be far from him. By the grace of God there is a fine preacher named Tom Allen that assured me he would give immediate and compassionate help to Cesar who only lives a short distance from him.

10   Tom not only preaches regularly, but also teaches Bible in a local Junior College as a Professor in the Department of Philosophy.   He said right now there is a Catholic student who comes to him after classes and asks serious questions about his soul, who now has started coming to church assemblies where he can learn more.

11 Praise God that Romans 8:28 is still true, that *all things are still working together for good to those who love God and who are being called by the gospel according to His purpose!*

12   Unfortunately millions are sad stories of those who wander aimlessly through life and never come to a knowledge of the only truth that can save from the everlasting fires of hell.

13   Cesar soon attended a few worship services where Tom Allen preaches and on January 18th he told Tom after a service that he wanted to be *'dipped into Christ."* The people that lingered came back in and witnessed his new birth into Christ which took place immediately.

14 He now continues regularly *in the apostles' doctrine, in fellowship, in the breaking of bread and in prayer,* Acts 21:42.   His son is the one who gave his father the book. Yes, the *written word is powerful in the heart of an honest man!* That is why God deposited

His word in a book and promised it would never pass away.

15   We will have to say with Paul Harvey, "Tune in next time for the rest of the story."   Our prayer is that it will be just as exciting as the first part.   Every man's life is like a story that is told, and some are happy ones like this.   Unfortunately millions are sad stories of those who wander aimlessly through life and never come to a knowledge of the only truth that can save from the everlasting fires of hell.

16 Let us pray that His grace will be sufficient to meet all of Cesar's needs and our needs. Joshua 1:9 is helpful at times like these: *"Be strong and courageous. Do not be terrified; do not be discouraged, for the Lord your God will be with you wherever you go."*

17   Praise God that Cesar has confessed his faith in Jesus of Nazareth, the King of kings and Lord of Lords!   We pray that Cesar and all of us will let the Word of God have plenty room in our hearts (Colossians 3:16), and that he will be faithful until death (Revelation 2:10).

18   When Paul asked that the books and parchments be brought to him in prison in Rome, perhaps he was asking for some he used in personal evangelism that he wanted on hand to give to his friends, some books that contrasted the *Word of God from the traditions of men!*

19 Since it is His strength that is working in us, we never brag but give glory to God in the church and in Christ Jesus, both now and evermore (cf. Ephesians 3:20-21)). One man plants, another waters, but God gives the increase.

20   May the Lord bless you always, and give you peace.

Written by Alvin Jennings, author of **Traditions of Men Vs. The Word of God**. It has been translated into several languages and has gone through many printings in English. Hundreds of thousands are in print. Reports have come from several continents similar to the story told here about Cesar who went on his way rejoicing and we saw him no more (see Acts 8:39).

Cesar Egurin

CHAPTER 21

FORTUNE FOUND
IN FAMILY
By Alvin Jennings

1 My story began with my grandmother back in 1912, seventeen years before I was born. Really it began at the cross, or even before the foundation of the world when God in love planned for the world to be saved from sin through the blood of His Son.

2 I feel I must begin with the part about my grandmother, Pearl Jennings. She was a godly person, always talking about the Lord as I reflect on those first visits to her house. I can remember her big radio playing the weekly program from the church of Christ and she never missed going to church where she lived at Tulia, Texas.

3 In her later years she talked more about arthritis, doctors and Campho-Phenique. It was about then that I asked her if she would answer some questions for me about her life and her conversion, because I wanted to preserve the story and she was getting "old and wore out," as she put it. When I asked her questions, I also recorded it on a cassette and then wrote it down in a little booklet that I called *Mother*. 4 She was 85 years old then (1967); she went to her eternal reward just five years later. So this story has become a treasure not only to me, but to many among our family and friends who have read it after it was printed.

5 When the booklet was printed it had a picture of her with four of her children, the oldest being my father, Herschel. Fortunately, a photograph was taken of her baptism in Tule Creek with several people standing in the water and horses and buggies on the bank and a crowd of people watching.

6 That photo was in the first edition of the booklet, but it got lost somehow--only one of the printed copies still exists. My grandmother, Pearl, knew the names of each of the baptismal candidates with her in the water that day, and of course told me the name of the preacher, too. He was A. D. Dyer.

7 She said she always loved the Bible even when she was a little girl. She went to Sunday School regularly even though she said her folks never went. She drove horseback nearly every Sunday. It was a Presbyterian church but met at the Methodist church because it was the only church house in town...one met one Sunday and the other the next.   8 When she was 19 a Baptist meeting was conducted so she went ... said the preacher was "a pretty good one." After that, she said she never went to a dance or anything like that because she "wanted to do what was right." Although they wanted her to be baptized and join the church, she declined because she thought she didn't know enough about the Bible.

9 Also she said she didn't think there was but one church right and she didn't know which one that was. An old Presbyterian friend told her, "It don't make no difference what church you join just so you join some church to show God whose side you're on!"

10 She thought, "If that was all there was to it, well, I wouldn't mind to go to and join some church but I told him, 'I want to be baptized right; I want to be immersed.'" He said he would immerse her if that's what she wanted, but he said the Bible didn't say anything about immersing

anybody.

11 She joined the Presbyterian church, but was not baptized. When she married, her husband, Otto, and his mother were Baptists, so she would go to his church one Sunday and to the Presbyterian the next.

First Hears of The Church

12 One day she was riding a train coming home from school in Decatur and she heard two women talking. One asked the other what church she was a member of and she replied, "I am a member of the church of Christ." My grandmother said to me, "That just thrilled me all over because it sounded correct and might just be the church I'm looking for."

13 She never heard of one like that being around her home town. But one day not long after that she heard there was going to be a meeting at the court house held by some people they called *Campbellites*. She went to hear them, too, since she wanted to learn all she could about the Bible. Otto went the first night and came home saying, "That man knows the Bible from cover to cover." She said, "Then that is the man I want to hear preach!" And she did the next night.

14 The preacher told everybody to bring a pencil and paper and check their Bibles at home. He also preached about the name of the church because she had told him she wanted to know why they called it a "Campbellite" church instead of the church of Christ. Brother Dyer even offered to come to her home to answer questions, so she invited a lot of her neighbors to write down their questions and come and ask him at her home. Her house was full to hear his answers the next day.

15 She was soon baptized in the creek, and Otto said, "Pearl, are you going to join every church that comes to town?" She told him, "Yes, as long as it is closer to the Bible." But she never changed again. She felt she had found *the pearl of great price.*

16 All of her six children became Christians except one, and he often promised her he would obey the gospel and become a preacher, but he never did. Most of her grandchildren and great-grandchildren and great great grandchildren have also followed her faith. I suppose the number would be well over a hundred now, maybe two hundred or more.

"The Faith that Was First in Grandmother and then in Mother"

17 Now you can understand how important my grandmother's faith and my parents' faith was in my own story about beginning to follow Christ. My father obeyed the gospel shortly after his mother did. When he later went to college he met Thelma, a country girl from Claude, whom he taught the gospel.

18 No doubt he shared some things about his mother's experience, too, in her search for the true way. Thelma respected the Bible, but like most farm people around her, she had not gone to church much. She was baptized after she married, in fact during the time she was pregnant with me inside her. I suppose it could be said that was quite an early infant baptism!

19 I did not learn from dad that he had been an outstanding college athlete, but later saw some old newspaper clippings that made me swell with pride that he had been such a football star...and that he had been so modest as to have never mentioned this to me.

20 My mother was special at the college also, but in a different way. Her interests were in the *field of literature,* not in *the field of football.* Even now at age 90 she rehearses by heart long poems of profound meaning that she had composed or memorized from other authors as a young lady...seventy years ago!

21 When dad finished school at West Texas there in Canyon where we lived, he got a Masters Degree and began teaching in the college. The family regularly attended the church every Sunday and Wednesday. If there was ever any discussion about whether to go to church or not on Sunday or Wedneday, I never heard it.

22 I grew up assuming that decision was made a long time ago, so did not have to be made again and again three times a week. In time, dad became an elder and since he was around the college a lot, he initiated inquiries into the idea of getting a Bible Chair started there.

23 I remember their first converted residence, a white frame house right next door to the fine brick Methodist Bible Chair. The first Bible Chair director was C. L. Kay. This project was blessed with growing interest, the classes grew and the building was enlarged and with the help of area churches of Christ, the building was bought from the Methodists to accomodate the needs.

24 Mother always supported dad in his leadership of the church and they often had groups to come to our house for dinner. I remember how we felt honored that occasionally our preacher would drop in for a visit. Some of the preachers I remember when growing up were Lyle Bonner, Joe Banks, Earl Craig, Virgil Jackson and Joe Watson.

Putting On Christ At Age Eleven

25 We always had a *"Gospel Meeting"* once or twice a year, when a visiting evangelist would come and preach every night for a week or two. One of these visiting evangelists was a notable young man, James D. Willeford, later to become the first speaker for the nationwide Herald of Truth (radio and television).

26 Dad liked him, because he seemed to appreciate it when corrections were offered on his use of English. Brother Willeford thanked him for the help in improving his preaching (dad was quite generous with such corrections but not all the preachers appreciated it--and by the way, the others were never asked to speak on nationwide radio or TV, either!).

27 Another preacher that came for a series of evening sermons was Raymond Kelcy, later to become chairman of the Bible Department at Oklahoma Christian University.

28 One night during brother Kelcy's series, my two brothers (Neal and Carl) and I were sitting with our parents as usual. Something was said in the sermon that moved me to decide it was time time to *"put Christ on"* in baptism. I remember stepping out into the aisle and walking to the front. That took a lot of courage for a shy eleven year old boy, but I was glad when I got to the front and sat down to see that my brothers had followed right behind me.

29 I know the exact date because the 3 x 5 card I signed is still preserved in my scrapbook, dated June 12, 1941. This is a copy of it. I carry it around in my billfold, because I consider it to be the most important document I have, verifying my new birth of the water and the spirit.

30 The baptistry underneath the pulpit was opened up by a swinging heavy floor attached by hinges hoisted by some of the stout men of the church. The church later had a sort of window behind the pulpit so people could see the baptisms in the pool that was behind the pulpit area, eliminating the need to raise the floor each time.

31 The little congregation encouraged us and taught us. As I began to mature through those years, I was given some responsibilities in leadership. The most important one that was given to me was the privilege of leading congregation in singing part of the time. That was during my High School days.

Conclusion

32 Later another brother was born in our family (Duke), then a girl (Donna). We all became Christians, all attended Christian colleges, all married Christian spouses and all have children (and some now have grandchildren) in the faith. All are continuing faithfully in Christ except my older brother who was murdered in 1988...his story was televised twice on *Unsolved Mysteries.*

33 I began preaching on Sundays while a student at Abilene Christian College. After graduation there and at Butler University School of Religion in Indianapolis, I preached in Canada and Vermont for fourteen years before becoming involved in Bible and Christian literature printing and publishing. In this non-profit business that my dad and I formed in 1963 and named *Star Bible Publications*, with the purpose of serving churches of Christ while

"publishing the word of the Lord throughout the region" (Acts 13:49).

34 I have authored a few books and several shorter works besides doing evangelistic work in radio and newspaper evangelism. Nothing could have been done without the mercies of God in giving *"bread for food and seed to the sower."* He has given abundant strength for our labors and to Him is ascribed all glory and praise for allowing this small part with Him in this *"ministry of reconciliation."*

35 In my own family, Ellen and I have five children who all married fine Christian spouses. They have given us sixteen grandchildren among whom seven have already become obedient to the faith. If the Bible says that *"the joy of old age is childrens' children,"* and it does, then how much greater is the joy when childrens' children are also children of God! We strive daily to write upon the tablets of their tender hearts the kindness and mercies of God as demonstrated through Jesus Christ and revealed by His Holy Spirit.

36 None of us is rich as the world would count it, but we consider ourselves wealthy because we are laying up treasures in heaven each day of our lives. We are also trying to share the good news with others and can count many children "in the faith" beyond our own physical family.

37 God faithfully blesses us each day and we continually thank and praise Him.

Written at age 67 on August 3, 1997, at the request of my friends Winston Bell and Bill Arnold at Richland Hills Church of Christ where Ellen and I and two of our childrens' families are members. I was reluctant to write this because it seemed that my own story, having its setting in a Christian family background for three generations, would be too ordinary. They thought, however, it would not be ordinary to most of the world.

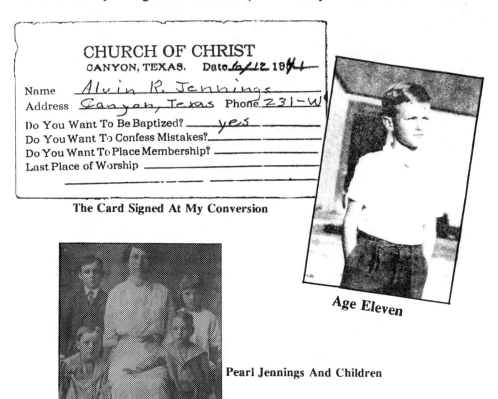

CHURCH OF CHRIST
CANYON, TEXAS.   Date 6/12 1941

Name   Alvin R. Jennings
Address Canyon, Texas   Phone 231-W
Do You Want To Be Baptized? _____yes_____
Do You Want To Confess Mistakes?_____
Do You Want To Place Membership? _____
Last Place of Worship _____
_____

The Card Signed At My Conversion

Age Eleven

Pearl Jennings And Children

BAPTISM IN 1912 NEAR TULIA, TEXAS
Preacher: A. D. Dyer. Ones being baptized: The Brown Boy, Pearl Jennings,
Mary E. Lemmon, Otto Jennings, and Mrs. Clayton.

CHAPTER 22

MUSLIM LEADER CONVERTS TO CHRIST

1 A public debate was conducted in Dallas, Texas, between Dr. Jack Evans, president of Southwestern Christian College, Terrell, Texas, and Minister Fard Muhammad of the Nation of Islam (Black Muslims), representing Mr. Louis Farrakhan, leader of the Nation of Islam.

2 It is reported that leader Farrakhan cautioned Minister Fard Muhammad about participating on the basis that Dr. Evans "had *two* books" (meaning he had a knowledge of both the Bible *and* the Koran), whereas the position of Islam would be represented by a man familiar with *only one* book (the Koran).

3 However, Minister Fard Muhammad had the confidence to proceed with the debate, with Mr. Farrakhan's advising him to enter it only after much prayer and fasting. The effects of the truth about Jesus presented in this debate prompted Minister Fard Muhammad to continue to study with Dr. Evans following the public discussion.

4 As a result of these studies which continued for eleven months, Minister Fard Muhammad submitted his resignation as a Muslim minister to Mr. Farrakhan and was baptized into Christ by Dr. Evans on Monday, July 14, 1997.

5 Now that he has been added by God to the church of Christ, Mr. Muhammad has stated that he is glad to be *free in Christ* and that he will be dropping the name Fard Muhammad which is the same as that of the founder of the Nation of Islam. He has assumed his original name, Jeremiah Cummings.

6 This new brother in Christ has become a catalyst to reaching many others in the Nation of Islam and the Muslim world. His desire now is to be a gospel minister. He announced that he would like to speak and write on the theme, *I Can See Clearly Now.*

7 Brother Jeremiah has been welcomed into the fellowship of churches of Christ and has been traveling nationally and internationally converting other Muslims to Christ. In only five and one half months since his conversion, he has baptized sixty-three persons into Christ, most of whom are from the Nation of Islam and Orthodox Islam.

8 What started out as a debate entitled **Showdown at the Bronco Bowl** in Dallas has now culminated in a great crusade for Christ among Muslims across America and abroad. Jeremiah Cummings is now telling the world that brother Evans is like his father and is a true friend in the cause of Christ.

9 Over sixty members of the Nation of Islam in Seattle, Washington, including the local Nation of Islam minister, listened intently at a meeting at the Southside Church of Christ that was packed and overflowing as Jeremiah developed his subject, "The Secret Is Out."

10 As hundreds looked on, Marilyn Muhammad, a local member of the Nation of Islam, stood up and began walking toward the baptismal pool. Brother Cummings asked her, "Are you ready to be baptized into Christ and His church?" and Ms. Muhammad replied very humbly, "Yes, sir."

11 Along with sister Marilyn, a person of Polish descent was baptized, Ms. Dee Przybylaki. All who were present at this service, including the members of the

Nation of Islam, seemed to be very pleased with the message and the Lord's messenger, brother Cummings.

12 From the opposite side of the United States, in Miami, Florida, Dr. Freeman Wyche of the Liberty City Church of Christ sent an invitation for brother Cummings to come there to tell his story and to preach. When Jeremiah arrived in Miami he preached during the night of a massive storm precipitated by El Nino which had winds clocked at 140 miles per hour.

13 To the surprise of all, the attendance at this meeting was still excellent. Even though brother Cummings had to continue to preach fifteen minutes without light and electricity, the Lord added four men that night to the church, some of whom were of the Muslim persuasion.

14 One of the loyal Muslims asked brother Cummings if it was his aim to convert *particularly* Muslims and those of the Nation of Islam, to which he replied that I Timothy 2:4 says that God's will is "that all men be saved and come into the knowledge of the truth," and the truth is that there is one Lord, one faith, one baptism and one church in the Bible...the one church that is built by Christ who is also "the head of the body, the church."

15 Brother Jeremiah tells his listeners, "These are not my words; these are the words of God."

16 Dr. Jack Evans likens brother Jeremiah to Apollos of the Bible as recorded in Acts 18:24-28. He believes that God has given the body of Christ an "open door" to the Muslim world through brother Jeremiah, a man who is willing and ready to speak anywhere on behalf of the Lord Jesus Christ.

This chapter is taken from a report written by Dr. Jack Evans. Jeremiah Cummings has written a book entitled **I CAN SEE CLEARLY NOW (817-516-7020).** The debate at the Bronco Bowl is also available on video tape. Contact Star Bible for information on how to obtain these and other materials that are being produced. This is the second public debate conducted by Dr. Evans with a representative of Islam.

Jeremiah Cummings

Dr. Jack Evans

CHAPTER 23

THE CONQUERING OF A STRONG MAN

By Larry Jones

1 The boy felt like there was something missing in his life. He was not truly happy for some reason that he could not quite understand. After a while, he and a friend decided they would try something new, something that everyone else was doing ... a *cool* thing to do.

2 So they got some marijuana from a friend and they got high. The boy was only 12 years old when he smoked his first joint and over the next few years his smoking went from occasional to frequent. Then something happened.

3 He entered High School and discovered an easier way to make a buck than the part-time jobs he hd been working. This new way was known as 'dealing.' Over the next four years the young man sold marijuana and speed to his friends while also working part-time jobs.

4 During these High School years he experimented with drugs such as cocaine, acid, heroin and crystal; burning his nostrils from snorting it, he began to 'shoot up.' He did this about once or twice a week for two years.

5 Eventually he graduated from High School (much to his surprise!) and he and his girlfriend moved in together. They had been sweethearts for three years and both of them felt it was time for them to leave home. All of a sudden he found out that he did not have the time or money for hard drugs anymore, so he just went back to smoking pot and drinking.

6 For some reason, when he stopped dealing, most of the friends he thought he had stopped coming around.

7 After living together a year, the couple got married and were able shortly afterwards to buy their first home. Things were going great: he had a beautiful wife, they both had good jobs. They were buying a nice house, they had nice clothes and furniture, cars, a motorcycle, family, pets and all! But somehow there was still something missing.

8 He decided that a hobby might be the answer so he started lifting weights. By training t wo hours each night, four nights a week, he gained fifty pounds and became much stronger in just the first year. At that time he began training in the Martial Arts as well, enjoying it just as much as he did lifting weights. After a year of this kind of discipline, he was in the best physical condition of his life.

9 He felt great and was very happy. His life was now complete...or was it?

10 There still seemed to be something missing, but he could not quite determine what it was. He had tried drugs; that was not it. He had tried drinking; that was not the answer either. He had a loving wife, a fine house, a good job, family, friends and hobbies. But there was still this void in his life when the answer suddenly hit him.

12 His parents had taken him to church as a boy and he had learned about Jesus and about God. This must be the answer. To merely know about Jesus and the Father in heaven was not enough now; he realized he must have a personal relationship with God. So he

thought the first step would be to get a Bible that would be esy to read, go through it and try to discover what God required of him.

13   And what a thrilling experience this was for him, to read for himself of the grace and mercy of God, and how Jesus was willing to come and to die for sinners like him - even while he was still an enemy of God. He knew he must respond to God's goodness that had been extended to him, and he noted as he continued to read what he must do to become obedient to what he had read in the Word of God.

14 He believed that Jesus was the Christ, the Son of God. He confessed his faith and professed his acceptance of Jesus as Lord and Savior of his life. He repented of his past sins and was baptized into the name of the Father and the Son and the Holy Spirit so his sins could be washed away in by the blood of Christ (Acts 22:16). What a happy day!

15   He was twenty-four years old when he turned his life over to the Lord. Now he tells others how he found true happiness in a personal relationship with Jesus Christ and what it is like not to just know about God but to love Him and to live for Him.

Larry Jones tells his own story in his own words in the third person. I did not know him until about three months after he had begun his serious search of the Scriptures. The day I met him it was about eleven o'clock in the morning when he came to my Bible booth in the flea market when I noticed him browsing through the books. He then began asking questions. His hunger and thirst for truth was an inspiration to me. He seemed startled when he looked at his watch and saw it was already 4:30 pm, that the 5 1/2 hours had flown by so rapidly!

We made an appointment to study further at his home on Saturday night, which we continued for several weeks. Larry always had friends present who had heard him tell about the wonderful things he had been learning. What a great day it was for Larry when I lowered him in the grave of baptism with Christ (Romans 6:3-4). His joy was almost uncontrollable (he could have called it *a high with no regrets!)* when his friend Michael Black followed in obedience after a home Bible study on December 21, 1987. Then on January 2, just like Andrew found his brother Peter, so also Larry first found and told his brother Ronnie. Larry immersed him into Christ on that date.

Thank you Larry for sharing about your weaknesses and failures, and of how your life was so empty without the Lord Jesus and His Holy Spirit to direct your life. I love you and am so glad you have learned that the gospel is God's power, and that you are not ashamed to tell it to others. I pray you will always be faithful until death, serving God in His church.

- Editor

LARRY JONES,

A STRONG MAN WITH A TENDER HEART

CHAPTER 24

SOMETHING HAPPENED
ON THE ROAD TO CANADA

1 Almost fifty years ago (in 1951) this evangelist went to Canada to preach. He had attended Abilene Christian University (then College) and Butler University School of Religion, had a B.A. in Bible and an M.A. in Church History, but still had no MRS. The Lord had not provided a companion from among the hundreds of Christian young ladies at ACC, so he went as a single man age 21 to Saskatoon, Saskatchewan.

2 A few disciples were meeting in the home of Martha Olson and her sons Roger, Roland and David. Soon the meetings were moved to the YMCA, then to the Hungarian Hall and for a time in a room above a store downtown. With a radio program, newspaper teaching, personal evangelism and tent meetings with evangelists and teams of campaigners from the states, the numbers grew to about forty.

3 Ellen and Ruby Kristianson of the Estevan church graduated from High School there then moved to Saskatoon to find jobs...to the great delight of this young preacher from Texas! Not only did this add numbers to the little church, but in time God (and the preacher) chose

Ellen for a wife. They married January 1, 1955. Of this marriage five children have been born and now there are sixteen grandchildren. Ellen and Alvin have lived in Texas where he devotes himself to producing and distributing gospel literature.

4 Both of Ellen's parents have gone to be with the Lord, but most of her family still reside in Canada. We travel the 1300 miles to visit them occasionally and Ellen worked for six months in writing and phoning all of our family urging them to come to a family reunion near Winnipeg, Manitoba, in July of 1995. By the grace of God, all of our five children with their families formed a caravan of 26 and we all headed north. It might remind a Bible student of Joseph who went alone to Egypt, then took a wife there and saw his family increase to a sizeable number.

5 Something happened on the road to Canada that seemed at the time to be a sad misfortune when the car I was driving had a mechanical failure. It was decided that Ellen should go on with one of our sons and that I should stay in Sioux Falls, South Dakota, and take care of the repair. And so it happened.

6 It was fairly late in the day and no mechanic was available. We did get a commitment from a

Chuck Loneman of CB Motors who said he could get on the job the first thing the next morning. And so it was. Chuck was a good man and before long had parts ordered and began the work. His wife frequently came in the mornings to help out, so while her husband worked I began talking with her about my occupation, etc.

7 There just happened to be several boxes of Bibles and Bible-related books from our publishing company in the trunk of the car, and our conversation soon led us to these books. Brenda showed unusual interest since she had been a student of the Bible for many years. We discussed various subjects such as the church, salvation, the sad state of confusion and division among professed followers of Christ. She said she was Lutheran and that Chuck was Catholic, that they four children, but that their little boy, Joshua, had tragically been killed in an accident not long before.

8 When Brenda learned that it would take a couple of hours to finish the repair on the car, she offered to take me for a drive to give me a tour of her city. She showed me the downtown area, the area where she worked, the park and other places of interest. When we returned to the garage, Chuck had just about finished the job. I had spoken to Brenda about

obedience to Christ and though she said she is not a regular church-goer, she had often felt a need to be baptized by what she called *"total immersion."*

9 I said, "Brenda, why not be baptized *today*?" She had often thought of doing this *sometime*, but wondered how it could be taken care of so quickly. We discussed Acts 8 where Philip baptized a man while on a road when they came to some water, and I asked, "Why couldn't we go to the lake in the beautiful park you showed to me?" She thought for a moment then agreed, but wanted to speak to Chuck first.

10 Chuck had no objection to Brenda being baptized, but when he was asked about his own obedience, said he was too busy and suggested that we go ahead without him.

11 We got in Brenda's car again and went by her house to get a towel and a change of clothing. Her little girl, Brianna, age 9, wanted to come along, too. When we got to the lake, we waded out in the rocky bottom to a depth of about three feet where she confessed her faith in Jesus as the Son of God, then was buried under the water and raised up out of the water. According to the promise in Acts 2:38, she now had forgiveness of sins and the gift of the Holy Spirit! God added her to

the body of Christ, His church (verse 42, 47). When we got back to the bank and walked to a place where we could sit and reflect on the wonders of what God did through Christ in taking away her sins, we took her picture then headed back to their shop.

12 I paid Chuck for the work, urged him to consider obeying the gospel also, left Brenda several books, said my fairwell and went on my way rejoicing (in my wet clothes) to Canada.

13 We have not seen Brenda or Chuck since then, but did receive a refreshing letter the next April which told of Dawna, their middle daughter, being immersed also! Brenda said Chuck was "a little upset and went on about why did she have to be baptized when she was *already* baptized?" The fact was, Brenda went on writing, "the first baptism was *our decision*, and now this is *her own decision*."

Chuck later acknowledged that "this was *Dawna's day!*"

14 "I am sure Brianna will be right behind her to profess her faith since she's the one that wanted to have you baptize her also," Brenda wrote. "See how your watering has grown in our family?"

Written three years later by Alvin Jennings. We have talked on the phone a few times, but have not seen them since that first day. Brenda promised to attend the church where she can break bread with the disciples each Lord's Day, and where the teaching is honored about baptism like she and Dawna have obeyed. Let us pray the Word will continue to be followed in their family and that Chuck and all the children will be added by God to the body of believers upon their obedience to Christ's command. It will be exciting to hear, as Paul Harvey would say, *the rest of the story!*

Brenda Loneman and daughter Brianna (age 9) on the date of Brenda's new birth into Christ, July 13, 1995.

CHAPTER 25

HIS LIFE HAD REDUCED TO "A PIECE OF BREAD"

1 He walked home from work last Friday, tired after a hard day laboring on a massive bridge on the Dallas North Tollway. He had an old car but had let it go into disrepair. Things generally had not been going well.

2 But this night the bottom fell out. When he reached his apartment he found the door had been broken in. Inside nothing was left but a couple of pieces of old furniture, a Gideon Bible taken from a motel some time back, a scripture poster stapled to the wall ... and part of a loaf of bread in the kitchen. Even the telephone was gone.

3 As he hurried from one room to another, he came across a note Dianne had left. "Dear Steve," it began, "I cannot take it any more." On three pages she poured out her sad story of fear, frustration and hopelessness. She pleaded for him not to attempt to find where she went or to try to get together again. She had left several times before, but this was to be the last time.

4 Dianne had a marriage fail earlier in life. Her husband had brought another woman into their home, acting shamefully even in the presence of her two small children. She got out, not really caring where she went and not being able to care for the children, left them too.

5 A divorce followed and sometime later she met Stephen (n a m e w i t h h e l d), a Checkoslovakian neighbor who showed her some friendship. Soon they were living together. Although Steve had some misgivings about living with a divorced woman "because of what Jesus said in the gospel of Matthew," they developed a love for each other. Dianne already had a bad liver caused by alcohol consumption, but against her better judgment would frequently drink when neighbors offered it to her.

6 This infuriated Steve at times, but later they would agree to drink together. When he struck her during one of these "happy hours," she became frightened of what he might do to her and she left him.

7 Steve went into deep depression. He went out and bought a cheap telephone and to drown his sorrows, bought two gallons of whiskey. When that was almost gone, he came across a brochure and a book that I had given to him a couple of Saturdays before at my Bible booth at Traders Village flea market. There had been something special about Steve that attracted me to him; I loved him immediately for his youthful zeal and enthusiasm about the things of God...though sadly weak and misguided.

8 It was about 11 pm Saturday night when he called my number that was printed on the church brochure. He began to pour out his life's miseries and how he felt there was no hope in the world for him. Not only his present troubles loomed before him, but the guilt of the "thousands murdered in bombings over Viet Nam, Laos and Cambodia."

9 In addition to that, his guilt as an adulterer grieved him ever since he began reading the Bible: "I discovered I have been living in sin; pray for me and my old lady. We both want to be Christians. I took her and immersed her in Lake Travis so she could be saved...into the name of the Father, Son and

the Holy Spirit. I had already been baptized in the Catholic Church but she never knew anything about religion or the Bible."

10 He went on to tell about his depression and how he prayed to St. Jude, the patron saint of all lost causes. It did not relieve his grief to learn that I Timothy chapter 2 affirms there "is only one mediator between God and men, the man Christ Jesus." He had thought Jesus was so busy there was no use praying to God through Him! This was the first real discomfort he felt about his religion. He later confessed his anger toward me for introducing this disturbing passage from the Bible.

11 A couple of days went by then my phone rang again. It was Steve saying he had been reading his Bible all day and also a book he was given at the Bible booth called **Bible Digest**. "I have believed and preached false doctrines all these years. I see now what I was never taught in parochial schools or in my church."

12 As he continued, it was evident he had read extensively in the Scriptures and that he remembered much of what he had read. He remembered the story of Saul's conversion and how "he had fallen off his horse and was blinded."

13 Steve told many things that had deeply cut to his heart. He really did have, despite all his woes, a good and honest heart that was now broken and contrite before God. He cried out and said he was not worthy that I even come to his house. Nevertheless, seeing a soul here in deep despair, I told him if he would promise to be there, I would come the next evening. I called my friend Dave Swenson to go along with me and sure enough, there Stephen was,

watching and waiting for us outside his apartment.

14 He pointed to a construction site nearby. As we began to walk he explained to us about his work on the tollway near the Galleria and about the moral corruption of his co-workers. "There is not a Christian on the whole job; even though I preach to everybody, I'm the worst of them all because I don't live what I preach to them and I have not been preaching *the truth* to them."

15 We walked back and while he sat on the floor of his empty apartment, he falteringly read Dianne's note through tear-filled eyes. He so wanted her to be saved! He said he would pay for a Bible to be mailed to her to be sent simply *"from your guardian angel."* We continued speaking of self control, righteousness, the judgment to come, the way of salvation through Jesus Christ and of the price of being a disciple of Jesus.

16 Dave and I warned of the shame of beginning and then turning back to sin like a washed pig to the mud or like a dog to its vomit. We told him it would be better to never start unless he resolved to surrender totally to Jesus as the Lord and Master of his life. Steve confessed his faith and vowed his determination to serve faithfully. He pleaded for us to immerse him that same night in a lake or in his bathtub or a swimming pool or anywhere there was enough water.

17 We could not "forbid the water," so made a call to Tim and Travis and they got the use of a baptistry tank in Garland near their home. It was about midnight when he was born of the water and the Spirit. We buried the old dead man of sin in the bottom of the tank and the new man arose rejoicing in the promise of God that his sins had been finally and fully washed away in the blood of Jesus. He embraced me and kissed me.

18 Several elders left their conference room and came to encourage him to live for God. We prayed together and wept for joy. Steve began reciting in emotional tones a prayer of St Francis of Assisi:

19 "Lord, make me an instrument
   of your peace.
Where there is hatred, let me sow
   love,
Where there is injury, pardon;
Where there is sadness, joy;
Where there is despair, hope;
Where there is darkness, light.

20 "Lord, grant that I not seek so
   much
To be consoled, as to console;
To be understood, as to understand,
And to be loved, as to love.

21 "For it is in giving that we
   recieve,
And it is in pardoning that we are
   pardoned,
And it is in dying that we are born to
   eternal life. Amen."

22 As we left him he was telling about his intention to share the good news about his new life in Christ with his co-workers the next day. He also resolved to spend every night reading the new Bible we gave to him.

23 He did share his new-found faith the next day with Bert and Ed and several others who marvelled at his happiness despite the troubles they knew he was experiencing. One mocked Steve with a vulgar jest: "Yeah, I guess you will now *masterbate* with your left hand instead of your right!" From this Steve turned away without making a response, perhaps remembering Proverbs 9:7,

24 "Whoever corrects a mocker invites insult; whoever rebukes a wicked man incurs abuse." However, two others gave him courage and hope ... they listened with concern about baptism into Christ and about the forgiveness of sins.

25 If Stephen had not suffered and been *reduced to a loaf of bread* (Proverbs 6:26) through a shameful life of drunkenness and adultery, he would likely never have felt a need for a Savior. But now he knows God included him in His marvellous plan of redemption. Like the prodigal son, he has returned to his Father and can now say with David: "It was good for me to be afflicted so that I might learn your decrees; now I obey your word" (Psalm 119:67-72).

26 Every man's life, when it is over, is like a story that is told (Psalm 90:9 KJV). God knows what Steve's full story will be and what kind of an instrument he will be to others in this life.

27 We pray he will be faithful unto death and that he will receive the crown of life on that last Great Day!

This true account was written in March of 1986 by Alvin Jennings who displays Bibles and Bible-related books each week at flea markets. Though he sells very little, his motivation is to be a *fisher of men*. He is alert through prayer to watch for "fish" like Steve and to cast the net in such a way as to bring men and women into the *Ship of*

Zion headed for eternity's shore. Over one hundred have been immersed through these contacts whose hearts God has opened at his "Gospel Chariot," a mobile Christian book display.

As for Steve (who has asked that his name be withheld), he now resides in a northeastern state with a loving Christian wife and two children. He assembles with the church there and breaks bread on the first day of each week with them whenever he is able.

"A Man Is Brought To A Piece of Bread"   -- Proverbs 6:26

"The Gospel Chariot"

CHAPTER 26

ONE OF THE MORMON'S "SEVENTIES" TURNS FROM FABLES TO CHRIST

1 During a public debate with Kenneth Farnsworth in the Liberty Park in Salt Lake City, Utah, conducted August 17-21, 1942, Bob Helsten from Burkley, California, was passing out invitations.

2 He invited a man who was pushing his wife in a wheelchair and asked him to come to hear the debate on the Mormon religion.

3 His name was Jacob C. Vandervis. Both he and his wife were baptized into Christ.

4 Vandervis was not only one of the "Seventies" in a Mormon Ward, but he also wore the "holy" garments. These "holy" garments were what all good Mormons wear constantly. The garments have a slit over the heart, each elbow and knee symbolizing that if one would leave the church, he would be killed.

5 The Danites were the revenge tribe in the Mormon Church.

6 Brother Vandervvis presented to Otis Gatewood his "holy under-garments." Prior to his conversion to Christ, he had been baptized according to Mormon tradition over 150 times in the Mormon Temple *for the dead*.

7 An invitation came to brother Vandervis from the State of Arizona to come for a speaking engagement. When he came back, his senses told him that something was wrong back home. Upon returning, he found his wife dead and blood all over the floor.

8 Everyone believed that the Danites killed her, a charge that has never been proven. It happened so soon; much sooner than we all expected, else we would have given Sister Vandervis special protection while Brother Vandervis was gone.

8 However, brother Vandervis was not going to be left defeated. He therefore wrote a pamphlet on *Why I Left The Mormon Church.*

9 He was originally from Holland. We took him one day to the Northside Church of Christ in Abilene, Texas, where I asked them to send Brother Vandervis back to Holland.

10 They agreed to do so. On September 14, 1946, *The Christian Chronicle* had an article about him which read in part: "Jacob C. Vandervis and Bill Phillips have arrived in Holland, Netherlands, where they are making their temporary headquarters for full-time evangelistic work in Holland. They arrived in Antwerp on August 23, 1946," which was before we arrived in Germany for our mission there later in 1947.

11 But the Danites were not finished with Brother Vandervis. They shadowed him until they found him alone in Florida and ran over him in a car and killed him. That was the conviction of many, although they had such a good cover-up, his death by them was never openly proved nor publicly known.

This article was contributed by Otis Gatewood who lived and preached among the Mormons in Salt Lake City, Utah, from 1939 till 1946. He was the first gospel preacher in Salt Lake City and helped build their meeting house. His famous debate with Farnsworth on Mormon doctrine was published in 1942, preceded in 1941 by another discussion with them on "Baptism for the Dead, Continuous Revelation, and Book of Mormon." In all, he had ten debates with Mormons in addition to public debates with Adventists and Baptists (1943). His power and persuasiveness as a public speaker was rare during those years, and his influence on other preachers and churches was outstanding.

Through his preaching in 1938 the first Mexican Penitente, Pete Olevias, was converted in Las Vegas, New Mexico.

When he went to Frankfurt, Germany, following the Second World War, the Lord used him under the support of the Broadway church in Lubbock, Texas, to accomplish marvellous things in winning former Nazi soldiers to Christ. He wrote of these experiences in a book, **Preaching in the Footsteps of Hitler.** He has written several other books including his first (which is still in print): **You Can Do Personal Work,** also **There Is A God In Heaven** and commentaries on **Acts** and on **Revelation.** These have been translated and circulated in several languages and nations.

A valuable source for this footnote material has come from **Preachers Of Today, Vol I,** The Christian Press, edited by Batsell Barrett Baxter and M. Norvel Young, Nashville. cir 1953.

He now resides (at the young age of 87) with his wife Irene at 160 West Avon Road, Rochester Hills, MI 48307. Nothing impressed this writer more profoundly than his exciting reports of God's working through him and fellow missionaries in Germany during the late 'forties at Abilene Christian College. And no compliment was ever offered that was appreciated more nor of which one could feel more unworthy than to have heard it said during our ministry in Canada six years later, *"Alvin Jennings is the Otis Gatewood of Canada."*
Editor

Otis Gatewood, 1948

Otis Gatewood, 1998

We regret that we have no photograph of Jacob Vandervis.

CHAPTER 27

AND THE TWO
BECAME AS ONE

1 *SHE* came from a loving home where her mother was a member of the Church of Christ. Her father was Italian, a Roman Catholic, but not active in his church. The father insisted that his wife take **Kathy** and her three brothers to church three times a week.

2 Kathy resented him for this and swore that when she was old enough, she would not go to church at all. She was rebellious, hard to handle and soon got involved with drugs.

3 *HE* came from a broken home. His parents divorced when he was eight. Both his mother and father remarried immediately, and he lived with his mother.

4 His mother's second husband was an alcoholic who supposed that he could support the family by writing bad checks. When the bad checks caught up with them, they moved. They moved often. **Mike** attended seven grade schools and three Jr. High Schools, but he never seemed to fit in anywhere.

5 At home he was being severely abused, both mentally and physically. During all this time, Mike never had a chance to see his father, whom he idolized. His father was too busy in his own world, and was always on the move. Mike was the oldest of four children and so became both mother and father to his younger siblings while their mother and stepfather went to bars or parties.

6 He enlisted in the Navy while still in high school just to get out from under the responsibility that weighed heavy on his shoulders at home. He was an angry, bitter young man. After serving two years in the Vietnam war, he was home, disillusioned, angry and confused. He had joined the Navy "to serve his country" and now his country was telling him he was a "baby-killer."

7 Because he was a Vietnam Vet it was difficult to find a job. He started using drugs and alcohol to ease the emptiness and loneliness he felt.

8 They met at a party where drugs and alcohol were abundant. Neither of them was looking for someone. Yet, their eyes met. He was there with another girl who was just *a body* to him. He drove her home and returned with his motorcycle hoping to entice Kathy. He did. He offered to give her a ride and she quickly accepted.

9 The thrill of being on that bike with this tall, strong, rebellious and handsome stranger was the dare she would gladly take because she too was lost, confused and alone. They knew very soon that they were meant for each other.

10 For the next two years they lived together in a small apartment in Boulder, Colorado. They used drugs on a daily basis as well as alcohol and tobacco. She knew better but didn't care. He was just living like the adults that surrounded him when he was young. Neither of them were happy but they did not know why, so they would get high to forget.

11 Mike was the road manager for a popular rock group and was on the road most of the time. Sometimes Kathy would go with him on these trips in a motor home with ten other people, all high on cocaine, pot, alcohol and anything

else that got thrown their way.

12 Neither of them had much to do with their families and most of the time their families didn't know where they were. That was fine with Mike; he had grown bitter and distant from having to overcome his unpleasant childhood. Kathy avoided her family at all costs because she knew deep inside that the life she was living was wrong, *so wrong*.

13 After a time of living this lifestyle, Kathy started having health problems and wound up in the hospital for exploratory abdominal surgery. Mike was self-absorbed and so lost emotionally he hardly found any time to visit her at the hospital. They were growing apart. Kathy had plenty of time to think about her situation while cooped up in the hospital bed. Her mom came to see her as well as her brothers. They all pleaded with her to come home. She was ready.

14 Having grown tired of being high and out of control all the time and wondering who Mike might be with and what he might be doing during those long weeks on the road, she made the decision to leave him and move back in with her mom and dad.

15 Kathy started going to church again...*and it felt so right.* Something huge had been missing in her life all those months away from God and her family. If anyone had told her that it was God she needed to fill that empty place, she would have denied it bitterly. It was only when she returned to Him that she realized what that huge void in her life had been.

16 Mike argued and pleaded with Kathy to come back to him. He loved her and was willing to do just about anything to get her back, or so he thought. Kathy was back in church, back in the Word and off of drugs. Her appearance changed, her language was clean and she was becoming transformed into the fragrant likeness of Jesus.

17 Her life was starting to make sense again and she was happy and fulfilled. But her love for Mike was strong and she missed him. He would call her and they would talk for hours. They both cried a lot and longed for each other; yet each time Kathy would drive to Boulder to see him, she would give in and get high or drunk, sometimes both just to be with him. Then the guilt would set in; she knew she must avoid him.

18 He decided that he would visit church with her and study the Bible because he *knew he could prove the Bible to be false!* The first Bible class Mike ever attended, he walked away from, saying to Kathy: "That old man doesn't have the slightest idea what he's talking about." That "old man" was Norman Gipson.

19 Eventually he asked her to marry him, but she replied that she would only marry a Christian. He said he would be baptized if that was what she wanted. She told him that simply being baptized would not change a thing.

20 For many months Mike continued to study the Bible diligently to prove to Kathy that it was all a farce. Gradually Mike was no longer able to deny that the message was getting to his heart and to his soul. Finally, after reading Acts 2:37 and its context (it reads, "Now when they heard this, they were pierced to the heart and said to Peter and the rest of the apostles, 'Brethren, what shall we do?'"), Mike was baptized into Christ. That was in December of 1972. A few weeks later, Kathy was *re*baptized so she could become a new creation in Christ.

21 They were married in February of 1973. Mike sold his guitar to buy Kathy's wedding ring. Mike and Kathy continued to study and grow; soon Mike felt like he needed some intense training in the Scriptures. That led him to enroll in the extension school of the Bear Valley School of Preaching, which in those days was known as the "Saturday School."

22 After several months of study and prayer, and with many long discussions with Kathy, he decided to become a full-time student at the School of Preaching. Mike observed that Norman Gipson, one of his instructors, had been able to learn a lot through the years.

23 He graduated from the school. Since that time, Mike has been enthusiastically received by the churches and has preached for congregations in Texas, Colorado, California and Arizona. He has served as a prison minister, a personal work minister, a police chaplain, a pulpit minister and a T.V. evangelist. He is well known thoughout the Western States as a television evangelist and also as the "sound man" for the Yosemite, Red River and Grand Canyon Family Encampments. He has been able to use his talents and experience of sound systems gained in the rock-and-roll bands of his former years in the world to serve in the Kingdom of God where all things have become new!

24 He is currently preaching at the Mt. Vernon church of Christ in Prescott, Arizona. Mike is speaker for the award winning weekly television program, *What Do The Scriptures Say?*, which is broadcast to over a million homes in Arizona and California.

25 He has established his own web site on the World Wide Web which gives him an opportunity to answer Bible questions from all over the world. The award winning web site receives thousands of visitors each month and Mike hopes to continue to expand its content and capabilities. The web site address is WWW.SCRPTURESSAY.COM where the gospel is preached twenty-four hours a day, seven days a week around the world in both Spanish and English.

26 Kathy typed out an entire book for the web so everyone can know of the church in the Bible; the title of the book is **Introducing The Church of Christ**, issued by Star Bible Publications in 1981. This book has also been added to his website in the Spanish language.

27 Mike and Kathy have been married for 25 years and have two adopted children, Jeremy age 23 and Jessica age 21.

Written by Kathy Scott, April 1, 1998. Photos are of Mike and Kathy in earlier years, of Mike in his church office and of the two of them together as servants of God. They are dearly loved by all who know them.

Kathy (18) & Mike (22)

First Anniversary

Mike Scott, preacher of the gospel, in his office
at the church building.

CHAPTER 28

AURELIO NORI, MAN OF COURAGE IN ITALY

1 The Bible speaks of men and women who walked by faith...they were heroic figures, larger than life to most of us. Yet, the faith they displayed in God is still seen in the lives of men and women of today.

2 When we consider how God *continues to work* through men and women today, as He did in the lives that were changed by the preaching of the gospel in the Book of Acts of **Apostles**, perhaps the book should rather have been called the *Acts of Christians.*

3 Take for example a man who had a place of prestige and security. Through diligent study and training he became a Catholic priest. But the more he studied, the more dissatisfied he became with his religion. The yearning for simple New Testament Christianity was in his heart.

4 He knew the personal losses he would sustain. It would mean giving up position, salary and retirement for an uncertain future. But like the man who found the pearl of great value, he was willing to give up everything in order to obtain this wonderful treasure.

5 This man was **Aurelio Nori**. Through the providence of God he would eventually meet Cline Paden and be baptized into Christ in January of 1951. Aurelio describes his baptism in this way:

6 *"It was in that moment that my life began as if I were born truly in that moment, and spiritually I felt a new man, having thrown behind my shoulders all the years of my youth passed in company with my mother and the other 18 years of study and service in the Catholic*

church. Rightly the old things became new, as teaches the Gospel."

7 The church of Christ at Sixth and Izard in Little Rock, Arkansas, has had the privilege of supporting Aurelio as the preacher for the church in Frascati, Italy, from those early days. It was here that he was destined to spend the rest of his life laboring with his good wife Natalina to become a blessing to so many.

8 On Thursday, June 26, 1997, the earthly existence of this significant life came to a close. He faithfully served his generation and diligently taught his children to love God and to keep His commandments. Nor did he neglect the public proclamation of the gospel of Christ. Thrilled with the wonderful discoveries he found in the Bible, he was eager to share the good tidings with all.

9 This couple lived their lives together above reproach, marked by a spirit of humility, love and service.

10 The genuineness of his faith, which marked every aspect of his life, preached a sermon far more eloquent and powerful than could be delivered from any pulpit.

11 *"Therefore, since we are surrounded by so great a cloud of witnesses, let us also lay aside every weight, and sin which clings so closely, and let us run with perseverance the race that is set before us, looking to Jesus the pioneer and perfecter of our faith"* (Hebrews 12:1-2).

ACROSS THE YEARS AND ACROSS THE MEDITERRANIAN SEA TO MOROCCO

12 The Concord Road church in Brentwwood, Tennessee, provided the funds for send Maurice and Marie Hall on a three week journey

to Morocco in 1995 with the promise from Jesus, "I will be with you."

13 This nation was chosen by the Halls due to their French ability and the fact tht it was one of thirty nations that had been targeted without a congregation of the church of Christ.

14 A French university student 24 years of age, fluent in English, French, Berber and Arabic, had written from Casablanca asking for help in finding the truth. A French soldier of World War II period had given Mahmoud's father a Gospel of John in Berber. Then in 1989 Mahmoud got the Gospel and began to read it.

15 This city is the commercial capital of thirty million Muslims. With prayer we journeyed from the known to the unknown from November 1 until our safe return on the 18th. Jesus was with us. With Foy Smith as our fellow-traveller joined us in finding the "Macedonian" Muslim who had already indicated his desire to obey the gospel of Christ.

16 With my picture in his hand, Mahmoud came to the airport and watched passengers until he found a face that resembled the picture on the card. Our prayers were further answered when the eyes of the baggage checker were closed to the 65 pounds of Christian literature that was now in the Muslim nation.

17 Following two nights of after work study at our hotel, the gentle, kind, intelligent Mahmoud became our brother in Christ. He was baptized in our hotel bathtub.

18 In a small rented Fiat we journeyed the 300 kilometres to his home to visit and teach the 16 members of his family.

19 The next day we went to the market of the mountain area village to find the makings of *couscous*, the Arabian staple food...a grainy like grits, a mixture of wheat and oil cooked over an open fire. On the same fire was a piece of mutton.

20 The patriarch tore the mutton into parts and in the ritual of the Berber people he gave to each guest his portion of meat. Their mountain house gave shelter to 6 sheep and 16 men, women and children. Normally a visitor is expected to remain 3 days.

21 Taking our leave, we set out to contact personally or by phone 16 listeners who had responded to Station KNLS, Alaska. One said he was "addicted" to this station. The young of the Muslim world gladly listen to Christian religion programs.

22 King Hassan II has openly declared a policy of tolerance. He practiced this when his monarchy joined the Allies in the Kuwait crisis. A teacher of English we met said he could teach 50 Bible classes daily in English if he had the time. Another American met at McDonald's (where a Big Mac costs a day's wages for them) has begun an English school to provide income while he seeks opportunity to tell the good news of Jesus.

23 At the American Consulate an official said, "I note that you are with Christian organizations. If you teach the Bible to Moraccans, you will go to prison." Juan Monroy of Spain had verified this also in a letter in which was enclosed a Madrid news article telling of several Moroccans going to prison, though international pressure had forced their early release.

We are indebted to John Gipson of Little Rock for this beautiful summary in verses 1-11, as well as to Cline

Paden, the Little Rock church and of course to God, Who gives all things and to Whom alone is due all glory and praise.

Verses 11 through 23 are from our dear friend, Maurice Hall in a February, 1996, report of the trip. He gladly gave permission to use this conversion story for the *Now* Book of Acts. He reflected on R.C. Bell's saying that Acts of Apostles would be better named "Acts of Christians"...and that the book was continuing on and on.

Perhaps the present volume can be Number One, to be followed by Number Two, etc. Several wonderful stories had to be eliminated in order to keep within the 28 chapters allotted so as to "match" the *Then* Book of Acts. You will notice that some chapters have more than one narrative, like in Acts 16 we read of the jailer and also about Lydia.

John Gipson

Aurelio & Natalina Nori

Maurice Hall   Cline Paden

PART TWO

THE BOOK OF ACTS

The *original* Book of Acts of Apostles
gives the inspired account of
conversions to Christ
in the first century

Peter

Paul

Portraits in oil by Kenneth Wyatt, by permission. Kenneth Wyatt Art Galleries, 310 Commanche Trail, Tulia, Texas, and Red River, New Mexico.

The *Then*
Book of Acts

Introduction

"The Acts of the Apostles" is the common designation of this book, although it is actually *only some* acts of *some* of the apostles. This book especially tells about the work of two of the apostles, Peter and Paul. Peter is the central person involved in the beginning of the church in Jerusalem in 33 AD and he continues in the forefront through chapter 12. Paul is the preacher who went out to nearby countries to tell others about Christ. Acts can also be called "The Acts of the Holy Spirit" because it tells about the coming and work of the Spirit. We shall call it the *then* book of Acts because it had to do with the first century of history.

In Luke's first book, he wrote to the "Friend of God" (Theophilus) by the inspiration of the Spirit (2 Timothy 3:16-17) "about all that Jesus began to do and to teach until the day he was taken up to heaven." In his second book, he writes to this same friend and to us all about what happened in the lives of Jesus' disciples after he was taken up before their very eyes, when the cloud hid him from their sight. In the second chapter he wrote of the receiving of power when the Holy Spirit came upon the twelve on the day of Pentecost, as had been promised in chapter one, verse eight.

In one of the most exciting books in all the Bible, he tells in one story after another of how men and women responded to the message of salvation through Jesus Christ, the Son of God. Some of these accounts are joyous because some "gladly received the word and were immersed," like on the birthday of the church when about 3,000 were added to their number on that day. As Peter and the other apostles warned and pleaded with the multitude of Jews gathered that day from every nation under heaven, Luke did not tell us how many did not believe and obey in baptism, hence were *not added;* instead they "made fun of" Peter as he stood up with the eleven and preached about the resurrection of the Christ whom they had crucified (read chapter two).

The Holy Spirit guided Luke to write about the most important thing that can happen in a man's life: how he or she will react when the gospel is preached to them. Luke's focus was on those who hearing, believed, turned from their sins and were baptized (immersed) and who then went on their way rejoicing and telling others about the treasure they had found worth more than life itself. Read in chapters 2, 8, 9, 10 and 16 for some of the more detailed cases of conversions.

We have no particular preference of what version to print among the many that were available. We are not qualified to make a judgment on which English translation is the best. The **Easy-To-Read Version** has been chosen because we want every person who reads to be able to understand God's Word. We acknowledge with gratitude the permission of our friends at the World Bible Translation Center, Inc., of Fort Worth, Texas, to use the Book of Acts from their English Easy-To-Read Version, copyright 1975 (Luke and Acts), 1978, 1981, 1982, 1987, 1990, 1993, 1997.

- Alvin Jennings

October 2, 1998

Acts

Luke Writes Another Book

1 Dear Theophilus,
The first book I wrote was about everything that Jesus did and taught. ²I wrote about the whole life of Jesus, from the beginning until the day he was carried up into heaven. Before this happened, Jesus talked to the apostles* he had chosen. With the help of the Holy Spirit,* Jesus told the apostles what they should do. ³This was after Jesus' death, but he showed the apostles that he was alive. Jesus proved this by doing many powerful things. The apostles saw Jesus many times during the 40 days after he was raised from death. Jesus spoke to the apostles about the kingdom of God. ⁴One time when Jesus was eating with them, he told them not to leave Jerusalem. Jesus said, "The Father has promised you something; I told you about it before. Wait here ⌊in Jerusalem⌋ to receive this promise. ⁵John baptized* people with water, but in a few days you will be baptized with the Holy Spirit.*"

Jesus Is Carried Up into Heaven

⁶The apostles* were all together. They asked Jesus, "Lord, is this the time for you to give the Jews their kingdom again?"

⁷Jesus said to them, "The Father is the only One who has the authority to decide dates and times. You cannot know these things. ⁸But the Holy Spirit* will come to you. Then you will receive power. You will be my witnesses—⌊you will tell people about me⌋. First, you will tell people in Jerusalem. Then you will tell people in all of Judea, in Samaria, and in every part of the world."

apostles The men Jesus chose to be his special helpers.
Holy Spirit Also called the Spirit of God, the Spirit of Christ, and the Comforter. Joined with God and Christ, he does God's work among people in the world.
baptized A Greek word meaning to immerse, dip, or bury a person or thing briefly under water.

⁹After Jesus told the apostles these things, he was lifted up into the sky. While the apostles were watching, Jesus went into a cloud, and they could not see him. ¹⁰Jesus was going away, and the apostles were looking into the sky. Suddenly, two men (angels) wearing white clothes stood beside them. ¹¹The two men said to the apostles, "Men from Galilee, why are you standing here looking into the sky? You saw Jesus carried away from you into heaven. He will come back in the same way you saw him go."

A New Apostle Is Chosen

¹²Then the apostles* went back to Jerusalem from the Mount of Olives. (This mountain is about one-half mile from Jerusalem.) ¹³The apostles entered the city. They went to the place where they were staying; this was in a room upstairs. The apostles were: Peter, John, James, Andrew, Philip, Thomas, Bartholomew, Matthew, James (the son of Alphaeus), Simon (known as the Zealot*), and Judas (the son of James).

¹⁴The apostles* were all together. They were constantly praying with the same purpose. Some women, Mary, the mother of Jesus, and his brothers were there with the apostles.

¹⁵After a few days there was a meeting of the believers. (There were about 120 of them.) Peter stood up and said, ¹⁶⁻¹⁷"Brothers, in the Scriptures* the Holy Spirit* said through David that something must happen. He was talking about Judas, one of our own group. Judas served together with us. The Spirit said that Judas would lead men to arrest Jesus."

¹⁸(Judas was paid money for doing this. His money was used to buy him a field. But Judas fell on his head, and his body broke open. All his intestines poured out. ¹⁹And all the people of Jerusalem learned about this. That is why they

Zealot The Zealots were a Jewish political group.
Scriptures Holy Writings—the Old Testament.

named that field Akeldama. In their language Akeldama means "field of blood.")

²⁰⌊Peter said,⌋ "In the book of Psalms, this is written ⌊about Judas⌋:

'People should not go
      near his land *(property)*;
No one should live there!'

Psalm 69:25

And it is also written:

'Let another man have his work.'

Psalm 109:8

²¹⁻²²So now another man must join us and become a witness of Jesus' resurrection *(rising from death)*. This man must be one of those men who were part of our group during all the time when the Lord Jesus was with us. This man must have been with us from the time John began to baptize* people until the day when Jesus was carried up from us into heaven."

²³The apostles* put two men before the group. One was Joseph Barsabbas. He was also called Justus. The other man was Matthias. ²⁴⁻²⁵The apostles prayed, "Lord, you know the minds of all men. Show us which one of these two men you choose to do this work. Judas turned away from it and went where he belongs. Lord, show us which man should take his place as an apostle!" ²⁶Then the apostles used lots* to choose one of the two men. The lots showed that Matthias was the one that the Lord wanted. So he became an apostle with the other eleven.

The Coming of the Holy Spirit

2 When the day of Pentecost* came, the apostles* were all together in one place. ²Suddenly a noise came from the sky. It sounded like a strong wind blowing. This noise filled the whole house where they were sitting. ³They saw something that looked like flames of fire. The flames were separated and stood over each person there. ⁴They were all filled with the Holy Spirit,*

and they began to speak different languages. The Holy Spirit was giving them the power to do this.

⁵There were some very religious Jewish men in Jerusalem at this time. These men were from every country in the world. ⁶A large group of these men came together because they heard the noise. They were surprised because the apostles* were speaking, and every man heard in his own language. ⁷The Jews were all amazed at this. They did not understand how the apostles could do this. They said, "Look! These men *(the apostles)* that we hear speaking are all from Galilee*! ⁸But we hear them in our own languages. How is this possible? We are from different places: ⁹Parthia, Media, Elam, Mesopotamia, Judea, Cappadocia, Pontus, Asia,* ¹⁰Phrygia, Pamphylia, Egypt, the areas of Libya near the city of Cyrene, Rome, ¹¹Crete and Arabia. Some of us were born Jews. Others are converts.* We are from these different countries. But we can hear these men in our own languages! We can all understand the great things they are saying about God." ¹²The people were all amazed and confused. They asked each other, "What is happening?" ¹³Other people were laughing at the apostles. These people thought the apostles were drunk from too much wine.

Peter Speaks to the People

¹⁴Then Peter stood up with the other eleven apostles.* He spoke loudly so that all the people could hear. He said, "My Jewish brothers and all of you who live in Jerusalem, listen to me. I will tell you something you need to know. Listen carefully. ¹⁵These men are not drunk like you think; it is only nine o'clock in the morning! ¹⁶But Joel the prophet* wrote about the things you see happening here today. This is what Joel wrote:

17   'God says: In the last days,
      I will pour out *(give)* my Spirit*
         on all people.
      Your sons and daughters will prophesy.*
      Your young men will see visions.*
      Your old men will have special dreams.

---

baptize A Greek word meaning to immerse, dip, or bury a person or thing briefly under water.

apostles The men Jesus chose to be his special helpers.

lots Rocks or sticks used like dice for making a choice.

Pentecost Jewish festival celebrating the wheat harvest. It was fifty days after Passover.

Spirit, Holy Spirit Also called the Spirit of God, the Spirit of Christ, and the Comforter. Joined with God and Christ, he does God's work among people in the world.

from Galilee The people thought men from Galilee could speak only their own language.

Asia The western part of Asia Minor.

converts People that changed their religion to become Jews.

prophet A prophet was a person who spoke for God.

prophesy To speak for God.

visions Something like dreams used by God to speak to people.

18 At that time I will pour out *(give)* my Spirit*
     on my servants, men and women,
     and they will prophesy.*
19 I will show amazing things in the sky above.
     I will give proofs on the earth below.
     There will be blood, fire, and thick smoke.
20 The sun will be changed into darkness,
     and the moon will become red like blood.
     Then the great and glorious day of the Lord
     will come.
21 And every person who trusts in the Lord
     will be saved.'

Joel 2:28-32

22"My Jewish brothers, listen to these words: Jesus from Nazareth was a very special man. God clearly showed this to you. God proved this by the powerful and amazing things he did through Jesus. You all saw these things. So you know this is true. 23Jesus was given to you, and you killed him. With the help of bad men you nailed Jesus to a cross. But God knew all this would happen. This was God's plan. God made this plan long ago. 24Jesus suffered the pain of death, but God made him free. God raised Jesus from death. Death could not hold Jesus. 25David said this about Jesus:

'I saw the Lord before me always;
     he is at my right side to keep me safe.
26 So my heart is glad,
     and my mouth speaks with joy.
     Yes, even my body will live with hope;
27   because you will not leave my soul
          in the place of death.*
     You will not let the body of your Holy One
          rot in the grave.
28 You taught me how to live.
     You will come close to me
     and give me great joy.'

Psalm 16:8-11

29"My brothers, I can tell you truly about David, our ancestor. He died and was buried. His grave is still here with us today. 30David was a prophet* and knew something God said. God promised David that he would make a person from David's family to be a king like David. 31David knew this before it happened. That is why David said this about that person:

'He was not left in the place of death.*
His body did not rot in the grave.'

David was talking about the Christ* rising from death. 32So Jesus is the One God raised from death, ⌊not David⌋! We are all witnesses of this. We saw him! 33Jesus was lifted up to heaven. Now Jesus is with God, at God's right side. The Father *(God)* has now given the Holy Spirit* to Jesus. The Holy Spirit is what God promised to give. So now Jesus is pouring out *(giving)* that Spirit. This is what you see and hear. 34David was not the one who was lifted up to heaven. ⌊It was Jesus who was lifted up to heaven⌋. David himself said:

'The Lord *(God)* said to my Lord:
     Sit at my right side,
35   until I put your enemies
               under your power.*'

Psalm 110:1

36"So, all the Jewish people should know this truly: God has made Jesus to be Lord and Christ.* He is the man you nailed to the cross!"

37When the people heard this, they felt very, very sorry. They asked Peter and the other apostles,* "Brothers, what should we do?"

38Peter said to them, "Change your hearts and lives and be baptized,* each one of you, in the name of Jesus Christ. Then God will forgive your sins, and you will receive the gift of the Holy Spirit.* 39This promise is for you. It is also for your children and for the people who are far away. It is for every person that the Lord our God calls to himself."

40Peter warned them with many other words; he begged them, "Save yourselves from the evil of the people that live now!" 41Then those people who accepted *(believed)* what Peter said were baptized.* On that day about 3,000 people were added to the group of believers. 42⌊The believers continued to meet together.⌋ They used their time to learn the teaching of the apostles.* The

---

Spirit, Holy Spirit Also called the Spirit of God, the Spirit of Christ, and the Comforter. Joined with God and Christ, he does God's work among people in the world.
prophesy To speak for God.
place of death Literally, "Hades."
prophet Person who spoke for God. He often told things that would happen in the future.

Christ The "anointed one" (Messiah) or chosen of God.
until I put ... power Literally, "until I make your enemies a footstool for your feet."
apostles The men Jesus chose to be his special helpers.
baptized A Greek word meaning to be immersed, dipped, or buried briefly under water.

believers shared with each other. They ate*
together and prayed together.

The Believers Share

43The apostles* were doing many powerful and
amazing things; and every person felt great
respect for God. 44All the believers stayed
together. They shared everything. 45The believers
sold their land and the things they owned. Then
they divided the money and gave it to those
people who needed it. 46The believers met
together in the temple* yard every day. They all
had the same purpose. They ate* together in their
homes. They were happy to share their food and
ate with joyful hearts. 47The believers praised
God, and all the people liked them. More and
more people were being saved every day; the Lord
was adding those people to the group ⌊of
believers⌋.

Peter Heals a Crippled Man

3 One day Peter and John went to the temple.* It
was three o'clock in the afternoon. This was
the time for the daily temple prayer service.
2When they were going into the temple yard, a
man was there. This man had been crippled all his
life. He could not walk, so some friends carried
him. His friends brought him to the temple every
day. They put the crippled man by one of the
gates outside the temple. It was called Beautiful
Gate. There the man begged for money from the
people going to the temple. 3⌊That day⌋ the man
saw Peter and John going into the temple yard. He
asked them for money. 4Peter and John looked at
the crippled man and said, "Look at us!" 5The
man looked at them; he thought they would give
him some money. 6But Peter said, "I don't have
any silver or gold, but I do have something else I
can give you: By the power of Jesus Christ from
Nazareth—stand up and walk!" 7Then Peter held
the man's right hand and lifted him up.
Immediately the man's feet and legs became
strong. 8The man jumped up, stood on his feet,
and began to walk. He went into the temple with
them. The man was walking and jumping, and he

was praising God. 9-10All the people recognized
him. The people knew he was the crippled man
who always sat by Beautiful Gate to beg for
money. Now they saw this same man walking and
praising God. The people were amazed. They
could not understand how this could happen.

Peter Speaks to the People

11The man was holding on to Peter and John.
All the people were amazed ⌊because the man was
healed⌋. They ran to Peter and John at Solomon's
Porch.* 12When Peter saw this, he said to the
people, "My Jewish brothers, why are you
surprised at this? You are looking at us like it was
our power that made this man walk. Do you think
this was done because we are good? 13No! God
did it! He is the God of Abraham, the God of
Isaac, and the God of Jacob.* He is the God of all
our fathers (ancestors). He gave glory to Jesus, his
special servant. But you gave Jesus to be killed.
Pilate decided to let Jesus go free. But you told
Pilate you did not want Jesus. 14Jesus was pure
and good (innocent), but you said you did not
want him. You told Pilate to give you a murderer*
instead of Jesus. 15And so you killed the One that
gives life! But God raised him from death. We are
witnesses of this—we saw this with our own eyes.
16It was the power of Jesus that made this crippled
man well. This happened because we trusted in
the power of Jesus. You can see this man, and you
know him. He was made completely well because
of trust in Jesus. You all saw it happen!

17"My brothers, I know you did those things to
Jesus because you did not understand what you
were doing. Your leaders also did not understand.
18God said that these things would happen. God
said through the prophets* that his Christ* would
suffer and die. I have told you how God made this
happen. 19So you must change your hearts and
lives! Come back to God and he will forgive your
sins. 20Then the Lord (God) will give you times of
spiritual rest. He will give you Jesus, the One he
chose to be the Christ. 21But Jesus must stay in
heaven until the time when all things will be made

---

ate   Literally, "broke bread." This may mean a meal or the
  Lord's Supper, the special meal Jesus told his followers to eat
  to remember him (Lk. 22:14-20).
apostles   The men Jesus chose to be his special helpers.
temple   The special building in Jerusalem for Jewish worship.
ate   (verse 46) Literally, "broke bread," the same as in verse 42.

Solomon's Porch   An area on the east side of the temple. It was
  covered by a roof.
Abraham, Isaac, Jacob   Three of the most important Jewish
  leaders during the time of the Old Testament.
murderer   Barabbas, the man the Jews asked Pilate to let go
  free instead of Jesus (Lk. 23:18).
prophets   People who spoke for God. Their writings are part of
  the Old Testament.
Christ   The "anointed one" (Messiah) or chosen one of God.

right again. God told about this time long ago when he spoke through his holy prophets. 22Moses said, 'The Lord your God will give you a prophet. That prophet will come from among your own people *(the Jews)*. He will be like me. You must obey everything that prophet tells you. 23And if any person refuses to obey that prophet, then that person will die, separated from God's people.'* 24Samuel, and all the other prophets who spoke for God after Samuel, talked about this time now. 25You have received the things the prophets talked about. You have received the agreement that God made with your fathers *(ancestors)*. God said to your father Abraham, 'Every nation on earth will be blessed through your descendants.'* 26God has sent his special servant *(Jesus)*. God sent him to you first. God sent Jesus to bless you. He does this by making each of you turn away from doing bad things."

Peter and John Before the Jewish Council

4 While Peter and John were speaking to the people, some men came to them. There were some Jewish priests, the captain of the soldiers that guarded the temple,* and some Sadducees.* 2They were upset because of what Peter and John were teaching the people. By telling people about Jesus, the two apostles* were teaching that people will rise from death. 3The Jewish leaders grabbed Peter and John and put them in jail. It was already night, so they kept Peter and John in jail until the next day. 4But many of the people that heard Peter and John preach believed the things they said. There were now about 5,000 men in the group of believers.

5The next day the Jewish leaders, the older Jewish leaders, and the teachers of the law met in Jerusalem. 6Annas (the high priest*), Caiaphas, John, and Alexander were there. Everyone from the high priest's family was there. 7They made Peter and John stand before all the people there. The Jewish leaders asked them many times, "How did you make this crippled man well? What power

did you use? With whose authority did you do this?"

8Then Peter was filled with the Holy Spirit.* He said to them. "Leaders of the people and you older leaders: 9Are you questioning us today about the good thing that was done to this crippled man? Are you asking us what made him well? 10We want all of you and all the Jewish people to know that this man was made well by the power of Jesus Christ from Nazareth! You nailed Jesus to a cross. God raised him from death. This man was crippled, but he is now well. He is able to stand here before you because of the power of Jesus! 11Jesus is

> 'the stone* that you builders
> thought was not important.
> But this stone has become
> the cornerstone.*'
>
> *Psalm 118:22*

12Jesus is the only One who can save people. His name is the only power in the world that has been given to save people. We must be saved through Jesus!"

13The Jewish leaders understood that Peter and John had no special training or education. But the leaders also saw that Peter and John were not afraid to speak. So the leaders were amazed. Then they realized that Peter and John had been with Jesus. 14They saw the crippled man standing there beside the two apostles.* They saw that the man was healed. So they could say nothing against the apostles. 15The Jewish leaders told them to leave the meeting. Then the leaders talked to each other about what they should do. 16They said, "What shall we do with these men *(the apostles)*? Every person in Jerusalem knows that they have done a great miracle.* This is clear. We cannot say it is not true. 17But we must make them afraid to talk to people about this man *(Jesus)*. Then this problem will not spread among the people."

18So the Jewish leaders called Peter and John in again. They told the apostles* not to say anything or to teach anything in the name of Jesus. 19But Peter and John answered them, "What do you think is right? What would God want? Should we obey you or God? 20We cannot be quiet. We must

---

'The Lord ... people' Quote from Deut. 18:15, 19.

descendants All the people born in a person's family after that person dies.

'Every ... descendants' Quote from Gen. 22:18; 26:24.

temple A building in Jerusalem for Jewish worship.

Sadducees A leading Jewish religious group. They accepted only the first five books of the Old Testament. They believed that people don't live again after death.

apostles Men Jesus chose to be his special helpers.

high priest Most important Jewish priest and leader.

Holy Spirit Also called the Spirit of God, the Spirit of Christ, and the Comforter. Joined with God and Christ, he does God's work among people in the world.

stone A picture or symbol meaning Jesus.

cornerstone First and most important rock of a building.

miracle(s) Miracles are amazing works done by God's power.

tell people about the things we saw and heard."
21-22The Jewish leaders could not find a way to
punish the apostles, because all the people were
praising God for what had been done. (This
miracle* was a proof from God. The man that was
healed was more than 40 years old!) So the Jewish
leaders warned the apostles again and let them go
free.

Peter and John Return to the Believers

23Peter and John left the meeting of Jewish
leaders and went to their own group. They told the
group everything that the leading priests and the
older Jewish leaders had said to them. 24When the
believers heard this, they all prayed to God. They
all wanted the same thing. They prayed, "Master,
you are the One who made the sky, the earth, the
sea, and everything in the world. 25Our father
(ancestor) David was your servant. With the help
of the Holy Spirit* he wrote these words:

'Why are the nations shouting?
Why are the people of the world
    planning things ˌagainst Godˌ?
It is hopeless!

26   The kings of the earth prepare
        themselves to fight,
    and the rulers all come together
        against the Lord (God)
        and against his Christ.*'

Psalm 2:1-2

27These things really happened when Herod,*
Pontius Pilate, the nations, and the Jewish people
all 'came together' against Jesus here in
Jerusalem. Jesus is your holy Servant. He is the
One you (God) made to be the Christ.* 28These
people that 'came together' against Jesus made
your plan happen; it happened because of your
power and your will. 29And now, Lord, listen to
what they are saying. They are trying to make us
afraid! Lord, we are your servants. Help us to
speak the things you want us to say without fear.
30Help us to be brave by showing us your power;
make sick people well, give proofs, and make
miracles* happen by the power of Jesus, your
holy servant."

31After the believers prayed, the place where
they were meeting shook. They were all filled
with the Holy Spirit,* and they continued to speak
God's message* without fear.

The Believers Share

32The group of believers were joined in their
hearts, and they had the same spirit. No person in
the group said that the things he had were his
own. Instead, they shared everything. 33With great
power the apostles* told the people that the Lord
Jesus was truly raised from death. And God
blessed all the believers very much. 34They all
received the things they needed. Everyone that
owned fields (land) or houses sold them for
money. They brought the money 35and gave it to
the apostles. Then each person was given the
things he needed.

36One of the believers was named Joseph. The
apostles* called him Barnabas. (This name means
"a person who helps others.") He was a Levite*
born in Cyprus. 37Joseph owned a field. He sold
the field, brought the money, and gave it to the
apostles.

Ananias and Sapphira

5There was a man named Ananias. His wife's
name was Sapphira. Ananias sold some land
that he had. 2But he gave only part of the money
to the apostles.* He secretly kept some of the
money for himself. His wife knew this, and she
agreed with it. 3Peter said, "Ananias, why did you
let Satan (the devil) rule your heart? You lied and
tried to deceive (fool) the Holy Spirit.* You sold
your field, but why did you keep part of the
money for yourself? 4Before you sold the field, it
belonged to you. And even after you sold it, you
could have used the money any way you wanted.
Why did you think of doing this bad thing? You
lied to God, not to men!" 5-6When Ananias heard
this, he fell down and died. Some young men
came and wrapped his body. They carried it out
and buried it. And every person that heard about
this was filled with fear.

7About three hours later his wife (Sapphira)
came in. Sapphira did not know about this thing
that had happened to her husband. 8Peter said to

---

miracle(s) Miracles are amazing works done by God's power.
Holy Spirit Also called the Spirit of God, the Spirit of Christ,
    and the Comforter. Joined with God and Christ, he does
    God's work among people in the world.
Christ The "anointed one" (Messiah) or chosen of God.
Herod Herod Antipas, tetrarch (ruler) of Galilee and Perea, son
    of Herod the Great.

God's message The news that God has made a way for people
    to have their sins forgiven and live with God forever.
apostles The men Jesus chose to be his special helpers.
Levite Levites were men from the family group of Levi who
    helped the Jewish priests in the temple.

her, "Tell me how much money you got for your field. Was it this much *(the amount Ananias had said)*?"

Sapphira answered, "Yes, that was all we got for the field."

⁹Peter said to her, "Why did you and your husband agree to test the Spirit of the Lord? Listen! Do you hear those footsteps? The men that buried your husband are at the door! They will carry you out in the same way." ¹⁰At that moment Sapphira fell down by his feet and died. The young men came in and saw that she was dead. The men carried her out and buried her beside her husband. ¹¹All the believers and all the other people who heard about these things were filled with fear.

Proofs from God

¹²The apostles* did many miracles* and powerful things. All the people saw these things. The apostles were together in Solomon's Porch*; they all had the same purpose. ¹³None of the other people felt worthy to stand with them. All the people were saying good things about the apostles. ¹⁴And more and more people believed in the Lord *(Jesus)*—many men and women were added to the group of believers. ¹⁵So the people brought their sick people into the streets. ⌐The people heard that⌐ Peter was coming by. So the people put their sick on little beds and mattresses. They thought that if the sick people could be close enough for Peter's shadow to touch them, it would be enough to heal them. ¹⁶People came from all the towns around Jerusalem. They brought their sick people and those that were bothered by evil spirits ⌐from the devil⌐. All of these people were healed.

The Jews Try to Stop the Apostles

¹⁷The high priest* and all his friends (a group called the Sadducees*) became very jealous. ¹⁸They grabbed the apostles* and put them in jail. ¹⁹But during the night, an angel of the Lord opened the doors of the jail. The angel led the apostles outside and said, ²⁰"Go and stand in the temple* yard. Tell the people everything about this new life ⌐in Jesus⌐." ²¹When the apostles heard this, they obeyed and went to the temple. It was early in the morning. The apostles began to teach the people.

The high priest* and his friends came ⌐to the temple*⌐. They called a meeting of the Jewish leaders and all the important older men of the Jews. They sent some men to the jail to bring the apostles* to them. ²²When the men went to the jail, they could not find the apostles there. So they went back and told the Jewish leaders about this. ²³The men said, "The jail was closed and locked. The guards were standing at the doors. But when we opened the doors, the jail was empty!" ²⁴The captain of the temple guards and the leading priests heard this. They were confused. They wondered, "What will happen because of this?" ²⁵Then another man came and told them, "Listen! The men you put in jail are standing in the temple yard. They are teaching the people!" ²⁶Then the captain and his men went out and brought the apostles back. But the soldiers did not use force, because they were afraid of the people. The soldiers were afraid that the people would ⌐become angry and⌐ kill them *(the soldiers)* with rocks.

²⁷The soldiers brought the apostles* to the meeting and made them stand before the Jewish leaders. The high priest* questioned the apostles. ²⁸He said, "We told you never to teach about this man *(Jesus)*! But look what you have done! You have filled Jerusalem with your teaching. You are trying to make us responsible *(guilty)* for the death of this man *(Jesus)*."

²⁹Peter and the other apostles* answered, "We must obey God, not you! ³⁰You killed Jesus. You hung him on a cross. But God, the same God our fathers *(ancestors)* had, raised Jesus up from death! ³¹Jesus is the One that God raised to his right side. God made Jesus our Leader and Savior. God did this so that all Jews can change their hearts and lives. Then God can forgive their sins. ³²We saw all these things happen, and we can say these things are true. The Holy Spirit* also shows that these things are true. God has given the Spirit to all people who obey him."

³³The Jewish leaders heard these words. They became very angry. They began to plan a way to

---

apostles The men Jesus chose to be his special helpers.

miracle(s) Miracles are amazing works done by God's power.

Solomon's Porch An area on the east side of the temple. It was covered by a roof.

high priest Most important Jewish priest and leader.

Sadducees A leading Jewish religious group. They accepted only the first five books of the Old Testament. They believed that people don't live again after death.

temple A building in Jerusalem for Jewish worship.

Holy Spirit Also called the Spirit of God, the Spirit of Christ, and the Comforter. Joined with God and Christ, he does God's work among people in the world.

kill the apostles.* [34]One of the Pharisees* in the meeting stood up. His name was Gamaliel. He was a teacher of the law, and all the people respected him. He told the men to make the apostles leave the meeting for a few minutes. [35]Then he said to them, "Men of Israel, be careful of what you are planning to do to these men! [36]Remember when Theudas appeared? He said that he was an important man. About 400 men joined him. But he was killed. And all who followed him were scattered and ran away. They were able to do nothing. [37]Later, a man named Judas came from Galilee. It was at the time of the registration.* He led a group of followers, too. He was also killed. And all his followers were scattered and ran away. [38]And so now I tell you: Stay away from these men. Leave them alone. If their plan comes from men, it will fail. [39]But if this is from God, then you will not be able to stop them. You might even be fighting against God himself!"

The Jewish leaders agreed with the thing that Gamaliel said. [40]They called the apostles* in again. They beat the apostles and told them not to talk to people about Jesus again. Then they let the apostles go free. [41]The apostles left the meeting. The apostles were happy because they were given the honor of suffering dishonor (shame) for the name ₁of Jesus₁. [42]The apostles did not stop teaching people. The apostles continued to tell the people the Good News—that Jesus is the Christ.* They did this every day in the temple* yard and in people's homes.

Seven Men Chosen for a Special Work

[6]More and more people were becoming followers of Jesus. But during this same time, the Greek-speaking followers had an argument with the other Jewish followers. They said that their widows* were not getting their share of the things that the followers received every day. [2]The twelve apostles* called the whole group of followers together. The apostles said to them, "Our work of teaching God's word has stopped. That's not good! It is better for us to continue

teaching God's word than to help people have something to eat. [3]So, brothers, choose seven of your own men. They must be men that people say are good. They must be full of wisdom and full of the Spirit.* We will give them this work to do. [4]Then we can use all our time to pray and to teach the word ₁of God₁."

[5]The whole group liked the idea. So they chose these seven men: Stephen (a man with great faith and full of the Holy Spirit*) Philip,* Prochorus, Nicanor, Timon, Parmenas, and Nicolaus (a man from Antioch, who had become a Jew). [6]Then they put these men before the apostles.* The apostles prayed and put their hands on* the men.

[7]The word of God was reaching more and more people. The group of followers in Jerusalem became larger and larger. Even a big group of Jewish priests believed and obeyed.

The Jews Against Stephen

[8]Stephen (one of the seven men) received a great blessing. God gave Stephen power to do miracles* and to show proofs from God to the people. [9]But some Jews came and argued with Stephen. These Jews were from a synagogue.* It was called a synagogue for Libertines.* (This synagogue was also for Jews from Cyrene, and for Jews from Alexandria.) Jews from Cilicia and Asia were with them. They all came and argued with Stephen. [10]But the Spirit* was helping Stephen speak with wisdom. His words were so strong that the Jews could not argue with him. [11]So the Jews paid some men to say, "We heard Stephen say bad things against Moses and against God!" [12]By doing this, these Jews upset the people, the older Jewish leaders, and the teachers of the law. They became so angry that they came and grabbed Stephen. They took him to a meeting of the Jewish leaders. [13]The Jews brought some men into the meeting. They told these men to tell lies about Stephen. The men said, "This man (Stephen) always says bad things about this holy

---

apostles   The men Jesus chose to be his special helpers.

Pharisees   The Pharisees were a Jewish religious group that claimed to follow carefully all Jewish laws and customs.

registration   A census or counting of all the people and the things they own.

Christ   The "anointed one" (Messiah) or chosen of God.

temple   A building in Jerusalem for Jewish worship.

widows   A widow is a woman whose husband has died.

Spirit, Holy Spirit   Also called the Spirit of God, the Spirit of Christ, and the Comforter. Joined with God and Christ, he does God's work among people in the world.

Philip   Not the apostle named Philip.

put their hands on   Here, doing this showed that these men were given a special work of God.

miracles   Amazing works done by the power of God.

synagogue   Synagogues were places where Jews gathered for prayer, study of the Scriptures, and other public meetings.

Libertines   Jews who had been slaves or whose fathers had been slaves, but were now free.

place *(the temple)*. And he always says bad things against the law ⌐of Moses⌐. ¹⁴We heard him say that Jesus from Nazareth will destroy this place. He also said that Jesus will change the things that Moses told us to do." ¹⁵All the people sitting in the meeting watched Stephen closely. His face looked like the face of an angel, and they saw it.

Stephen's Speech

7 The high priest* said to Stephen, "Are these things true?" ²Stephen answered, "My Jewish fathers and brothers, listen to me. Our glorious God appeared to Abraham, our father *(ancestor)*. Abraham was in Mesopotamia. This was before he lived in Haran. ³God said to Abraham, 'Leave your country and your people, and go to the country I will show you.'* ⁴So Abraham left the country of Chaldea.* He went to live in Haran. After Abraham's father died, God sent him to this place here, where you live now. ⁵But God did not give Abraham any of this land. God did not give him even a foot of it. But God promised that in the future he would give Abraham this land for himself and for his children. (This was before Abraham had any children.) ⁶This is what God said to him: 'Your descendants* will live in another country. They will be strangers. The people there will make them slaves and do bad things to them for 400 years. ⁷But I will punish the nation that made them slaves.'* And God also said, 'After those things happen, your people will come out of that country. Then your people will worship me here in this place.'* ⁸God made an agreement with Abraham; the sign for this agreement was circumcision.* And so when Abraham had a son, he circumcised his son when he was eight days old. His son's name was Isaac. Isaac also circumcised his son Jacob. And Jacob did the same for ⌐his sons. These sons later became⌐ the twelve fathers.*

high priest Most important Jewish priest and leader.
'Leave ... show you' Quote from Gen. 12:1.
Chaldea Or Babylonia, a land in the southern part of Mesopotamia. See verse 2.
descendants A person's children and all their future families.
'Your ... slaves' Quote from Gen. 15:13-14.
'After those ... place' Quote from Gen. 15:14; Ex. 3:12.
circumcision Cutting off the foreskin. This was done to every Jewish baby boy. It was a mark of the agreement God made with Abraham (Gen. 17:9-14).
fathers Important ancestors of the Jews; the leaders of the twelve Jewish family groups.

⁹"These fathers became jealous of Joseph *(their younger brother)*. They sold Joseph to be a slave in Egypt. But God was with Joseph. ¹⁰Joseph had many troubles there, but God saved him from all those troubles. Pharaoh was the king of Egypt. He liked Joseph and respected him because of the wisdom that God gave Joseph. Pharaoh gave Joseph the job of being a governor of Egypt. He even let Joseph rule over all the people in Pharaoh's house. ¹¹But all the land of Egypt and of Canaan became dry. It became so dry that food could not grow there. This made the people suffer very much. Our fathers* could not find anything to eat. ¹²But Jacob heard that there was food ⌐stored⌐ in Egypt. So he sent our fathers *(Jacob's sons)* there. (This was their first trip to Egypt.) ¹³Then they went there a second time. This time, Joseph told his brothers who he was. And Pharaoh learned about Joseph's family. ¹⁴Then Joseph sent some men to invite Jacob, his father, to come to Egypt. He also invited all his relatives (75 persons altogether). ¹⁵So Jacob went down to Egypt. Jacob and our fathers *(ancestors)* ⌐lived there until they⌐ died. ¹⁶Later their bodies were moved to Shechem. They were put in a grave there. (It was the same grave that Abraham had bought in Shechem from the sons of Hamor. He paid them with silver.)

¹⁷"The number of Jewish people in Egypt grew. There were more and more of our people there. (The promise that God made to Abraham was soon to come true.) ¹⁸Then a different king began to rule Egypt. He knew nothing about Joseph. ¹⁹This king tricked *(deceived)* our people. He was bad to our fathers *(ancestors)*. The king made them put their children outside to die. ²⁰This was the time when Moses was born. He was a very fine child. For three months they took care of Moses in his father's house. ²¹When they put Moses outside, Pharaoh's daughter took him. She raised him like he was her own son. ²²The Egyptians taught Moses about all the things they knew. He was powerful in the things he said and did.

²³"When Moses was about 40 years old, he thought it would be good to visit his brothers, the Jewish people. ²⁴Moses saw an Egyptian man doing wrong to a Jew. So he defended the Jew. Moses punished the Egyptian for hurting the Jew; Moses hit him so hard that he died. ²⁵Moses thought that his Jewish brothers would understand that God was using him to save them. But they did not understand. ²⁶The next day, Moses saw two Jewish men fighting. He tried to make peace

between them. He said, 'Men, you are brothers! Why are you doing wrong to each other?' ²⁷The man who was doing wrong to the other man pushed Moses away. He said to Moses, 'Did anyone say you could be our ruler and judge? No! ²⁸Will you kill me like you killed the Egyptian man yesterday?'* ²⁹When Moses heard him say this, he left Egypt. He went to live in the land of Midian. He was a stranger there. While Moses lived in Midian, he had two sons.

³⁰"After 40 years Moses was in the desert near Mount Sinai. An angel appeared to him in the flame of a burning bush. ³¹When Moses saw this, he was amazed. He went near to look closer at it. Moses heard a voice; it was the Lord's *(God's)*. ³²The Lord said, 'I am the same God your fathers *(ancestors)* had—the God of Abraham, the God of Isaac, and the God of Jacob*.'* Moses began to shake with fear. He was afraid to look at the bush. ³³The Lord said to him, 'Take off your shoes, because the place where you are now standing is holy ground. ³⁴I have seen my people suffer much in Egypt. I have heard my people crying. I have come down to save them. Come now, ⌊Moses,⌋ I am sending you back to Egypt.'*

³⁵"This Moses was the same man the Jews said they did not want. They had said to him, 'Did anyone say you could be our ruler and judge? No!' Moses is the same man that God sent to be a ruler and savior. God sent Moses with the help of an angel. This was the angel Moses saw in the ⌊burning⌋ bush. ³⁶So Moses led the people out. He did powerful things and miracles.* Moses did these things in Egypt, at the Red Sea, and then in the desert for 40 years. ³⁷This is the same Moses that said these words to the Jewish people: 'God will give you a prophet.* That prophet will come from among your own people. He will be like me.'* ³⁸This is the same Moses who was with the gathering ⌊of the Jews⌋ in the desert. He was with the angel that spoke to him at Mount Sinai, and he was with our fathers *(ancestors)*. Moses received

commands ⌊from God⌋ that give life. Moses gave us those commands.

³⁹"But our fathers *(ancestors)* did not want to obey Moses. They rejected him. They wanted to go back to Egypt again. ⁴⁰Our fathers said to Aaron, 'Moses led us out of the country of Egypt. But we don't know what has happened to him. So make some gods to go before us and lead us.'* ⁴¹So the people made an idol that looked like a calf. Then they brought sacrifices *(gifts)* to it. The people were very happy with what they had made with their own hands! ⁴²But God turned against them. God finished trying to stop them from worshiping the army ⌊of false gods⌋ in the sky. This is what is written in the book of the prophets*: God says,

> 'You Jewish people did not bring me blood
>   offerings and sacrifices*
>   in the desert for 40 years;
> ⁴³ You carried with you the tent *(place of
>   worship)* for Moloch *(a false god)*
>   and the image of the star of your god
>   Rephan.
> These were the idols you made to worship.
> So I will send you away beyond Babylon.'
>   *Amos 5:25-27*

⁴⁴"The Holy Tent* was with our fathers *(ancestors)* in the desert. God told Moses how to make this tent. He made it like the plan that God showed him. ⁴⁵Later, Joshua led our fathers to capture the lands of the other nations. Our people went in and God made the other people go out. When our people went into this new land, they took with them this same tent. Our people received this tent from their fathers, and our people kept it until the time of David. ⁴⁶God was very pleased with David. David asked God to let him build a house *(temple*)* for him, the God of Jacob. ⁴⁷But Solomon *(David's son)* was the person who built the temple.

'Did anyone ... yesterday?'   Quote from Ex. 2:14.

Abraham, Isaac, Jacob   Three of the most important Jewish leaders during the time of the Old Testament.

'I am ... Jacob'   Quote from Ex. 3:6.

'Take off ... Egypt'   Quote from Ex. 3:5-10.

miracle(s)   Miracles are amazing works done by God's power.

prophet   Person who spoke for God.

'God will give ... me'   Quote from Deut. 18:15.

'Moses led us out ... lead us'   Quote from Ex. 32:1.

prophets   People who spoke for God. Their writings are part of the Old Testament.

sacrifices   Offerings or gifts to God.

Holy Tent   Literally, "Tent of the Testimony," the movable tent where the Ten Commandments were kept and where God lived among his people in the time of Moses.

temple   A building in Jerusalem for Jewish worship.

48"But the Most High *(God)* does not live in houses that men build with their hands. This is what the prophet* writes:

'The Lord says,
    Heaven is my throne.
49   The earth is a place to rest my feet.
    What kind of house can you build for me?
    There is no place where I need to rest!
50   Remember, I made all these things!'"

Isaiah 66:1-2

51˻Then Stephen said,˼ "You stubborn Jewish leaders! You have not given your hearts to God! You won't listen to him! You are always against what the Holy Spirit* is trying to tell you. Your fathers *(ancestors)* did this, and you are just like them! 52Your fathers persecuted* every prophet* that ever lived. Those prophets said long ago that the Righteous One *(Christ)* would come. But your fathers killed those prophets. And now you have turned against the Righteous One and killed him. 53You are the people that received the law ˻of Moses˼. God gave you this law through his angels. But you don't obey this law!"

Stephen Is Killed

54The Jewish leaders heard Stephen say these things. They became very angry. The Jewish leaders were so mad that they were grinding their teeth at Stephen. 55But Stephen was full of the Holy Spirit.* Stephen looked up into the sky. He saw the Glory of God. He saw Jesus standing at God's right side. 56Stephen said, "Look! I see heaven open. And I see the Son of Man *(Jesus)* standing at God's right side!"

57Then the Jewish leaders all shouted with a loud voice. They closed *(covered)* their ears with their hands. They all ran at Stephen together. 58They took him out of the city and threw rocks at him until he was dead. The men who told lies against Stephen gave their coats to a young man named Saul. 59Then they threw rocks at Stephen. But Stephen was praying. He said, "Lord Jesus, receive my spirit!" 60He fell on his knees and shouted, "Lord, don't blame them for this sin!" After Stephen said this, he died.

8 Saul agreed that the killing of Stephen was a good thing.

Trouble for the Believers

2-3Some good *(religious)* men buried Stephen. They cried very loudly for him. On that day the Jews began to persecute* the group of believers in Jerusalem. The Jews made them suffer very much. Saul was also trying to destroy the group. Saul went into their houses. He dragged out men and women and put them in jail. All the believers left Jerusalem. Only the apostles* stayed. The believers went to different places in Judea and Samaria. 4The believers were scattered everywhere. Every place the believers went they told people the Good News.*

Philip Preaches in Samaria

5Philip* went to the city of Samaria. He preached about the Christ.* 6The people there heard Philip and saw the miracles* he was doing. They all listened carefully to the things Philip said. 7Many of these people had evil spirits ˻from the devil˼ inside them. But Philip made the evil spirits leave them. The spirits made a loud noise when they came out. There were also many weak and crippled people there. Philip made these people well, too. 8The people in that city were very happy because of this.

9But there was a man named Simon in that city. Before Philip came there, Simon did magic tricks. He amazed all the people of Samaria with his tricks. Simon boasted and called himself a great man. 10All the people—the least important and the most important—believed the things Simon said. The people said, "This man has the power of God that is called 'the Great Power'!" 11Simon amazed the people with his magic tricks so long that the people became his followers. 12But Philip told the people the Good News* about the kingdom of God and the power of Jesus Christ. Men and women believed Philip. They were baptized.* 13Simon himself also believed and was baptized. Simon stayed very close to Philip. He saw the

---

prophet   Isaiah, who spoke for God about 740-700 B.C.
Holy Spirit   Also called the Spirit of God, the Spirit of Christ, and the Comforter. Joined with God and Christ, he does God's work among people in the world.
persecute(d)   To persecute is to hurt or do bad things to.
prophet   Person who spoke for God.

apostles   The men Jesus chose to be his special helpers.
Good News   The news that God has made a way for people to have their sins forgiven and live with God forever.
Philip   Not the apostle named Philip.
Christ   The "anointed one" (Messiah) or chosen of God.
miracle(s)   Miracles are amazing works done by God's power.
baptized   A Greek word meaning to be immersed, dipped, or buried briefly under water.

miracles* and the very powerful things that Philip did. Simon was amazed.

¹⁴The apostles* were still in Jerusalem. They heard that the people of Samaria had accepted the word of God. So the apostles sent Peter and John to the people in Samaria. ¹⁵When Peter and John arrived, they prayed for the Samaritan believers to receive the Holy Spirit.* ¹⁶These people had been baptized* in the name of the Lord Jesus. But the Holy Spirit had not yet come down on any of them. This is why Peter and John prayed. ¹⁷The two apostles put their hands on* the people. Then the people received the Holy Spirit.

¹⁸Simon saw that the Spirit* was given to people when the apostles* put their hands on them. So Simon offered the apostles money. ¹⁹Simon said, "Give me this power so that when I put my hands on a person, he will receive the Holy Spirit.*"

²⁰Peter said to Simon, "You and your money should both be destroyed! You thought you could buy God's gift with money. ²¹You cannot share with us in this work. Your heart is not right before God. ²²Change your heart! Turn away from this bad thing you have done. Pray to the Lord *(God)*. Maybe he will forgive you for thinking this. ²³I see that you are full of bitter jealousy and ruled by sin."

²⁴Simon answered, "Both of you pray for me to the Lord *(God)*. Pray that the things you have said will not happen to me!"

²⁵Then the two apostles* told the people the things they had seen ⌊Jesus do⌋. The apostles told the people the message* of the Lord. Then they went back to Jerusalem. On the way they went through many Samaritan towns and preached the Good News* to the people.

Philip Teaches a Man from Ethiopia

²⁶An angel of the Lord spoke to Philip.* The angel said, "Get ready and go south. Go to the road that leads down to Gaza from Jerusalem—the road that goes through the desert." ²⁷So Philip got ready and went. On the road he saw a man from Ethiopia. This man was a eunuch.* He was an important officer in the service of Candace, the queen of the Ethiopians. He was responsible for taking care of all her money. This man had gone to Jerusalem to worship. ²⁸Now he was on his way home. He was sitting in his chariot* and reading from the book of Isaiah, the prophet.* ²⁹The Spirit* said to Philip, "Go to that chariot and stay near it." ³⁰So Philip went toward the chariot, and he heard the man reading. He was reading from Isaiah, the prophet. Philip said to him, "Do you understand what you are reading?"

³¹The man said, "How can I understand? I need some person to explain it to me!" Then he invited Philip to climb in and sit with him. ³²The part of Scripture* that he was reading was this:

> "He was like a sheep when it is taken
>   to be killed.
> He was like a lamb that makes no sound
>   when someone cuts off its wool.
> He says nothing.
> ³³ He was shamed, and all his rights
>   were taken away.
> His life on earth was ended;
>   There will be no story
>   about his family *(descendants)*."
>   *Isaiah 53:7-8*

³⁴The officer said to Philip, "Please, tell me, who is the prophet* talking about? Is he talking about himself or about someone else?" ³⁵Philip began to speak. He started with this same Scripture and told the man the Good News* about Jesus.

³⁶While they were traveling down the road, they came to some water. The officer said, "Look!

---

miracle(s) Miracles are amazing works done by God's power.
apostles The men Jesus chose to be his special helpers.
Holy Spirit, Spirit Also called the Spirit of God, the Spirit of Christ, and the Comforter. Joined with God and Christ, he does God's work among people in the world.
baptized A Greek word meaning to be immersed, dipped, or buried briefly under water.
put their hands on Here, doing this showed that the apostles had God's authority or power to give people the special powers of the Holy Spirit.
message, Good News The news that God has made a way for people to have their sins forgiven and live with God forever.

Philip Not the apostle named Philip.
eunuch Man whose testicles have been removed. Rulers often gave such men important positions.
chariot Something like a wagon pulled by horses.
prophet Person who spoke for God. He often told things that would happen in the future.
Scripture A part of the Holy Writings—the Old Testament.

Here is water! What is stopping me from being baptized*?" 37* 38Then the officer commanded the chariot to stop. Both Philip and the officer went down into the water, and Philip baptized him. 39When they came up out of the water, the Spirit* of the Lord took Philip away; the officer never saw him again. The officer continued on his way home. He was very happy. 40But Philip appeared in a city called Azotus. He was going to the city of Caesarea. He preached the Good News* in all the towns on the way from Azotus to Caesarea.

Saul Is Converted

9 In Jerusalem Saul was still trying to scare and kill the followers of the Lord (Jesus) all the time. So he went to the high priest.* 2Saul asked him to write letters to the Jews of the synagogues* in the city of Damascus. Saul wanted the high priest to give him the authority to find people in Damascus who were followers of Christ's Way. If he found any believers there, men or women, he would arrest them and bring them back to Jerusalem.

3So Saul went to Damascus. When he came near the city, a very bright light from the sky suddenly shined around him. 4Saul fell to the ground. He heard a voice saying to him: "Saul, Saul! Why are you doing these bad things to me?"

5Saul said, "Who are you, Lord?"

The voice answered, "I am Jesus. I am the One you are trying to hurt. 6Get up now and go into the city. Someone there will tell you what you must do."

7The men traveling with Saul stood there. They said nothing. The men heard the voice, but they saw no one. 8Saul got up from the ground. He opened his eyes, but he could not see. So the men with Saul held his hand and led him into

Damascus. 9For three days Saul could not see; he did not eat or drink.

10There was a follower of Jesus in Damascus. His name was Ananias. The Lord (Jesus) spoke to Ananias in a vision.* The Lord said, "Ananias!"

Ananias answered, "Here I am, Lord."

11The Lord said to Ananias, "Get up and go to the street called Straight Street. Find the house of Judas.* Ask for a man named Saul from the city of Tarsus. He is there now, praying. 12Saul has seen a vision.* In this vision a man named Ananias came to him and put his hands on him. Then Saul could see again."

13But Ananias answered, "Lord (Jesus), many people have told me about this man (Saul). They told me about the many bad things this man did to your holy people in Jerusalem. 14Now he (Saul) has come here to Damascus. The leading priests have given him the power to arrest all people who believe in you.*"

15But the Lord (Jesus) said to Ananias, "Go! I have chosen Saul for an important work. He must tell about me to kings, to the Jewish people, and to other nations. 16I will show Saul the things he must suffer for my name."

17So Ananias left and went to the house of Judas. He put his hands on Saul and said, "Saul, my brother, the Lord Jesus sent me. He is the One you saw on the road when you came here. Jesus sent me so that you can see again and so that you can be filled with the Holy Spirit.* 18Immediately, something that looked like fish scales fell off Saul's eyes. Saul was able to see again! Saul got up and was baptized.* 19Then he ate some food and began to feel strong again.

Saul Preaches in Damascus

Saul stayed with the followers of Jesus in Damascus for a few days. 20Soon he began to preach about Jesus in the synagogues.* He told the people, "Jesus is the Son of God!"

21All the people who heard Saul were amazed. They said, "This is the same man that was in Jerusalem. He was trying to destroy the people that trust in this name (Jesus)! He (Saul) has come here to do the same thing. He came here to arrest

---

baptized A Greek word meaning to be immersed, dipped, or buried briefly under water.

Verse 37 Some late copies of Acts add verse 37: "Philip answered, 'If you believe with all your heart, you can.' The officer said, 'I believe that Jesus Christ is the Son of God.'"

Spirit, Holy Spirit Also called the Spirit of God, the Spirit of Christ, and the Comforter. Joined with God and Christ, he does God's work among people in the world.

Good News The news that God has made a way for people to have their sins forgiven and live with God forever.

high priest Most important Jewish priest and leader.

synagogues Synagogues were places where Jews gathered for prayer, study of the Scriptures, and other public meetings.

vision Something like a dream used by God to speak to people.

Judas This is not either of the apostles named Judas.

believe in you Literally, "call on your name," meaning to show faith in Jesus by worshiping him or praying to him.

the followers ⌊of Jesus⌋ and take them back ⌊to Jerusalem⌋ to the leading priests."

²²But Saul became more and more powerful. He proved that Jesus is the Christ.* His proofs were so strong that the Jews who lived in Damascus could not argue with him.

Saul Escapes from the Jews

²³After many days, the Jews made plans to kill Saul. ²⁴The Jews were watching the city gates day and night, ⌊waiting for Saul⌋. They wanted to kill him. But Saul learned about their plan. ²⁵One night some followers that Saul had taught helped him leave the city. The followers put Saul in a basket. They put the basket through a hole in the city wall and lowered him down.

Saul in Jerusalem

²⁶Then Saul went to Jerusalem. He tried to join the group of followers (believers), but they were all afraid of him. They did not believe that Saul was really a follower ⌊of Jesus⌋. ²⁷But Barnabas accepted Saul and brought him to the apostles.* Barnabas told the apostles that Saul had seen the Lord (Jesus) on the road ⌊to Damascus⌋. Barnabas explained to the apostles how the Lord had spoken to Saul. Then he told the apostles that Saul preached for the Lord (Jesus) without fear to the people in Damascus.

²⁸And so Saul stayed with the followers. He went everywhere in Jerusalem, preaching for the Lord (Jesus) without fear. ²⁹Saul often talked with the Jews that spoke Greek. He had arguments with them. But they were trying to kill him. ³⁰When the brothers (believers) learned about this, they took Saul to the city of Caesarea. From Caesarea they sent Saul to the city of Tarsus.

³¹The church (believers) everywhere in Judea, Galilee, and Samaria had a time of peace. With the help of the Holy Spirit,* the group became stronger. The believers showed that they respected the Lord by the way they lived. Because of this, the group of believers grew larger and larger.

Peter in Lydda and Joppa

³²Peter traveled through all the towns ⌊around Jerusalem⌋. He visited the believers* who lived in Lydda. ³³In Lydda he met a paralyzed (crippled) man named Aeneas. Aeneas had not been able to leave his bed for the past eight years. ³⁴Peter said to him, "Aeneas, Jesus Christ heals you. Stand up and make your bed! You can do this for yourself now!" Aeneas stood up immediately. ³⁵All the people living in Lydda and on the plain of Sharon saw him. These people turned to (believed in) the Lord ⌊Jesus⌋.

³⁶In the city of Joppa there was a follower ⌊of Jesus⌋ named Tabitha. (Her Greek name, Dorcas, means "a deer.") She always did good things for people. She always gave money to people who needed it. ³⁷While Peter was in Lydda, Tabitha became sick and died. They washed her body and put it in a room upstairs. ³⁸The followers in Joppa heard that Peter was in Lydda. (Lydda is near Joppa.) So they sent two men to Peter. They begged him, "Hurry, please come quickly!" ³⁹Peter got ready and went with them. When he arrived, they took him to the room upstairs. All the widows* stood around Peter. They were crying. They showed Peter the coats and other clothes that Dorcas (Tabitha) had made when she was still alive. ⁴⁰Peter sent all the people out of the room. He kneeled and prayed. Then he turned to Tabitha's body and said, "Tabitha, stand up!" She opened her eyes. When she saw Peter, she sat up. ⁴¹He gave her his hand and helped her stand up. Then he called the believers* and the widows into the room. He showed them Tabitha; she was alive! ⁴²People everywhere in Joppa learned about this. Many of these people believed in the Lord (Jesus). ⁴³Peter stayed in Joppa for many days. He stayed with a man named Simon who was a leatherworker.*

Peter and Cornelius

10In the city of Caesarea there was a man named Cornelius. He was an army officer* in the "Italian" group ⌊of the Roman army⌋. ²Cornelius was a good (religious) man. He and all

---

Christ   The "anointed one" (Messiah) or chosen of God.

apostles   The men Jesus chose to be his special helpers.

Holy Spirit   Also called the Spirit of God, the Spirit of Christ, and the Comforter. Joined with God and Christ, he does God's work among people in the world.

believers   Literally, "holy ones," a name for people that believe in Jesus.

widows   A widow is a woman whose husband has died.

leatherworker   Man who made leather from animal skins.

army officer   A centurion, a Roman army officer who had authority over 100 soldiers.

the other people who lived in his home worshiped the true God. He gave much of his money to the poor people. Cornelius prayed to God always. [3]One afternoon about three o'clock, Cornelius saw a vision.* He saw it clearly. In the vision an angel from God came to him and said, "Cornelius!"

[4]Cornelius looked at the angel. He became afraid and said, "What do you want, sir?"

The angel said to Cornelius, "God has heard your prayers. He has seen the things you give to the poor people. God remembers you. [5]Send some men now to the city of Joppa. Send your men to bring back a man named Simon. Simon is also called Peter. [6]Simon is staying with a man, also named Simon, who is a leatherworker.* He has a house beside the sea." [7]The angel who spoke to Cornelius left. Then Cornelius called two of his servants and a soldier. This soldier was a good (religious) man. The soldier was one of Cornelius' close helpers. [8]Cornelius explained everything to these three men. Then he sent them to Joppa.

[9]The next day these men came near Joppa. At that time, Peter was going up to the roof to pray. It was about noon. [10]Peter was hungry. He wanted to eat. But while they were preparing the food for Peter to eat, a vision* came to him. [11]He saw something coming down through the open sky. It looked like a big sheet coming down to the ground. It was being lowered to the ground by its four corners. [12]Every kind of animal was in it— animals that walk, animals that crawl on the ground, and birds that fly in the air. [13]Then a voice said to Peter, "Get up, Peter; kill any of these animals and eat it."

[14]But Peter said, "I would never do that, Lord! I have never eaten food that is unholy or not pure."

[15]But the voice said to him again, "God has made these things clean (pure). Don't call them 'unholy'!" [16]This happened three times. Then the whole thing was taken back up into the sky.

[17]Peter wondered what this vision* meant. The men that Cornelius sent had found Simon's house. They were standing at the door. [18]They asked, "Is Simon Peter staying here?"

[19]Peter was still thinking about the vision.* But the Spirit* said to him, "Listen! Three men are looking for you. [20]Get up and go downstairs. Go with these men and don't ask questions. I have sent them to you." [21]So Peter went downstairs to the men. He said, "I am the man you are looking for. Why did you come here?"

[22]The men said, "A holy angel told Cornelius to invite you to his house. Cornelius is an army officer.* He is a good (righteous) man; he worships God. All the Jewish people respect him. The angel told Cornelius to invite you to his house so that he can listen to the things you have to say." [23]Peter asked the men to come in and stay for the night.

The next day Peter got ready and went away with the three men. Some of the brothers (believers) from Joppa went with Peter. [24]The next day they came into the city of Caesarea. Cornelius was waiting for them. He had already gathered his relatives and close friends ⌊at his house⌋. [25]When Peter entered the house, Cornelius met him. Cornelius fell down at Peter's feet and worshiped him. [26]But Peter told him to get up. Peter said, "Stand up! I am only a man like you." [27]Peter continued talking with Cornelius. Then Peter went inside and saw a large group of people together there. [28]Peter said to the people, "You people understand that it is against our Jewish law for a Jew to associate with or visit any person who is not a Jew. But God has shown me that I should not call any person 'unholy' or 'not clean.' [29]That is why I did not argue when the men asked me to come here. Now, please tell me why you sent for me."

[30]Cornelius said, "Four days ago, I was praying in my house. It was at this same time—three o'clock in the afternoon. Suddenly, there was a man (angel) standing before me. He was wearing bright, shiny clothes. [31]The man said, 'Cornelius! God has heard your prayer. God has seen the things you give to the poor people. God remembers you. [32]So send some men to the city of Joppa. Ask Simon Peter to come. Peter is staying in the house of a man, also named Simon, who is a leatherworker.* His house is beside the sea.' [33]So I sent for you immediately. It was very good of you to come here. Now we are all here before God to hear everything the Lord has commanded you to tell us."

vision Something like a dream used by God to speak to people.
leatherworker Man who made leather from animal skins.
Spirit Also called the Spirit of God, the Spirit of Christ, and the Comforter. Joined with God and Christ, he does God's work among people in the world.

army officer A centurion, a Roman army officer who had authority over 100 soldiers.

Peter Speaks in the House of Cornelius

34Peter began to speak: "I really understand now that to God every person is the same. 35And God accepts any person who worships him and does what is right. It is not important what country a person comes from. 36God has spoken to the Jewish people. God sent them the Good News* that peace has come through Jesus Christ. Jesus is the Lord *(Ruler)* of all people! 37You know what has happened all over Judea. It began in Galilee after John* preached to the people about baptism.* 38You know about Jesus from Nazareth. God made him the Christ* by giving him the Holy Spirit* and power. Jesus went everywhere doing good things for people. Jesus healed the people who were ruled by the devil. This showed that God was with Jesus. 39We saw all the things that Jesus did in Judea and in Jerusalem. We are witnesses. But Jesus was killed. They put him on a cross made of wood. 40But, on the third day ₍after his death₎, God raised Jesus to life! God let people see Jesus clearly. 41But Jesus was not seen by all the people. Only the witnesses that God had already chosen saw him. We are those witnesses! We ate and drank with Jesus after he was raised from death. 42Jesus told us to preach to the people. He told us to tell people that he is the One that God chose to be the Judge of all people who are living and all people who are dead. 43Every person who believes *(trusts)* in Jesus will be forgiven. God will forgive the sins of that person through the name of Jesus. All the prophets* say this is true."

The Holy Spirit Comes to Non-Jews

44While Peter was still speaking these words, the Holy Spirit* came down on all those people who were listening to his speech. 45The Jewish believers who came with Peter were amazed. They were amazed that the Holy Spirit was poured out *(given)* to the non-Jewish people too. 46These Jewish believers heard them speaking different languages and praising God. Then Peter said, 47"We cannot refuse to allow these people to be baptized* in water. They have received the Holy Spirit the same as we did!" 48So Peter commanded that Cornelius and his relatives and friends be baptized in the name of Jesus Christ. Then the people asked Peter to stay with them for a few days.

Peter Returns to Jerusalem

11 The apostles* and the brothers in Judea heard that non-Jewish people had accepted God's teaching too. 2But when Peter came to Jerusalem, some Jewish believers* argued with him. 3They said, "You went into the homes of people that are not Jews and are not circumcised*! You even ate with them!"

4So Peter explained the whole story to them. 5Peter said, "I was in the city of Joppa. While I was praying, a vision* came to me. In the vision I saw something coming down from the sky. It looked like a big sheet. It was being lowered to the ground by its four corners. It came down and stopped very close to me. 6I looked inside it. I saw animals, both tame and wild. I saw animals that crawl and birds that fly in the air. 7I heard a voice say to me, 'Get up, Peter. Kill any of these animals and eat it!' 8But I said, 'I would never do that, Lord! I have never eaten anything that is unholy or not pure.' 9But the voice from the sky answered again, 'God has made these things clean *(pure)*. Don't call them unholy!' 10This happened three times. Then the whole thing was taken back into the sky. 11Then three men came to the house where I was staying. These three men were sent to me from the city of Caesarea. 12The Spirit* told me to go with them without doubting. These six brothers *(believers)* here also went with me. We went to the house of Cornelius. 13Cornelius told us about the angel he saw standing in his house. The

---

Good News The news that God has made a way for people to have their sins forgiven and live with God forever.

John John the Baptizer, who preached to people about Christ's coming (Mt. 3; Lk. 3).

baptism A Greek word meaning to be immersed, dipped, or buried briefly under water.

Christ The "anointed one" (Messiah) or chosen of God.

Spirit, Holy Spirit Also called the Spirit of God, the Spirit of Christ, and the Comforter. Joined with God and Christ, he does God's work among people in the world.

prophets People who spoke for God. Their writings are part of the Old Testament.

baptized A Greek word meaning to be immersed, dipped, or buried briefly under water.

apostles The men Jesus chose to be his special helpers.

Jewish believers Literally, "those of circumcision." This may mean Jews who thought that all Christians must be circumcised and obey the law of Moses (See Gal. 2:12).

circumcised To have the foreskin cut off. This was done to every Jewish baby boy. It was a mark of the agreement God made with Abraham (Gen. 17:9-14).

vision Something like a dream used by God to speak to people.

angel said to Cornelius, 'Send some men to Joppa. Invite Simon Peter to come. [14]He will speak to you. The things he will say will save you and all your family.' [15]After I began my speech, the Holy Spirit* came on them the same as he *(the Spirit)* came on us at the beginning.* [16]Then I remembered the words of the Lord *(Jesus)*. The Lord said, 'John baptized* people in water, but you will be baptized in the Holy Spirit!' [17]God gave to these people the same gift that he gave to us who believed in the Lord Jesus Christ. So could I stop the work of God? No!"

[18]When the Jewish believers heard these things, they stopped arguing. They praised God and said, "So God is allowing the non-Jewish people to change their hearts and have life the same as us!"

The Good News Comes to Antioch

[19]The believers were scattered by the persecution* that happened after Stephen was killed. Some of the believers went to places far away like Phoenicia, Cyprus, and Antioch. The believers told the Good News* in these places; but they told it only to Jews. [20]Some of these believers were men from Cyprus and Cyrene. When these men came to Antioch, they also spoke to Greeks *(non-Jews)*. They told these Greek people the Good News about the Lord Jesus. [21]The Lord was helping the believers. And a large group of people believed and started following the Lord *(Jesus)*.

[22]The church *(group of believers)* in Jerusalem heard about these new believers ⌊in Antioch⌋. So the believers in Jerusalem sent Barnabas to Antioch. [23-24]Barnabas was a good man. He was full of the Holy Spirit* and full of faith. When Barnabas went to Antioch, he saw that God had blessed those people very much. This made Barnabas very happy. He encouraged all the believers in Antioch. He told them, "Never lose your faith. Always obey the Lord with all your hearts." Many, many people became followers of the Lord ⌊Jesus⌋.

[25]Then Barnabas went to the city of Tarsus. He was looking for Saul. [26]When he found Saul, Barnabas brought him to Antioch. Saul and Barnabas stayed there a whole year. Every time the group of believers came together, Saul and Barnabas met with them and taught many people. In Antioch the followers ⌊of Jesus⌋ were called "Christians" for the first time.

[27]About that same time some prophets* went from Jerusalem to Antioch. [28]One of these prophets was named Agabus. In Antioch, Agabus stood up and spoke. With the help of the Holy Spirit* he said, "A very bad time is coming to the whole world. There will be no food for people to eat." (This time without food happened when Claudius was emperor.*) [29]The believers decided that they would all try to help their brothers ⌊and sisters⌋ who lived in Judea. Each believer planned to send them as much as he could. [30]They gathered the money and gave it to Barnabas and Saul. Then Barnabas and Saul brought it to the elders* in Judea.

Herod Agrippa Hurts the Church

12 During that same time King Herod* began to persecute* some of the people who belonged to the church *(group of believers)*. [2]Herod ordered James to be killed with a sword. James was the brother of John. [3]Herod saw that the Jews liked this. So he decided to arrest Peter, too. (This happened during the time of the Jewish holiday called the Passover.*) [4]Herod arrested Peter and put him in jail. A group of 16 soldiers guarded Peter. Herod wanted to wait until after the Passover festival. Then he planned to bring Peter before the people. [5]So Peter was kept in jail. But the church was constantly praying to God for Peter.

Spirit, Holy Spirit Also called the Spirit of God, the Spirit of Christ, and the Comforter. Joined with God and Christ, he does God's work among people in the world.

beginning The beginning of the church on the day of Pentecost. (Read Acts 2).

baptize(d) A Greek word meaning to immerse, dip, or bury a person or thing briefly under water.

persecution A time when the Jews were punishing people who believed in Christ (Acts 8:1-4).

Good News The news that God has made a way for people to have their sins forgiven and live with God forever.

prophets People who spoke for God.

emperor The ruler (leader) of the Roman empire.

elders Men chosen to lead a church. Also called "overseers" and "pastors" ("shepherds"), they have the work of caring for God's people (Acts 20:17,28; Eph. 4:11; Tit. 1:7,9).

Herod Herod Agrippa I, grandson of Herod the Great.

persecute To persecute is to hurt or do bad things to.

Passover Important Jewish holy day. They ate a special meal on this day every year to remember that God freed them from slavery in Egypt in the time of Moses.

Peter Leaves the Jail

[6]Peter was sleeping between two of the soldiers. He was bound with two chains. More soldiers were guarding the door of the jail. It was at night, and Herod planned to bring Peter out before the people the next day. [7]Suddenly, an angel of the Lord stood there. A light shined in the room. The angel touched Peter on the side and woke him up. The angel said, "Hurry, get up!" The chains fell off Peter's hands. [8]The angel said to Peter, "Get dressed and put on your shoes." And so Peter did this. Then the angel said, "Put on your coat and follow me." [9]So the angel went out and Peter followed. Peter did not know if the angel was really doing this. He thought he might be seeing a vision.* [10]Peter and the angel went past the first guard and the second guard. Then they came to the iron gate that separated them from the city. The gate opened itself for them. Peter and the angel went through the gate and walked about a block. Then the angel suddenly left.

[11]Peter realized then what had happened. He thought, "Now I know that the Lord really sent his angel to me. He rescued *(saved)* me from Herod. The Jewish people thought that bad things would happen to me. But the Lord saved me from all these things."

[12]When Peter realized this, he went to the home of Mary. She was the mother of John. (John was also called Mark.) Many people were gathered there. They were all praying. [13]Peter knocked on the outside door. A servant girl named Rhoda came to answer it. [14]Rhoda recognized Peter's voice, and she was very happy. She even forgot to open the door. She ran inside and told the group, "Peter is at the door!" [15]The believers said to Rhoda, "You are crazy!" But she continued to say that it was true. So they said, "It must be Peter's angel."

[16]But Peter continued to knock. When the believers opened the door, they saw Peter. They were amazed. [17]Peter made a sign with his hand to tell them to be quiet. He explained to them how the Lord led him out of the jail. He said, "Tell James and the other brothers what happened." Then Peter left to go to another place.

[18]The next day the soldiers were very upset. They wondered what happened to Peter. [19]Herod looked everywhere for Peter but could not find

him. So Herod questioned the guards. Then he ordered that the guards be killed.

The Death of Herod Agrippa

Later Herod* moved from Judea. He went to the city of Caesarea and stayed there a while. [20]Herod was very angry with the people from the cities of Tyre and Sidon. Those people all came in a group to Herod. They were able to get Blastus on their side. Blastus was the king's personal servant. The people asked Herod for peace because their country needed food from Herod's country.

[21]Herod decided a day to meet with them. On that day Herod was wearing a beautiful royal robe. He sat on his throne and made a speech to the people. [22]The people shouted, "This is the voice of a god, not a man!" [23]Herod ₁accepted this praise and₁ did not give the glory to God. So an angel of the Lord caused him to become sick. He was eaten by worms inside him, and he died.

[24]The message* of God was spreading and influencing more and more people. The group of believers became larger and larger.

[25]After Barnabas and Saul finished their work in Jerusalem, they returned to Antioch. John Mark was with them.

Barnabas and Saul Given a Special Work

13 In the church *(group of believers)* at Antioch there were some prophets* and teachers. They were: Barnabas, Simeon (also called Niger), Lucius (from the city of Cyrene), Manaen (who had grown up with Herod,* the ruler) and Saul. [2]These men were all serving the Lord and fasting.* The Holy Spirit* said to them, "Give Barnabas and Saul to me to do a special work. I have chosen them to do this work."

[3]So the church fasted* and prayed. They put their hands on* Barnabas and Saul and sent them out.

Herod   Herod Agrippa I, grandson of Herod the Great.

message   The news that God has made a way for people to have their sins forgiven and live with God forever.

prophets   People who spoke for God.

fasting, fasted   To fast is to live without food for a special time of prayer and worship to God.

Holy Spirit   Also called the Spirit of God, the Spirit of Christ, and the Comforter. Joined with God and Christ, he does God's work among people in the world.

put their hands on   Here, this was a sign to show that these men were given a special work of God.

vision   Something like a dream used by God to speak to people.

Barnabas and Saul in Cyprus

[4]Barnabas and Saul were sent out by the Holy Spirit.* They went to the city of Seleucia. Then they sailed from Seleucia to the island of Cyprus. [5]When Barnabas and Saul came to the city of Salamis, they preached the message* of God in the Jewish synagogues.* (John ⌊Mark⌋ was with them to help.)

[6]They went across the whole island to the city of Paphos. In Paphos they met a Jewish man who did magic tricks. His name was Barjesus. He was a false prophet.* [7]Barjesus always stayed close to Sergius Paulus, the governor. Sergius Paulus was a wise man. He asked Barnabas and Saul to come to him. He wanted to hear the message* of God. [8]But Elymas, the magician, was against Barnabas and Saul. (Elymas is the name for Barjesus in the Greek language.) Elymas tried to stop the governor from believing ⌊in Jesus⌋. [9]But Saul was filled with the Holy Spirit.* Paul (Saul's other name) looked at Elymas (Barjesus) [10]and said, "You son of the devil! You are an enemy of everything that is right! You are full of evil tricks and lies. You always try to change the Lord's truths into lies! [11]Now the Lord will touch you and you will be blind. For a time you will not be able to see anything—not even the light from the sun."

Then everything became dark for Elymas. He walked around lost. He was trying to find someone to lead him by the hand. [12]When the governor (Sergius Paulus) saw this, he believed. He was amazed at the teaching about the Lord.

Paul and Barnabas Leave Cyprus

[13]Paul and those people with him sailed away from Paphos. They came to Perga, a city in Pamphylia. But John ⌊Mark⌋ left them; he returned to Jerusalem. [14]They continued their trip from Perga and went to Antioch, a city near Pisidia. In Antioch on the Sabbath day* they went into the Jewish synagogue* and sat down. [15]The law of Moses and the writings of the prophets* were read. Then the leaders of the synagogue sent a message to Paul and Barnabas: "Brothers, if you have something to say that will help the people here, please speak!"

[16]Paul stood up. He raised his hand* and said, "My Jewish brothers and you other people who also worship the true God, please listen to me! [17]The God of Israel (the Jews) chose our fathers (ancestors). God helped his people to have success during the time they lived in Egypt as strangers. God brought them out of that country with great power. [18]And God was patient with them for 40 years in the desert. [19]God destroyed seven nations in the land of Canaan. He gave their land to his people. [20]All this happened in about 450 years.

"After this, God gave ⌊our people⌋ judges (leaders) until the time of Samuel* the prophet. [21]Then the people asked for a king. God gave them Saul, the son of Kish. Saul was from the family group of Benjamin. He was king for 40 years. [22]After God took Saul away, God made David their king. This is what God said about David: 'David, the son of Jesse, is a man who is like me in his thinking. He will do all the things I want him to do.' [23]God has brought one of David's descendants to Israel (the Jews) to be their Savior.* That descendant is Jesus. God promised to do this. [24]Before Jesus came, John* preached to all the Jewish people. John told the people to be baptized* to show they wanted to change their lives. [25]When John was finishing his work, he said, 'Who do you think I am? I am not the Christ.* He is coming later. I am not worthy to untie his shoes.'

[26]"My brothers, sons in the family of Abraham, and you non-Jews who also worship the true God, listen! The news about this salvation has been sent to us. [27]The ⌊Jews⌋ living in Jerusalem and the Jewish leaders did not realize that ⌊Jesus⌋ was the

---

Holy Spirit Also called the Spirit of God, the Spirit of Christ, and the Comforter. Joined with God and Christ, he does God's work among people in the world.

message The news that God has made a way for people to have their sins forgiven and live with God forever.

synagogue(s) Synagogues were places where Jews gathered for prayer, study of the Scriptures, and other public meetings.

false prophet A person who says he speaks for God but does not really speak God's truth.

Sabbath day The seventh day of the Jewish week. It was a special religious day for the Jews.

prophets People who spoke for God. Their writings are part of the Old Testament.

raised his hand A sign to make the people listen.

Samuel Last judge and first prophet of Israel.

Savior The One that God promised to send to save his people from punishment for their sins.

John John the Baptizer, who preached to people about Christ's coming (Mt. 3; Lk 3).

baptized A Greek word meaning to be immersed, dipped, or buried briefly under water.

Christ The "anointed one" (Messiah) or chosen of God.

Savior. The words that the prophets* wrote ₍about Jesus₎ were read to the Jews every Sabbath day,* but they did not understand. The Jews condemned Jesus. When they did this, they made the words of the prophets come true! 28They could not find any real reason why Jesus should die, but they asked Pilate to kill him. 29These Jews did all the bad things that the Scriptures* said would happen to Jesus. Then they took Jesus down from the cross and put him in a grave. 30But God raised him up from death! 31After this, for many days, the people who had gone with Jesus from Galilee to Jerusalem saw Jesus. These people are now his witnesses to the people. 32We tell you the Good News* about the promise God made to our fathers (ancestors). 33We are their children (descendants), and God has made this promise come true for us. God did this by raising Jesus from death. We also read about this in Psalm 2:

'You are my Son.
Today I have become your Father.'
Psalm 2:7

34God raised Jesus from death. Jesus will never go back to the grave and become dust. So God said:

'I will give you the true and holy promises that
I made to David.'
Isaiah 55:3

35But in another place God says:

'You will not let ₍the body of₎ your Holy One
rot in the grave.'
Psalm 16:10

36David did God's will during the time when he lived. Then he died. David was buried with his fathers. And his body did rot in the grave! 37But the One (Jesus) that God raised from death did not rot in the grave. 38-39Brothers, you must understand what we are telling you: You can have forgiveness of your sins through this One (Jesus). The law of Moses could not free you from your sins. But every person who believes ₍in Jesus₎ is free from all his sins through him (Jesus). 40The prophets* said some things would happen. Be

careful! Don't let these things happen to you. The prophets said:

41 'Listen, you people who doubt!
You can wonder, but then go away and die;
because during your time,
I (God) will do something
that you will not believe.
You will not believe it,
even if someone explains it to you!'"
Habakkuk 1:5

42While Paul and Barnabas were leaving ₍the synagogue,₎* the people asked Paul and Barnabas to ₍come again₎ on the next Sabbath day* and tell them more about these things. 43After the meeting, many of the Jews followed Paul and Barnabas from that place. With the Jews there were many converts* to the Jewish religion. These converts also worshiped the true God. Paul and Barnabas were persuading them to continue trusting in God's grace (kindness).

44On the next Sabbath day,* almost all the people in the city came together to hear the word of the Lord. 45The Jews saw all these people there. So the Jews became very jealous. They said some very bad things and argued against the words that Paul said. 46But Paul and Barnabas spoke very boldly. They said, "We must speak the message* of God to you Jews first. But you refuse to listen. You are making yourselves lost—not worthy of having eternal life! So we will now go to the people of other nations! 47This is what the Lord (God) told us to do. The Lord said:

'I have made you to be a light
for other nations,
so that you can show the way of salvation
to people all over the world.'"
Isaiah 49:6

48When the non-Jewish people heard Paul say this, they were happy. They gave honor to the message* of the Lord. And many of the people believed the message. These were the people chosen to have life forever.

49And so the message* of the Lord was being told through the whole country. 50But the Jews

---

prophets People who spoke for God. Their writings are part of the Old Testament.

Sabbath day The seventh day of the Jewish week. It was a special religious day for the Jews.

Scriptures Holy Writings—the Old Testament.

Good News The news that God has made a way for people to have their sins forgiven and live with God forever.

synagogue Synagogues were places where Jews gathered for prayer, study of the Scriptures, and other public meetings.

converts People that changed their religion to become Jews.

message The news that God has made a way for people to have their sins forgiven and live with God forever.

caused some of the important religious women and the leaders of the city to become angry and to be against Paul and Barnabas. These people did things against Paul and Barnabas and threw them out of town. [51]So Paul and Barnabas shook the dust off their feet.* Then they went to the city of Iconium. [52]But the followers ⌊of Jesus in Antioch⌋ were happy and full of the Holy Spirit.*

Paul and Barnabas in Iconium

14Paul and Barnabas went to the city of Iconium. They entered the Jewish synagogue.* (This is what they did in every city.) They spoke to the people there. Paul and Barnabas spoke so well that many Jews and Greeks (non-Jews) believed what they said. [2]But some of the Jews did not believe. These Jews excited the non-Jewish people and made them think bad things about the brothers (believers). [3]So Paul and Barnabas stayed in Iconium a long time, and they spoke bravely for the Lord. Paul and Barnabas preached about God's grace (kindness). The Lord proved that what they said was true by helping the apostles* (Paul and Barnabas) do miracles and wonders.* [4]But some of the people in the city agreed with the Jews. Other people in the city believed Paul and Barnabas. So the city was divided.

[5]Some non-Jewish people, some Jews, and their Jewish leaders tried to hurt Paul and Barnabas. These people wanted to kill them with rocks. [6]When Paul and Barnabas learned about this, they left that city. They went to Lystra and Derbe, cities in Lycaonia, and to the areas around those cities. [7]They told the Good News* there too.

Paul in Lystra and Derbe

[8]In Lystra there was a man who had something wrong with his feet. He had been born crippled; he had never walked. [9]This man was sitting and listening to Paul speak. Paul looked at him. Paul saw that the man believed that God could heal him. [10]So Paul shouted, "Stand up on your feet!" The man jumped up and began walking around. [11]When the people saw what Paul did, they shouted in their own Lycaonian language. They said, "The gods have become like men! They have come down to us!" [12]The people began to call Barnabas "Zeus."* They called Paul "Hermes,"* because he was the main speaker. [13]The temple of Zeus was near the city. The priest of this temple brought some bulls and flowers to the city gates. The priest and the people wanted to give an offering to ⌊worship⌋ Paul and Barnabas.

[14]But when the apostles,* Barnabas and Paul, understood what the people were doing, they tore their own clothes.* Then they ran in among the people and shouted to them: [15]"Men, why are you doing these things? We are not gods! We have the same feelings as you have! We came to tell you the Good News.* We are telling you to turn away from these worthless things. Turn to the true living God. He is the One who made the sky, the earth, the sea, and everything that is in them. [16]In the past, God let all the nations do what they wanted. [17]But God did things that prove he is real: He does good things for you. He gives you rain from the sky. He gives you good harvests at the right times. He gives you plenty of food, and he fills your hearts with joy." [18]Paul and Barnabas told the people these things. But still Paul and Barnabas almost could not stop the people from offering sacrifices to ⌊worship⌋ them.

[19]Then some Jews came from Antioch and Iconium. They persuaded the people to be against Paul. And so the people threw rocks at Paul and dragged him out of the town. The people thought that they had killed Paul. [20]The followers ⌊of Jesus⌋ gathered around Paul and he got up and went back into the town. The next day, he and Barnabas left and went to the city of Derbe.

The Return to Antioch in Syria

[21]Paul and Barnabas told the Good News* in the city of Derbe too. Many people became followers ⌊of Jesus⌋. Paul and Barnabas returned to

---

shook the dust off their feet A warning. It showed that they were finished talking to these people.

Holy Spirit Also called the Spirit of God, the Spirit of Christ, and the Comforter. Joined with God and Christ, he does God's work among people in the world.

synagogue Synagogues were places where Jews gathered for prayer, study of the Scriptures, and other public meetings.

apostles The men Jesus chose to be his special helpers.

miracles and wonders Amazing works or great things done by the power of God.

Good News The news that God has made a way for people to have their sins forgiven and live with God forever.

Zeus The most important of the many Greek gods.

Hermes Another Greek god. The Greeks believed he was a messenger for the other gods.

tore ... clothes This showed they were very angry.

the cities of Lystra, Iconium, and Antioch. [22]In those cities Paul and Barnabas made the followers ⌊of Jesus⌋ stronger. They helped them to stay in the faith. Paul and Barnabas said, "We must suffer many things on our way into God's kingdom." [23]Paul and Barnabas chose elders* for each church (group of believers). They fasted* and prayed for these elders. These elders were men who had trusted the Lord ⌊Jesus.⌋ So Paul and Barnabas put them in the Lord's care.

[24]Paul and Barnabas went through the country of Pisidia. Then they came to the country of Pamphylia. [25]They preached the message* ⌊of God⌋ in the city of Perga, and then they went down to the city of Attalia. [26]And from there Paul and Barnabas sailed away to Antioch ⌊in Syria⌋. This is the city where the believers had put them into God's care and sent them to do this work. Now they had finished the work.

[27]When Paul and Barnabas arrived, they gathered the church (group of believers) together. Paul and Barnabas told them about all the things God had done with them. They said, "God opened a door so that the people of other nations (non-Jews) could also believe!" [28]Paul and Barnabas stayed there a long time with the followers ⌊of Christ⌋.

The Meeting at Jerusalem

15 Then some men came ⌊to Antioch⌋ from Judea. They began teaching the non-Jewish brothers: "You cannot be saved if you are not circumcised.* Moses taught us to do this." [2]Paul and Barnabas were against this teaching. They argued with these men about it. So the group decided to send Paul, Barnabas, and some other men to Jerusalem. These men were going there to talk more about this with the apostles* and elders.*

[3]The church helped the men leave on the trip. These men went through the countries of Phoenicia and Samaria. In these countries they told all about how the non-Jewish people had turned to the true God. This made all the brothers very happy. [4]Paul, Barnabas, and the others arrived in Jerusalem. The apostles,* the elders,* and the whole group of believers welcomed them. Paul, Barnabas, and the others told about all the things that God had done with them. [5]Some of the believers ⌊in Jerusalem⌋ had belonged to the Pharisees.* They stood up and said, "The non-Jewish believers must be circumcised.* We must tell them to obey the law of Moses!"

[6]Then the apostles* and the elders* gathered to study this problem. [7]There was a long debate. Then Peter stood up and said to them, "My brothers, I know that you remember what happened in the early days. God chose me then from among you to preach the Good News* to the non-Jewish people. They heard the Good News from me and they believed. [8]God knows the thoughts of all men, and he accepted these non-Jewish people. God showed this to us by giving them the Holy Spirit* the same as he did to us. [9]To God, those people are not different from us. When they believed, God made their hearts pure. [10]So now, why are you putting a heavy burden* around the necks of the non-Jewish brothers? Are you trying to make God angry? We and our fathers (ancestors) were not strong enough to carry that burden! [11]No, we believe that we and these people will be saved by the grace (mercy) of the Lord Jesus!"

[12]Then the whole group became quiet. They listened to Paul and Barnabas speak. Paul and Barnabas told about all the miracles and wonders* that God did through them among the non-Jewish people. [13]Paul and Barnabas finished speaking. Then James spoke. He said, "My brothers, listen to me. [14]Simon (Peter) has told us how God showed his love for the non-Jewish people. For the first time, God accepted the non-Jewish people and made them his people. [15]The words of the prophets* agree with this too:

---

elders   A group of men chosen to lead a church. Also called "overseers" and "pastors" (shepherds), they have the work of caring for God's people (Acts 20:17,28; Eph. 4:11; Tit.1:7,9).

fasted   To fast is to live without food for a special time of prayer.

message, Good News   The news that God has made a way for people to have their sins forgiven and live with God forever.

circumcised   To have the foreskin cut off. This was done to every Jewish baby boy. It was a mark of the agreement that God made with Abraham (Gen. 17:9-14).

apostles   The men Jesus chose to be his special helpers.

Pharisees   A Jewish religious group that claimed to follow carefully all Jewish laws and customs.

Holy Spirit   Also called the Spirit of God, the Spirit of Christ, and the Comforter. Joined with God and Christ, he does God's work among people in the world.

burden   The Jewish law. Some of the Jews tried to make the non-Jewish believers follow this law.

miracles and wonders   Amazing works or great things done by the power of God.

prophets   People who spoke for God. Their writings are part of the Old Testament.

16 'I *(God)* will return after this.
      I will build David's house again.
        It has fallen down.
      I will build again the parts of his house that
        have been pulled down.
      I will make his house new.
17 Then all other people will look for
        the Lord *(God)*—
      all the non-Jewish people that are
        my people too.
      The Lord *(God)* said this.
      And he is the One who does
        all these things.
18 These things have been known
        from the beginning of time.'
                                        Amos 9:11-12

19"So I think we should not bother the non-Jewish brothers who have turned to God. 20Instead, we should write a letter to them. We should tell them these things:

> Don't eat food that has been given to idols.*
>   (This makes the food unclean.)
> Don't do any kind of sexual sin.
> Don't taste *(eat)* blood.
> Don't eat animals that have been
>   strangled *(choked)*.

21They should not do these things, because there are still men *(Jews)* in every city who teach the law of Moses. The words of Moses have been read in the synagogue* every Sabbath day* for many years."

The Letter to the Non-Jewish Believers

22The apostles,* the elders,* and the whole church *(group of believers)* wanted to send some men with Paul and Barnabas to Antioch. The group decided to choose some of their own men. They chose Judas (also called Barsabbas) and Silas. These men were respected by the brothers ⌊in Jerusalem⌋. 23The group sent the letter with these men. The letter said:

> From the apostles and elders, your brothers.
> To all the non-Jewish brothers
>   in the city of Antioch and in the
>   countries of Syria and Cilicia:

Dear Brothers,

24We have heard that some men have come to you from our group. The things they said troubled and upset you. But we did not tell them to do this! 25We have all agreed to choose some men and send them to you. They will be with our dear friends, Barnabas and Paul. 26Barnabas and Paul have given their lives to serve our Lord Jesus Christ. 27So we have sent Judas and Silas with them. They will tell you the same things. 28The Holy Spirit* thinks that you should have no more burdens, and we agree. You need to do only these things:

29   Don't eat food that has been given
        to idols.*
      Don't taste *(eat)* blood.
      Don't eat animals that have been
        strangled *(choked)*.
      Don't do any kind of sexual sin.

If you stay away from these things, you will do well.

We say good-bye now.

30So Paul, Barnabas, Judas, and Silas left Jerusalem. They went to Antioch. In Antioch they gathered the group of believers and gave them the letter. 31When the believers read it, they were happy. The letter comforted them. 32Judas and Silas were also prophets.* They said many things to help the brothers *(believers)* and make them stronger. 33After Judas and Silas stayed there for a while, they left. They received a blessing of peace from the brothers. Judas and Silas went back to the brothers ⌊in Jerusalem⌋ who had sent them. 34*

---

idols The false gods that the non-Jewish people worshiped.

synagogue Synagogues were places where Jews gathered for prayer, study of the Scriptures, and other public meetings.

Sabbath day The seventh day of the Jewish week. It was a special religious day for the Jews.

apostles The men Jesus chose to be his special helpers.

elders Men chosen to lead a church. Also called "overseers" and "pastors" (shepherds), they have the work of caring for God's people (Acts 20:17,28; Eph. 4:11; Tit. 1:7,9).

Holy Spirit Also called the Spirit of God, the Spirit of Christ, and the Comforter. Joined with God and Christ, he does God's work among people in the world.

prophets Men who spoke for God.

Verse 34 Some Greek copies of Acts add verse 34: "... but Silas decided to remain there."

[35]But Paul and Barnabas stayed in Antioch. They and many others told the Good News* and taught the people the message* of the Lord.

Paul and Barnabas Separate

[36]A few days later, Paul said to Barnabas, "We told the message* of the Lord in many towns. We should go back to all those towns to visit the brothers ⌊and sisters⌋ and see how they are doing." [37]Barnabas wanted to bring John Mark with them too. [38]But ⌊on their first trip⌋ John Mark had left them at Pamphylia; he did not continue with them in the work. So Paul did not think it was a good idea to take him. [39]Paul and Barnabas had a big argument about this. They separated and went different ways. Barnabas sailed to Cyprus and took Mark with him. [40]Paul chose Silas to go with him. The brothers ⌊in Antioch⌋ put Paul into the Lord's care and sent him out. [41]Paul and Silas went through the countries of Syria and Cilicia, helping the churches* grow stronger.

Timothy Goes with Paul and Silas

16 Paul went to the cities of Derbe and Lystra. A follower ⌊of Christ⌋ named Timothy was there. Timothy's mother was a Jewish believer. His father was a Greek *(not a Jew)*. [2]The believers in the cities of Lystra and Iconium respected Timothy. They said good things about him. [3]Paul wanted Timothy to travel with him. But all the Jews living in that area knew that Timothy's father was Greek *(not Jewish)*. So Paul circumcised* Timothy to please the Jews. [4]Then Paul and the men with him traveled through other cities.* They gave the believers the rules and decisions from the apostles* and elders* in Jerusalem. They told the believers to obey these rules. [5]So the churches *(groups of believers)* were

becoming stronger in the faith and were growing bigger every day.

Paul Is Called out of Asia

[6]Paul and the men with him went through the countries of Phrygia and Galatia. The Holy Spirit* did not allow them to preach the Good News* in the country of Asia.* [7]Paul and Timothy went near the country of Mysia. They wanted to go into the country of Bithynia. But the Spirit of Jesus did not let them go in. [8]So they passed by Mysia and went to the city of Troas. [9]That night Paul saw a vision.* In this vision, a man from the country of Macedonia came to Paul. The man stood there and begged, "Come across to Macedonia. Help us!" [10]After Paul had seen the vision, we immediately prepared to leave for Macedonia. We understood that God had called us to tell the Good News to those people.

The Conversion of Lydia

[11]We left Troas in a ship, and we sailed to the island of Samothrace. The next day we sailed to the city of Neapolis. [12]Then we went to Philippi. Philippi is an important city in that part of Macedonia. It is a city for Romans. We stayed in that city for a few days. [13]On the Sabbath day* we went out the city gate to the river. At the river we thought we might find a special place for prayer. Some women had gathered there. So we sat down and talked with them. [14]There was a woman named Lydia from the city of Thyatira. Her job was selling purple cloth. She worshiped the true God. Lydia listened to Paul. The Lord opened her heart. She believed the things Paul said. [15]She and all the people living in her home were baptized.* Then Lydia invited us into her home. She said, "If you think I am truly a believer in the Lord Jesus, then come stay in my house." She persuaded us to stay with her.

Good News, message The news that God has made a way for people to have their sins forgiven and live with him forever.

churches Groups of believers in the towns where Paul and Barnabas went before.

circumcised To have the foreskin cut off. This was done to every Jewish baby boy. It was a mark of the agreement God made with Abraham (Gen. 17:9-14).

cities The cities where there were groups of believers.

apostles The men Jesus chose to be his special helpers.

elders Men chosen to lead a church. Also called "overseers" and "pastors" (shepherds), they have the work of caring for God's people (Acts 20:17,28; Eph. 4:11; Tit. 1:7,9).

Holy Spirit Also called the Spirit of God, the Spirit of Christ, and the Comforter. Joined with God and Christ, he does God's work among people in the world.

Asia The western part of Asia Minor.

vision Something like a dream used by God to speak to people.

Sabbath day The seventh day of the Jewish week. It was a special religious day for the Jews.

baptized A Greek word meaning to be immersed, dipped, or buried briefly under water.

Paul and Silas in Jail

16One time something happened to us while we were going to the place for prayer. A servant girl met us. She had a special spirit* in her. This spirit gave her the power to tell what would happen in the future. By doing this she earned a lot of money for the men who owned her. 17This girl followed Paul and us. She said loudly, "These men are servants of the Most High God! They are telling you how you can be saved!" 18She continued doing this for many days. This bothered Paul, so he turned and said to the spirit, "By the power of Jesus Christ, I command you to come out of her!" Immediately, the spirit came out.

19The men that owned the servant girl saw this. These men knew that now they could not use her to make money. So they grabbed Paul and Silas and dragged them into the meeting place of the city. The city officials were there. 20The men brought Paul and Silas to the leaders and said, "These men are Jews. They are making trouble in our city. 21They are telling the people to do things that are not right for us. We are Roman citizens and cannot do these things." 22The people were against Paul and Silas. Then the leaders tore the clothes of Paul and Silas and told some men to beat Paul and Silas with rods. 23The men beat Paul and Silas many times. Then the leaders put Paul and Silas in jail. The leaders told the jailer, "Guard them very carefully!" 24The jailer heard this special order. So he put Paul and Silas far inside the jail. He tied their feet between large blocks of wood.

25About midnight Paul and Silas were praying and singing songs to God. The other prisoners were listening to them. 26Suddenly, there was a big earthquake. It was so strong that it shook the foundation of the jail. Then all the doors of the jail opened. All the prisoners were freed from their chains. 27The jailer woke up. He saw that the jail doors were open. He thought that the prisoners had already escaped. So the jailer got his sword and was ready to kill himself.* 28But Paul shouted, "Don't hurt yourself! We are all here!"

29The jailer told someone to bring a light. Then he ran inside. He was shaking. He fell down in front of Paul and Silas. 30Then he brought them outside and said, "Men, what must I do to be saved?"

31They said to him, "Believe in the Lord Jesus and you will be saved—you and all the people living in your house." 32So Paul and Silas told the message* of the Lord to the jailer and all the people in his house. 33It was late at night, but the jailer took Paul and Silas and washed their wounds. Then the jailer and all his people were baptized.* 34After this the jailer took Paul and Silas home and gave them some food. All the people were very happy because they now believed in God.

35The next morning, the leaders sent some soldiers to tell the jailer, "Let these men *(Paul and Silas)* go free!"

36The jailer said to Paul, "The leaders have sent these soldiers to let you go free. You can leave now. Go in peace."

37But Paul said to the soldiers, "Your leaders did not prove that we did wrong. But they beat us in front of the people and put us in jail. We are Roman citizens,* ⌊so we have rights⌋. Now the leaders want to make us go quietly. No! The leaders must come and bring us out!"

38The soldiers told the leaders what Paul said. When the leaders heard that Paul and Silas were Roman citizens,* they were afraid. 39So they came and told Paul and Silas they were sorry. They took Paul and Silas out of jail and asked them to leave the city. 40But when Paul and Silas came out of the jail, they went to Lydia's house. They saw some of the believers there and comforted them. Then Paul and Silas left.

Paul and Silas in Thessalonica

17 Paul and Silas traveled through the cities of Amphipolis and Apollonia. They came to the city of Thessalonica. In that city there was a Jewish synagogue.* 2Paul went into this synagogue to see the Jews. This is what he always did. Every Sabbath day* for three weeks Paul talked with the Jews about the Scriptures.* 3Paul

---

message The news that God has made a way for people to have their sins forgiven and live with God forever.

baptized A Greek word meaning to be immersed, dipped, or buried briefly under water.

Roman citizens Roman law said that Roman citizens must not be beaten before they had a trial.

synagogue Synagogues were places where Jews gathered for prayer, study of the Scriptures, and other public meetings.

Sabbath day The seventh day of the Jewish week. It was a special religious day for the Jews.

Scriptures Holy Writings—the Old Testament.

---

spirit A spirit from the devil that gave special knowledge.

kill himself He thought the leaders would kill him for letting the prisoners escape.

explained these Scriptures to the Jews. He showed that the Christ* must die and then rise from death. Paul said "This man Jesus that I am telling you about is the Christ." ⁴Some of the Jews there believed Paul and Silas and decided to join them. Also there were some Greek men who worshiped the true God and some important women. A large group of the men and many of the women also joined Paul and Silas.

⁵But the Jews ₗthat did not believeₗ became jealous. They hired some bad men from the city. These bad men gathered many people and made trouble in the city. They went to Jason's house, looking for Paul and Silas. They wanted to bring Paul and Silas out before the people. ⁶But they did not find Paul and Silas. So the people dragged Jason and some of the other believers to the leaders of the city. The people all yelled, "These men *(Paul and Silas)* have made trouble everywhere in the world. And now they have come here too! ⁷Jason is keeping them in his house. They all do things against the laws of Caesar.* They say there is another king called Jesus."

⁸The leaders of the city and the other people heard these things. They became very upset. ⁹They made Jason and the other believers pay a fine. Then they let the believers go free.

Paul and Silas Go to Berea

¹⁰That same night the believers sent Paul and Silas to another city named Berea. In Berea, Paul and Silas went to the Jewish synagogue.* ¹¹These Jews were better people than the Jews in Thessalonica. These Jews were very happy to listen to the things Paul and Silas said. These Jews in Berea studied the Scriptures* every day. They wanted to know if these things were true. ¹²Many of these Jews believed. Many important Greek men and Greek women also believed. ¹³But when the Jews in Thessalonica learned that Paul was telling the word of God in Berea, they came to Berea too. The Jews from Thessalonica upset the people in Berea and made trouble. ¹⁴So the believers sent Paul away quickly to the sea. But Silas and Timothy stayed in Berea. ¹⁵The believers that went with Paul took him to the city of Athens. These brothers carried a message from Paul back to Silas and Timothy. The message said, "Come to me as soon as you can."

Paul in Athens

¹⁶Paul was waiting for Silas and Timothy in Athens. Paul was troubled because he saw that the city was full of idols.* ¹⁷In the synagogue,* Paul talked with the Jews and the Greeks who worshiped the true God. Paul also talked with some people in the business area of the city. Paul did this every day. ¹⁸Some of the Epicurean and Stoic philosophers* argued with him.

Some of them said, "This man doesn't really know what he is talking about. What is he trying to say?" Paul was telling them the Good News about Jesus' rising from death. So they said, "He seems to be telling us about some other gods." ¹⁹They got Paul and took him to a meeting of the Areopagus council.* They said, "Please explain to us this new idea that you have been teaching. ²⁰The things that you are saying are new to us. We have never heard these things before. We want to know what this teaching means." ²¹(All the people of Athens and the people from other countries who lived there always used their time talking about all the newest ideas.)

²²Then Paul stood before the meeting of the Areopagus council.* Paul said, "Men of Athens, I can see that you are very religious in all things. ²³I was going through your city and I saw the things you worship. I found an altar that had these words written on it: 'TO THE GOD WHO IS NOT KNOWN.' You worship a god that you don't know. This is the God I am telling you about! ²⁴He is the God who made the whole world and everything in it. He is the Lord *(Ruler)* of the land and the sky. He does not live in temples* that men build! ²⁵This God is the One who gives life, breath, and everything else to people. He does not need any help from people. God has everything he needs. ²⁶God began by making one man *(Adam)*. From him God made all the different people. God made them to live everywhere in the world. God decided exactly when and where they must live. ²⁷God wanted the people to look for him. Maybe

---

Christ The "anointed one" (Messiah) or chosen of God.

Caesar The name given to the emperor (ruler) of Rome.

synagogue Synagogues were places where Jews gathered for prayer, study of the Scriptures, and other public meetings.

Scriptures Holy Writings—the Old Testament.

idols The false gods that the non-Jewish people worshiped.

philosophers People who study and talk about their own ideas and the ideas and teachings of other people.

Areopagus council A group of important leaders in Athens. They were like judges.

temples Buildings where people go to worship.

they could search all around for him and find him. But he is not far from any of us:

28 'We live with him.
We walk with him.
We are with him.'

Some of your own writers have said:

'For we are his children.'

29We are God's children. So, you must not think that God is like something that people imagine or make. He is not like gold, silver, or rock. 30In the past, people did not understand God, but God ignored this. But now, God tells every person in the world to change his heart and life. 31God has decided a day when he will judge all the people in the world. He will be fair. He will use a man (Jesus) to do this. God chose this man long ago. And God has proved this to every person; God proved it by raising that man from death!"

32When the people heard about ⌊Jesus⌋ being raised from death, some of them laughed. The people said, "We will hear more about this from you later." 33Paul went away from them. 34But some of the people believed Paul and joined him. One of the people who believed was Dionysius. He was a member of the Areopagus council.* Another person who believed was a woman named Damaris. There were also some other people who believed.

Paul in Corinth

18 Later, Paul left Athens and went to the city of Corinth. 2In Corinth Paul met a Jewish man named Aquila. Aquila was born in the country of Pontus. But Aquila and his wife, Priscilla, had recently moved ⌊to Corinth⌋ from Italy. They left Italy because Claudius* commanded that all Jews must leave Rome. Paul went to visit Aquila and Priscilla. 3They were tentmakers, the same as Paul. Paul stayed with them and worked with them. 4Every Sabbath day* Paul talked with the Jews and Greeks in the synagogue.* Paul tried to persuade these people ⌊to believe in Jesus⌋.

5Silas and Timothy came from Macedonia to Paul in Corinth. After this, Paul used all his time telling people the Good News.* He showed the Jews that Jesus is the Christ.* 6But the Jews would not accept Paul's teaching. The Jews said some very bad things. So Paul shook off the dust from his clothes.* He said to the Jews, "If you are not saved, it will be your own fault! I have done all I can do! After this, I will go only to non-Jewish people!" 7Paul left the synagogue* and moved into the home of Titius Justus. This man worshiped the true God. His house was next to the synagogue. 8Crispus was the leader of that synagogue. Crispus and all the people living in his house believed in the Lord (Jesus). Many other people in Corinth also listened to Paul. They too believed and were baptized.*

9During the night, Paul had a vision.* The Lord said to him, "Don't be afraid! Continue talking to people and don't stop! 10I am with you. No one will be able to hurt you. Many of my people are in this city." 11Paul stayed there for a year and a half, teaching God's truth to the people.

Paul Is Brought Before Gallio

12Gallio became the governor of the country of Achaia. At that time, some of the Jews came together against Paul. They took Paul to the court. 13The Jews said to Gallio, "This man is teaching people to worship God in a way that is against our ⌊Jewish⌋ law!"

14Paul was ready to say something, but Gallio spoke to the Jews. Gallio said, "I would listen to you Jews if you were complaining about a bad crime or some wrong. 15But the things you Jews are saying are only questions about words and names—arguments about your own ⌊Jewish⌋ law. So you must solve this problem yourselves. I don't want to be a judge of these things!" 16Then Gallio made them leave the court.

17Then they all grabbed Sosthenes. (Sosthenes was ⌊now⌋ the leader of the synagogue.*) They beat Sosthenes before the court. But this did not bother Gallio.

Areopagus council A group of important leaders in Athens. They were like judges.
Claudius The emperor (ruler) of Rome, 41-54 A.D.
Sabbath day The seventh day of the Jewish week. It was a special religious day for the Jews.
synagogue Synagogues were places where Jews gathered for prayer, study of the Scriptures, and other public meetings.

Good News The news that God has made a way for people to have their sins forgiven and live with God forever.
Christ The "anointed one" (Messiah) or chosen of God.
shook off the dust from his clothes This was a warning. It showed that Paul was finished talking to the Jews.
baptized A Greek word meaning to be immersed, dipped, or buried briefly under water.
vision Something like a dream used by God to speak to people.

Paul Returns to Antioch

[18]Paul stayed with the brothers for many days. Then he left and sailed for Syria. Priscilla and Aquila were also with him. At Cenchrea, Paul cut off his hair.* ⌊This showed that⌋ he had made a promise (vow) to God. [19]Then they went to the city of Ephesus. This is where Paul left Priscilla and Aquila. While Paul was in Ephesus, he went into the synagogue* and talked with the Jews. [20]The Jews asked Paul to stay longer, but he refused. [21]Paul left them and said, "I will come back to you again if God wants me to." And so Paul sailed away from Ephesus.

[22]Paul went to the city of Caesarea. Then he went and said hello to the church (group of believers) ⌊in Jerusalem⌋. After that, Paul went to the city of Antioch. [23]Paul stayed in Antioch for a while. Then he left Antioch and went through the countries of Galatia and Phrygia. Paul traveled from town to town in these countries. He made all the followers ⌊of Jesus⌋ stronger.

Apollos in Ephesus and Achaia (Corinth)

[24]A Jew named Apollos came to Ephesus. Apollos was born in the city of Alexandria. He was an educated man. He knew very much about the Scriptures.* [25]Apollos had been taught about the Lord (Jesus). Apollos was always very excited when he talked to people about Jesus. The things Apollos taught about Jesus were right. But the only baptism* that Apollos knew about was the baptism that John* taught. [26]Apollos began to speak very boldly in the synagogue.* Priscilla and Aquila heard him speak. They took him to their home and helped him understand the way of God better. [27]Apollos wanted to go to the country of Achaia. So the brothers ⌊in Ephesus⌋ helped him. They wrote a letter to the followers ⌊of Jesus in Achaia⌋. In the letter they asked these followers to accept Apollos. These followers ⌊in Achaia⌋ had believed in Jesus because of God's grace (kindness). When Apollos went there, he helped them very much. [28]He argued very strongly against the Jews before all the people. Apollos clearly proved that the Jews were wrong. He used the Scriptures* and showed that Jesus is the Christ.*

Paul in Ephesus

19 While Apollos was in the city of Corinth, Paul was visiting some places on the way to the city of Ephesus. In Ephesus Paul found some followers ⌊of John⌋.* [2]Paul asked them, "Did you receive the Holy Spirit* when you believed?"

These followers said to him, "We have never even heard of a Holy Spirit!"

[3]So Paul asked them, "What kind of baptism* did you have?"

They said, "It was the baptism that John* taught."

[4]Paul said, "John told people to be baptized to show they wanted to change their lives. John told people to believe in the One who would come after him. That person is Jesus."

[5]When these followers ⌊of John⌋ heard this, they were baptized in the name of the Lord Jesus. [6]Then Paul put his hands on them* and the Holy Spirit* came into them. They began speaking different languages and prophesying.* [7]There were about twelve men in this group.

[8]Paul went into the synagogue* and spoke very boldly. Paul continued doing this for three months. He talked with the Jews and persuaded them to accept the things he said about the kingdom of God. [9]But some of the Jews became stubborn. They refused to believe. These Jews said some very bad things about the Way ⌊of God⌋. All the people heard these things. So Paul left those Jews and took the followers ⌊of Jesus⌋ with him. Paul went to a place where a man named Tyrannus had a school. There Paul talked with people every day. [10]Paul did this for two years. Because of this work, every Jew and Greek (non-Jew) in the country of Asia* heard the word of the Lord.

---

cut off his hair Jews did this to show that the time of a special promise to God was finished.

synagogue Synagogues were places where Jews gathered for prayer, study of the Scriptures, and other public meetings.

Scriptures Holy Writings—the Old Testament.

baptism A Greek word meaning to be immersed, dipped, or buried briefly under water.

John John the Baptizer, who preached to people about Christ's coming (Mt. 3; Lk. 3).

Christ The "anointed one" (Messiah) or chosen of God.

Holy Spirit Also called the Spirit of God, the Spirit of Christ, and the Comforter. Joined with God and Christ, he does God's work among people in the world.

put his hands on them Here, doing this was a sign to show that Paul had God's authority or power to give these people special powers of the Holy Spirit.

prophesying Speaking or teaching things from God.

Asia The western part of Asia Minor.

The Sons of Sceva

[11]God used Paul to do some very special miracles.* [12]Some people carried away handkerchiefs and clothes that Paul had used. The people put these things on sick people. When they did this, the sick people were healed, and evil spirits [from the devil] left them.

[13-14]Some Jews also were traveling around and making evil spirits go out of people. The seven sons of Sceva were doing this. (Sceva was a high priest.*) These Jews tried to use the name of the Lord Jesus to make the evil spirits go out of people. They all said, "By the same Jesus that Paul talks about, I order you to come out!"

[15]But one time an evil spirit said to these Jews, "I know Jesus, and I know about Paul, but who are you?"

[16]Then the man, who had the evil spirit [from the devil] inside him, jumped on these Jews. He was much stronger than all of them. He beat them up and tore their clothes off. These Jews ran away from that house. [17]All the people in Ephesus, Jews and Greeks (non-Jews), learned about this. They all began to have great respect [for God]. And the people gave great honor to the name of the Lord Jesus. [18]Many of the believers began to confess and tell all the bad things they had done. [19]Some of the believers had used magic. These believers brought their magic books and burned them before everyone. Those books were worth about 50,000 silver coins.* [20]This is how the word of the Lord was influencing more and more people in a powerful way. And more and more people believed.

Paul Plans a Trip

[21]After these things, Paul made plans to go to Jerusalem. Paul planned to go through the countries of Macedonia and Achaia, and then go to Jerusalem. Paul thought, "After I visit Jerusalem, I must also visit Rome." [22]Timothy and Erastus were two of Paul's helpers. Paul sent them ahead to the country of Macedonia. Paul stayed in Asia* for a while.

Trouble in Ephesus

[23]But during that time, there was some bad trouble in Ephesus. This trouble was about the Way [of God]. This is how it all happened: [24]There was a man named Demetrius. He worked with silver. He made little silver models that looked like the temple* of the goddess Artemis.* The men that did this work made much money. [25]Demetrius had a meeting with these men and some other men who did the same kind of work. Demetrius told them, "Men, you know that we make much money from our business. [26]But look at what this man Paul is doing! Listen to what he is saying! Paul has influenced and changed many people. He has done this in Ephesus and all over the country of Asia.* Paul says the gods that men make are not real. [27]These things that Paul says might turn the people against our work. But there is also another problem: People will begin to think that the temple of the great goddess Artemis is not important! Her greatness will be destroyed. Artemis is the goddess that everyone in Asia and the whole world worships."

[28]When the men heard this, they became very angry. They shouted, "Artemis,* the goddess of the city of Ephesus, is great!" [29]All the people in the city became upset. The people grabbed Gaius and Aristarchus. (These two men were from Macedonia and were traveling with Paul.) Then all the people ran to the stadium. [30]Paul wanted to go in and talk to the people, but the followers [of Jesus] did not let him go. [31]Also, some leaders of the country were friends of Paul. These leaders sent him a message. They told Paul not to go into the stadium. [32]Some people were yelling one thing and other people were yelling other things. The meeting was very confused. Most of the people did not know why they had come there. [33]The Jews made a man named Alexander stand before the people. The people told him what to do. Alexander waved his hand because he wanted to explain things to the people. [34]But when the people saw that Alexander was a Jew, they all began shouting the same thing. They continued shouting for two hours. The people said, "Great is Artemis* of Ephesus! Great is Artemis of Ephesus! Great is Artemis...!"

[35]Then the city clerk persuaded the people to be quiet. He said, "Men of Ephesus, all people know that Ephesus is the city that keeps the temple* of the great goddess Artemis.* All people know that

---

miracle(s) Miracles are amazing works done by God's power.
high priest Most important Jewish priest and leader.
silver coins Probably drachmas. One coin was enough to pay a man for working one day.
Asia The western part of Asia Minor.

temple The special building in Ephesus where the people worshiped the false goddess Artemis.
Artemis Greek goddess worshiped by the people of Asia Minor. The Romans called her Diana.

we also keep her holy rock.* [36]No person can say that this is not true. So you should be quiet. You must stop and think before you do anything. [37]You brought these men,* but they have not said anything bad against our goddess. They have not stolen anything from her temple. [38]We have courts of law and there are judges. Do Demetrius and those men that work with him have a charge against anyone? They should go to the courts! That is where they can argue with each other! [39]Is there something else you want to talk about? Then come to the regular town meeting of the people. It can be decided there. [40]I say this because some person might see this trouble today and say that we are rioting (making trouble). We could not explain all this trouble, because there is no real reason for this meeting." [41]After the city clerk said these things, he told the people to go home. And all the people left.

Paul Goes to Macedonia and Greece

20 When the trouble stopped, Paul invited the followers ⌊of Jesus⌋ to come visit him. He said things to comfort them and then told them good-bye. Paul left and went to the country of Macedonia. [2]He said many things to strengthen the followers ⌊of Jesus⌋ in the different places on his way through Macedonia. Then Paul went to Greece (Achaia). [3]He stayed there three months. He was ready to sail for Syria, but some Jews were planning something against him. So Paul decided to go back through Macedonia to Syria. [4]Some men were with him. They were: Sopater, the son of Pyrrhus, from the city of Berea, Aristarchus and Secundus, from the city of Thessalonica, Gaius, from the city of Derbe, Timothy, and Tychicus and Trophimus, two men from Asia.* [5]These men went first, ahead of Paul. They waited for us in the city of Troas. [6]We sailed from the city of Philippi after the ⌊Jewish⌋ Festival of Unleavened Bread.* We met these men in Troas five days later. We stayed there seven days.

Paul's Last Visit to Troas

[7]On Sunday,* we all met together to eat ⌊the Lord's Supper⌋.* Paul talked to the group. He was planning to leave the next day. Paul continued talking until midnight. [8]We were all together in a room upstairs, and there were many lights in the room. [9]There was a young man named Eutychus sitting in the window. Paul continued talking, and Eutychus became very, very sleepy. Finally, Eutychus went to sleep and fell out of the window. He fell to the ground from the third floor. When the people ⌊went and⌋ lifted him up, he was dead. [10]Paul went down to Eutychus. He kneeled down and hugged Eutychus. Paul said to the other believers, "Don't worry. He is alive now." [11]Paul went upstairs again. He divided the bread and ate. Paul spoke to them a long time. When he finished talking, it was early morning. Then Paul left. [12]The people took the young man (Eutychus) home. He was alive, and the people were very much comforted.

The Trip from Troas to Miletus

[13]We sailed for the city of Assos. We went first, ahead of Paul. He planned to meet us in Assos and join us on the ship there. Paul told us to do this because he wanted to go to Assos by land. [14]Later, we met Paul at Assos, and then he came on the ship with us. We all went to the city of Mitylene. [15]The next day, we sailed away from Mitylene. We came to a place near the island of Chios. Then the next day, we sailed to the island of Samos. A day later, we came to the city of Miletus. [16]Paul had already decided not to stop at Ephesus. He did not want to stay too long in Asia.* He was hurrying because he wanted to be in Jerusalem on the day of Pentecost* if possible.

Paul Speaks to the Elders from Ephesus

[17]In Miletus Paul sent a message back to Ephesus. Paul invited the elders* (leaders) of the church in Ephesus to come to him. [18]When the elders came, Paul said to them, "You know about

---

holy rock   Probably a meteorite or rock that the people worshiped because they thought it looked like Artemis.

men   Gaius and Aristarchus, the men traveling with Paul.

Asia   The western part of Asia Minor.

Festival of Unleavened Bread   An important Jewish holiday week. In the Old Testament it began the day after Passover, but by this time the two holidays had become one.

Sunday   Literally, "first day of the week," which for the Jews began at sunset on Saturday. But if Luke is using Greek time here, then the meeting was Sunday night.

to eat the Lord's Supper   Literally, "to break bread." This may mean a meal or the Lord's Supper, the special meal Jesus told his followers to eat to remember him (Lk. 22:14-20).

Pentecost   Jewish festival celebrating the wheat harvest.

elders   Men chosen to lead a church. Also called "overseers" and "pastors" (shepherds), they have the work of caring for God's people (Acts 20:17,28; Eph. 4:11; Tit. 1:7,9).

my life from the first day I came to Asia.* You know the way I lived all the time I was with you. [19]The Jews planned things against me. This gave me much trouble, and I often cried. But you know that I always served the Lord. I never thought about myself first. [20]I always did what was best for you. I told you the Good News* about Jesus in public before the people and also taught in your homes. [21]I told all people—Jewish people and Greek (non-Jewish) people—to change their hearts and turn to God. I told them all to believe in our Lord Jesus. [22]But now I must obey the Holy Spirit* and go to Jerusalem. I don't know what will happen to me there. [23]I know only that in every city the Holy Spirit tells me that troubles and even jail wait for me ⌊in Jerusalem⌋. [24]I don't care about my own life. The most important thing is that I finish my work. I want to finish the work that the Lord Jesus gave me to do—to tell people the Good News about God's grace (kindness).

[25]"And now listen to me. I know that none of you will ever see me again. All the time I was with you, I told you the Good News* about the kingdom of God. [26]So today I can tell you one thing that I am sure of: God will not blame me if some of you are not saved! [27]I can say this because I know that I told you everything that God wants you to know. [28]Be careful for yourselves and for all the people that God has given you. The Holy Spirit* gave you the work of caring for this flock (God's people). You must be like shepherds to the church (people) of God.* This is the church that God bought with his own blood.* [29]I know that after I leave, some men will come into your group. They will be like wild wolves. They will try to destroy the flock (group). [30]Also, men from your own group will become bad leaders. They will begin to teach things that are wrong. They will lead some followers ⌊of Jesus⌋ away from the truth. [31]So be careful! Always remember this: I was with you for three years. During this time, I never stopped warning you. I taught you night and day. I often cried for you.

[32]"Now I am giving you to God. I am depending on the message* about God's grace

(kindness) to make you strong. That message is able to give you the blessings that God gives to all his holy people. [33]When I was with you, I never wanted anyone's money or fine clothes. [34]You know that I always worked to take care of my own needs and the needs of the people that were with me. [35]I always showed you that you should work like I did and help people that are weak. I taught you to remember the words of the Lord Jesus. Jesus said, 'You will be happier when you give than when you receive.'"

[36]When Paul finished saying these things, he kneeled down and they all prayed together. [37-38]They all cried and cried. The men were very sad because Paul had said that they would never see him again. They hugged Paul and kissed him. They went with him to the ship to say good-bye.

Paul Goes to Jerusalem

21 We all said good-bye to the elders.* Then we sailed away. We sailed straight to Cos island. The next day, we went to the island of Rhodes. From Rhodes we went to Patara. [2]At Patara we found a ship that was going to the area of Phoenicia. We went on the ship and sailed away. [3]We sailed near the island of Cyprus. We could see it on the north side, but we did not stop. We sailed to the country of Syria. We stopped at the city of Tyre because the ship needed to unload its cargo there. [4]We found some followers ⌊of Jesus⌋ in Tyre, and we stayed with them for seven days. They warned Paul not to go to Jerusalem because of what the Holy Spirit* had told them. [5]But when we finished our visit, we left. We continued our trip. All the followers ⌊of Jesus⌋, even the women and children, came outside the city with us to say good-bye. We all kneeled down on the beach and prayed. [6]Then we said good-bye and got on the ship. The followers went home.

[7]We continued our trip from Tyre and went to the city of Ptolemais. We greeted the brothers (believers) there and stayed with them one day. [8]The next day we left Ptolemais and went to the city of Caesarea. We went into the home of Philip and stayed with him. Philip had the work of telling the Good News.* He was one of the seven helpers.* [9]He had four daughters who were not married. These daughters had the gift of

---

Asia The western part of Asia Minor.

Good News, message The news that God has made a way for people to have their sins forgiven and live with him forever.

Holy Spirit Also called the Spirit of God, the Spirit of Christ, and the Comforter. Joined with God and Christ, he does God's work among people in the world.

of God Some Greek copies say, "of the Lord."

his own blood Or, "the blood of his own son."

elders Men chosen to lead a church. Also called "overseers" and "pastors" (shepherds), they have the work of caring for God's people (Acts 20:17,28; Eph. 4:11; Tit. 1:7,9).

helpers Men chosen for a special work. Read Acts 6:1-6.

prophesying.* [10]After we had been there for many days, a prophet* named Agabus came from Judea. [11]He came to us and borrowed Paul's belt. Then Agabus used the belt to tie his own hands and feet. Agabus said, "The Holy Spirit* tells me, 'This is how the Jews in Jerusalem will tie the man who wears this belt.* Then they will give him to the non-Jewish people.'"

[12]We all heard these words. So we and the other followers ⌊of Jesus⌋ there begged (asked) Paul not to go to Jerusalem. [13]But Paul said, "Why are you crying? Why are you making me so sad? I am ready to be tied in Jerusalem. I am also ready to die for the name of the Lord Jesus!"

[14]We could not persuade him to stay away from Jerusalem. So we stopped begging him and said, "We pray that what the Lord wants will be done."

[15]After this, we got ready and left for Jerusalem. [16]Some of the followers ⌊of Jesus⌋ from Caesarea went with us. These followers took us to the home of Mnason, a man from Cyprus. Mnason was one of the first people to be a follower ⌊of Jesus⌋. They took us to his home so that we could stay with him.

Paul Visits James

[17]In Jerusalem the believers were very happy to see us. [18]The next day, Paul went with us to visit James. All the elders (church leaders) were there too. [19]Paul greeted all of them. Then he told them about how God used him to do many things among the non-Jewish people. He told them all the things that God did through him. [20]When the leaders heard these things, they praised God. Then they said to Paul, "Brother, you can see that thousands of Jews have become believers. But they think it is very important to obey the law of Moses. [21]These Jews have heard about your teaching. They heard that you tell the Jews who live in other countries among non-Jews to leave the law of Moses. They heard that you tell those Jews not to circumcise* their children and not to obey Jewish customs. [22]What should we do? The Jewish believers here will learn that you have come. [23]So we will tell you what to do: Four of our men have made a vow* (promise) to God. [24]Take these men with you and share in their cleansing (washing) ceremony.* Pay their expenses. Then they can shave their heads.* Do this and it will prove to everyone that the things they have heard about you are not true. They will see that you obey the law of Moses in your own life. [25]We have already sent a letter to the non-Jewish believers. The letter said:

> 'Don't eat food that has been given to idols.*
> Don't taste (eat) blood.
> Don't eat animals that have been
>   strangled (choked).
> Don't do any kind of sexual sin.'"

[26]Then Paul took the four men with him. The next day, Paul shared in the cleansing (washing) ceremony.* Then he went to the temple.* Paul announced the time when the days of the cleansing ceremony would be finished. On the last day an offering would be given for each of the men.

[27]The seven days were almost finished. But some Jews from Asia* saw Paul at the temple.* They caused all the people to be upset, and they grabbed Paul. [28]They shouted, "You Jewish men, help us! This is the man who is teaching things that are against the law of Moses, against our people, and against this place (the temple). This man is teaching these things to all people everywhere. And now he has brought some Greek (non-Jewish) men into the temple yard! He has made this holy place unclean!" [29](The Jews said this because they had seen Trophimus with Paul in Jerusalem. Trophimus was a ⌊Greek⌋ man from Ephesus. The Jews thought that Paul had taken him into the holy area of the temple.)

[30]All the people in Jerusalem became very upset. They all ran and grabbed Paul. They dragged him out of the holy area of the temple.* The temple gates were closed immediately. [31]The

---

prophesying Speaking or teaching things from God.

prophet Person who spoke for God. He often told things that would happen in the future.

Holy Spirit Also called the Spirit of God, the Spirit of Christ, and the Comforter. Joined with God and Christ, he does God's work among people in the world.

belt Paul's belt; so Agabus means that the Jews in Jerusalem will tie (arrest) Paul.

circumcise To cut off the foreskin. This was done to every Jewish baby boy. It was a mark of the agreement God made with Abraham (Gen. 17:9-14).

vow Probably a Nazirite vow, a time of special service that Jews promised to give to God.

cleansing ceremony The special things the Jews did to end the Nazirite vow.

shave their heads To show their vow was finished.

idols The false gods that the non-Jewish people worship.

temple The special building in Jerusalem for Jewish worship.

Asia The western part of Asia Minor.

people were trying to kill Paul. The commander of the Roman army in Jerusalem learned that there was trouble in the whole city. [32]Immediately the commander went to the place where the people were. He brought some army officers* and soldiers with him. The people saw the commander and his soldiers. So they stopped beating Paul. [33]The commander went to Paul and arrested him. The commander told his soldiers to tie Paul with two chains. Then the commander asked, "Who is this man? What has he done wrong?" [34]Some people there were yelling one thing and other people were yelling other things. Because of all this confusion and shouting, the commander could not learn the truth about what had happened. So the commander told the soldiers to take Paul to the army building. [35-36]All the people were following them. When the soldiers came to the steps, they had to carry Paul. They did this ˻to protect Paul˼, because the people were ready to hurt him. The people shouted, "Kill him!"

[37]The soldiers were ready to take Paul into the army building. But Paul spoke to the commander. Paul asked, "Do I have the right to say something to you?"

The commander said, "Oh, you speak Greek? [38]Then you are not the man I thought you were? I thought you were the Egyptian man who started some trouble against the government not long ago. That Egyptian man led 4,000 killers out to the desert."

[39]Paul said, "No, I am a Jewish man from Tarsus. Tarsus is in the country of Cilicia. I am a citizen of that important city. Please, let me speak to the people."

[40]The commander let Paul speak to the people. So Paul stood on the steps. He made signs with his hands so that the people would be quiet. The people became quiet and Paul spoke to them. He used the Jewish language.*

Paul Speaks to the People

22 Paul said, "My brothers and my fathers, listen to me! I will make my defense to you." [2]The Jews heard Paul speaking the Jewish language.* So they became very quiet. Paul said, [3]"I am a Jew. I was born in Tarsus in the country of Cilicia. I grew up in this city (Jerusalem). I was

a student of Gamaliel.* He carefully taught me everything about the law of our fathers (ancestors). I was very serious about serving God, the same as all of you here today. [4]I persecuted* the people who followed the Way ˻of Jesus˼. Some of them were killed because of me. I arrested men and women. I put them in jail. [5]The high priest* and the whole council of older Jewish leaders can tell you that this is true! One time these leaders gave me some letters. The letters were to the Jewish brothers in the city of Damascus. I was going there to arrest the followers of Jesus and bring them back to Jerusalem for punishment.

Paul Tells About His Conversion

[6]"But something happened to me on my way to Damascus. It was about noon when I came close to Damascus. Suddenly a bright light from the sky shined all around me. [7]I fell to the ground. I heard a voice saying to me: 'Saul, Saul, why are you doing these bad things to me?' [8]I asked, 'Who are you, Lord?' The voice said, 'I am Jesus from Nazareth. I am the One you are persecuting.' [9]The men who were with me did not understand the voice. But the men saw the light. [10]I said, 'What shall I do, Lord?' The Lord (Jesus) answered, 'Get up and go into Damascus. There you will be told all the things I have planned for you to do.' [11]I could not see, because the bright light had made me blind. So the men led me into Damascus.

[12]"In Damascus a man named Ananias* came to me. Ananias was a religious man; he obeyed the law ˻of Moses˼. All the Jews who lived there respected him. [13]Ananias came to me and said, 'Brother Saul, see again!' Immediately I was able to see him. [14]Ananias told me, 'The God of our fathers (ancestors) chose you long ago. God chose you to know his plan. He chose you to see the Righteous One (Jesus) and to hear words from him. [15]You will be his witness to all people. You will tell men about the things you have seen and heard. [16]Now, don't wait any longer. Get up, be baptized* and wash your sins away. Do this, trusting in him (Jesus) ˻to save you.'˼

Gamaliel A very important teacher of the Pharisees, a Jewish religious group (See Acts 5:34).

persecuted To persecute is to hurt or do bad things to.

high priest Most important Jewish priest and leader.

Ananias In Acts there are three men with this name. See Acts 5:1 and 23:2 for the other two.

baptized A Greek word meaning to be immersed, dipped, or buried briefly under water

---

army officers Centurions, Roman army officers who had authority over 100 soldiers.

Jewish language Probably Aramaic, a language like Hebrew that was spoken by the Jews in the first century.

[17]"Later, I came back to Jerusalem. I was praying in the temple* yard, and I saw a vision.* [18]I saw Jesus, and Jesus said to me: 'Hurry! Leave Jerusalem now! The people here will not accept the truth about me.' [19]I said, 'But Lord, the people know that I was the one who put the believers in jail and beat them. I went through all the synagogues* to find and arrest the people who believe in you. [20]The people also know that I was there when Stephen, your witness, was killed. I stood there and agreed that they should kill Stephen. I even held the coats of the men who were killing him!' [21]But Jesus said to me, 'Leave now. I will send you far away to the non-Jewish people.'"

[22]The people stopped listening when Paul said this last thing ⌊about going to the non-Jewish people⌋. They all shouted, "Kill him! Get him out of the world! A man like this should not be allowed to live!" [23]They yelled and threw off their coats.* They threw dust into the air.* [24]Then the commander told the soldiers to take Paul into the army building. He told the soldiers to beat Paul. He wanted to make Paul tell why the people were shouting against him like this. [25]So the soldiers were tying Paul, preparing to beat him. But Paul said to an army officer* there, "Do you have the right to beat a Roman citizen* who has not been proven guilty?"

[26]When the officer heard this, he went to the commander and told him about it. The officer said, "Do you know what you are doing? This man *(Paul)* is a Roman citizen!"

[27]The commander came to Paul and said, "Tell me, are you really a Roman citizen?"

Paul answered, "Yes."

[28]The commander said, "I paid much money to become a Roman citizen."

But Paul said, "I was born a citizen."

[29]The men who were preparing to question Paul moved away from him immediately. The commander was afraid because he had already tied Paul, and Paul was a Roman citizen.*

Paul Speaks to the Jewish Leaders

[30]The next day the commander decided to learn why the Jews were speaking against Paul. So he commanded the leading priests and the Jewish council to meet together. The commander took Paul's chains off. Then he brought Paul out and stood Paul before their meeting.

23 Paul looked at the Jewish council meeting and said, "Brothers, I have lived my life in a good way before God. I have always done what I thought was right." [2]Ananias,* the high priest,* was there. Ananias heard Paul and told the men who were standing near Paul to hit him on his mouth. [3]Paul said to Ananias, "God will hit you too! You are like a ⌊dirty⌋ wall that has been painted white! You sit there and judge me, using the law ⌊of Moses⌋. But you are telling them to hit me, and that is against the law ⌊of Moses⌋."

[4]The men standing near Paul said to him, "You cannot talk like that to God's high priest.* You are insulting him!"

[5]Paul said, "Brothers, I did not know this man was the high priest. It is written in the Scriptures,* 'You must not say bad things about a leader of your people.'*"

[6]Some of the men in the meeting were Sadducees* and some others were Pharisees.* So Paul had an idea: He shouted to them, "My brothers, I am a Pharisee and my father was a Pharisee! I am on trial here because I hope *(believe)* that people will rise from death!"

[7]When Paul said this, there was a big argument between the Pharisees* and the Sadducees.* The group was divided. [8](The Sadducees believe that after people die, they will not live again as an angel or as a spirit. But the Pharisees believe in both.) [9]All these Jews began shouting louder and louder. Some of the teachers of the law, who were Pharisees, stood up and argued, "We find nothing wrong with this man! Maybe an angel or a spirit did speak to him ⌊on the road to Damascus⌋!"

---

temple   The special building in Jerusalem for Jewish worship.

vision   Something like a dream used by God to speak to people.

synagogues   Synagogues were places where Jews gathered for prayer, study of the Scriptures, and other public meetings.

threw off their coats   This showed that the Jews were very angry at Paul.

threw dust into the air   This also showed very strong anger.

army officer   A centurion, a Roman army officer who had authority over 100 soldiers.

Roman citizen   Roman law said that Roman citizens must not be beaten before their trial.

Ananias   Not the same man named Ananias in Acts 22:12.

high priest   Most important Jewish priest and leader.

Scriptures   Holy Writings—the Old Testament.

'You must not say ... people'   Quote from Ex. 22:28.

Sadducees   A leading Jewish religious group. They accepted only the first five books of the Old Testament.

Pharisees   The Pharisees were a Jewish religious group that claimed to follow carefully all Jewish laws and customs.

[10]The argument became a fight. The commander was afraid that the Jews would tear Paul to pieces. So the commander told the soldiers to go down and take Paul away from these Jews and to put him in the army building.

[11]The next night the Lord ⌊Jesus⌋ came and stood by Paul. He said, "Be brave! You have told people in Jerusalem about me. You must also go to Rome to tell people there about me!"

[12]The next morning some of the Jews made a plan. They wanted to kill Paul. The Jews made a promise *(vow)* to themselves that they would not eat or drink anything until they had killed Paul. [13]There were more than 40 Jews who made this plan. [14]These Jews went and talked to the leading priests and the older Jewish leaders. The Jews said, "We have made a serious promise to ourselves. We promised that we will not eat or drink until we have killed Paul! [15]So this is what we want you to do: Send a message to the commander from you and all the Jewish leaders. Tell the commander you want him to bring Paul out to you. Tell the commander that you want to ask Paul more questions. We will be waiting to kill Paul while he is on the way here."

[16]But Paul's nephew heard about this plan. He went to the army building and told Paul about the plan. [17]Then Paul called one of the army officers* and said to him, "Take this young man to the commander. He has a message for him." [18]So the army officer brought Paul's nephew to the commander. The officer said, "The prisoner, Paul, asked me to bring this young man to you. He wants to tell you something."

[19]The commander led the young man to a place where they could be alone. The commander asked, "What do you want to tell me?"

[20]The young man said, "The Jews have decided to ask you to bring Paul down to their council meeting tomorrow. The Jews want you to think that they plan to ask Paul more questions. [21]But don't believe them! There are more than 40 Jews who are hiding and waiting to kill Paul. They have all promised *(vowed)* not to eat or drink until they have killed him! Now they are waiting for you to say yes."

[22]The commander sent the young man away. The commander told him, "Don't tell anyone that you have told me about their plan."

Paul Is Sent to Caesarea

[23]Then the commander called two army officers.* He said to them, "I need some men to go to Caesarea. Get 200 soldiers ready. Also, get 70 soldiers on horses and 200 men to carry spears. Be ready to leave at nine o'clock tonight. [24]Get some horses for Paul to ride. He must be taken to Governor Felix safely." [25]The commander wrote a letter. This is what the letter said:

[26]From Claudius Lysias
To the Most Excellent Governor Felix:

Greetings.

[27]The Jews had taken this man *(Paul)*, and they planned to kill him. But I learned that he is a Roman citizen, so I went with my soldiers and saved him. [28]I wanted to know why they were accusing him. So I brought him before their council meeting. [29]This is what I learned: The Jews said Paul did some things that were wrong. But these charges were about their own Jewish laws. And none of these things were worthy of jail or death. [30]I was told that some of the Jews were making a plan to kill Paul. So I send him to you. I also told those Jews to tell you the things they have against him.

[31]The soldiers did the things they were told. The soldiers got Paul and took him to the city of Antipatris that night. [32]The next day the soldiers on horses went with Paul to Caesarea. But the other soldiers and the spearmen went back to the army building ⌊in Jerusalem⌋. [33]The soldiers on horses entered Caesarea and gave the letter to the governor *(Felix)*. Then they gave Paul to him. [34]The governor read the letter. Then he asked Paul, "What country are you from?" The governor learned that Paul was from Cilicia. [35]The governor said, "I will hear your case when the Jews who are against you come here too." Then the governor gave orders for Paul to be kept in the palace. (This building had been built by Herod.*)

The Jews Accuse Paul

24 Five days later Ananias went to the city of Caesarea. Ananias was the high priest.* Ananias also brought some of the older Jewish leaders and a lawyer named Tertullus. They went to Caesarea to make charges against Paul before

---

army officer(s) A centurion, a Roman army officer who had authority over 100 soldiers.

Herod Herod I (the Great), ruler of Judea, 40 B.C. to 4 B.C.
high priest Most important Jewish priest and leader.

the governor. [2]Paul was called into the meeting, and Tertullus began to make his charges.

Tertullus said, "Most Excellent Felix! Our people enjoy much peace because of you, and many wrong things in our country are being made right through your wise help. [3]We are very thankful to accept these things from you. We accept these things always and in every place. [4]But I don't want to take any more of your time. So I will say only a few words. Please be patient. [5]This man (Paul) is a troublemaker. He makes trouble with the Jews everywhere in the world. He is a leader of the Nazarene group. [6]Also, he was trying to make the temple* unclean, but we stopped him. [8]* You can decide if all these things are true. Ask him some questions yourself." [9]The other Jews agreed. They said, "These things are really true!"

[10]The governor made a sign for Paul to speak. So Paul answered, "Governor Felix, I know that you have been a judge over this nation (Israel) for a long time. So I am happy to defend myself before you. [11]I went to worship in Jerusalem only twelve days ago. You can learn for yourself that this is true. [12]These Jews who are accusing me did not find me arguing with anyone at the temple.* I was not making trouble with the people. And I was not making trouble or arguing in the synagogues* or any other place in the city. [13]These Jews cannot prove the things they are saying against me now. [14]But I will tell you this: I worship the God of our fathers (ancestors) as a follower of the Way ⌊of Jesus⌋. The Jews say that the Way ⌊of Jesus⌋ is not the right way. But I believe everything that is taught in the law of Moses. And I believe everything that is written in the books of the prophets.* [15]I have the same hope in God that these Jews have—the hope that all people, good and bad, will be raised from death. [16]This is why I always try to do what I believe is right before God and men.

[17]"I was away ⌊from Jerusalem⌋ for many years. I went back there to bring money to my people and to give some offerings (gifts). [18]I was doing this when some Jews saw me at the temple.* I had finished the cleansing (washing) ceremony.* I had not made any trouble; no people were gathering around me. [19]But some Jews from Asia* were there. They should be here, standing before you. If I have really done anything wrong, those Jews from Asia are the ones who should accuse me. They were there! [20]Ask these Jews here if they found any wrong in me when I stood before the Jewish council meeting in Jerusalem. [21]I did say one thing when I stood before them: I said, 'You are judging me today because I believe that people will rise from death!'"

[22]Felix already understood a lot about the Way ⌊of Jesus⌋. He stopped the trial and said, "When commander Lysias comes here, I will decide about these things." [23]Felix told the army officer* to keep Paul guarded. But he told the officer to give Paul some freedom and to let Paul's friends bring the things that Paul needed.

Paul Speaks to Felix and His Wife

[24]After a few days Felix came with his wife, Drusilla. She was a Jew. Felix asked for Paul to be brought to him. Felix listened to Paul talk about believing in Christ Jesus. [25]But Felix became afraid when Paul spoke about things like living right, self-control, and the judgment that will come in the future. Felix said, "Go away now! When I have more time, I will call you." [26]But Felix had another reason for talking with Paul. Felix hoped that Paul would pay him a bribe.* So Felix sent for Paul often and talked with him.

[27]But after two years, Porcius Festus became governor. So Felix was no longer governor. But Felix left Paul in prison, because Felix wanted to do something to please the Jews.

Paul Asks to See Caesar

25 Festus became governor, and three days later he went from Caesarea to Jerusalem. [2]The leading priests and the important Jewish leaders made charges against Paul before Festus. [3]They asked Festus to do something for them; the Jews wanted Festus to send Paul back to Jerusalem. They had a plan to kill Paul on the

---

temple   The special building in Jerusalem for Jewish worship.

Verses 6-8   Some Greek copies add 6b-8a: "And we wanted to judge him by our own law. [7]But the officer Lysias came and used much force to take him from us. [8]And Lysias commanded his people to come to you to accuse us."

synagogues   Synagogues were places where Jews gathered for prayer, study of the Scriptures, and other public meetings.

prophets   People who spoke for God. Their writings are part of the Old Testament.

cleansing ceremony   The special things Jews did to end the Nazirite vow.

Asia   The western part of Asia Minor.

army officer   A centurion, a Roman army officer who had authority over 100 soldiers.

bribe   Money to pay for Paul's freedom.

way. [4]But Festus answered, "No! Paul will be kept in Caesarea. I myself will go to Caesarea soon. [5]Some of your leaders should go with me. They can accuse the man (Paul) there in Caesarea, if he has really done something wrong."

[6]Festus stayed in Jerusalem another eight or ten days. Then he went back to Caesarea. The next day Festus told the soldiers to bring Paul before him. Festus was seated on the judgment seat. [7]Paul came into the room. The Jews who had come from Jerusalem stood around him. The Jews said that Paul had done many wrong things. But they could not prove any of these things. [8]This is what Paul said to defend himself: "I have done nothing wrong against the Jewish law, against the temple,* or against Caesar.*"

[9]But Festus wanted to please the Jews. So he asked Paul, "Do you want to go to Jerusalem? Do you want me to judge you there on these charges?"

[10]Paul said, "I am standing at Caesar's* judgment seat now. This is where I should be judged! I have done nothing wrong to the Jews; you know this is true. [11]If I have done something wrong, and the law says I must die, then I agree that I should die. I don't ask to be saved from death. But if these charges are not true, then no person can give me to these Jews. No! I want Caesar* to hear my case!"

[12]Festus talked about this with his advisers. Then he said, "You have asked to see Caesar,* so you will go to Caesar!"

Paul Before Herod Agrippa

[13]A few days later King Agrippa* and Bernice* came to Caesarea to visit Festus. [14]They stayed there many days. Festus told the king about Paul's case. Festus said, "There is a man that Felix left in prison. [15]When I went to Jerusalem, the leading priests and the older Jewish leaders there made charges against him. These Jews wanted me to order his death. [16]But I answered, 'When a man is accused of doing something wrong, Romans don't give the man to other people to judge. First, the man must face the people who are accusing him. And he must be allowed to defend himself against their charges.' [17]So these Jews came here to Caesarea for the trial. And I did not waste time. The next day I sat on the judgment seat and commanded that the man (Paul) be brought in. [18]The Jews stood up and accused him. But the Jews did not accuse him of any bad crimes. I thought they would. [19]The things they said were about their own religion and about a man named Jesus. Jesus died, but Paul said that he is still alive. [20]I did not know much about these things, so I did not ask questions. But I asked Paul, 'Do you want to go to Jerusalem and be judged there?' [21]But Paul asked to be kept in Caesarea. He wants a decision from the Emperor (Caesar*). So I commanded that Paul be held until I could send him to Caesar in Rome."

[22]Agrippa* said to Festus, "I would like to hear this man, too."

Festus said, "Tomorrow you can hear him!"

[23]The next day Agrippa* and Bernice* appeared. They dressed and acted like very important people. Agrippa and Bernice, the army leaders, and the important men of Caesarea went into the judgment room. Festus commanded the soldiers to bring Paul in. [24]Festus said, "King Agrippa and all of you men gathered here with us, you see this man (Paul). All the Jewish people, here and in Jerusalem, have complained to me about him. When they complain about him, they shout that he should be killed. [25]When I judged him, I could find nothing wrong. I found no reason to order his death. But he asked to be judged by Caesar.* So I decided to send him to Rome. [26]But I don't really know what to tell Caesar that this man has done wrong. So I have brought him before all of you—especially you, King Agrippa. I hope that you can question him and give me something to write to Caesar. [27]I think it is foolish to send a prisoner to Caesar without making some charges against him."

Paul Before King Agrippa

26 Agrippa* said to Paul, "You may now speak to defend yourself."

Then Paul raised his hand* and began to speak. [2]He said, "King Agrippa, I will answer all the charges that the Jews say against me. I think it is a blessing that I can stand here before you today and do this. [3]I am very happy to talk to you, because you know much about all the Jewish customs and the things that the Jews argue about. Please listen to me patiently.

---

temple The special building in Jerusalem for Jewish worship.
Caesar The name given to the emperor (ruler) of Rome.
Agrippa Herod Agrippa II, great-grandson of Herod the Great.
Bernice Agrippa's sister. She was the oldest daughter of Herod Agrippa I.

raised his hand A sign to make the people listen

[4]"All the Jews know about my whole life. They know the way I lived from the beginning in my own country and later in Jerusalem. [5]These Jews have known me for a long time. If they want to, they can tell you that I was a good Pharisee.* And the Pharisees obey the laws of the Jewish religion more carefully than any other group of Jewish people. [6]Now I am on trial because I hope for the promise that God made to our fathers (ancestors). [7]This is the promise that all the twelve tribes (family groups) of our people hope to receive. For this hope the Jews serve God day and night. My king, the Jews have accused me because I hope for this same promise! [8]Why do you people think it is impossible for God to raise people from death?

[9]"⌊When I was a Pharisee⌋, even I thought I should do many things against the name of Jesus from Nazareth. [10]And in Jerusalem I did many things against the believers.* The leading priests gave me the power to put many of these people (believers) in jail. When the followers of Jesus were being killed, I agreed that it was a good thing. [11]In every synagogue,* I punished them. I tried to make them say bad things against* ⌊Jesus⌋. I was so angry against these people (believers) that I went to other cities to find them and hurt them.

Paul Tells About Seeing Jesus 5-28

[12]"One time the leading priests gave me permission and the power to go to the city of Damascus. [13]I was on the way to Damascus. It was noon. I saw a light from the sky. The light was brighter than the sun. The light shined all around me and the men who were traveling with me. [14]We all fell to the ground. Then I heard a voice talking to me in the Jewish language.* The voice said, 'Saul, Saul, why are you doing these bad things to me? You are only hurting yourself by fighting me.' [15]I said, 'Who are you, Lord?' The Lord said, 'I am Jesus. I am the One you are persecuting. [16]Stand up! I have chosen you to be

my servant. You will be my witness—you will tell people the things that you have seen about me today and the things that I will show you. This is why I have come to you today. [17]I will not let ⌊your own⌋ people (the Jews) hurt you. And I will keep you safe from the non-Jewish people too. I am sending you to these people. [18]You will show the people the Truth. The people will turn away from darkness (sin) to the light (good). They will turn away from the power of Satan, and they will turn to God. Then their sins can be forgiven. They can have a share with those people who have been made holy* by believing in me.'"

Paul Tells About His Work

[19]Paul continued speaking: "King Agrippa,* after I had this vision* from heaven, I obeyed it. [20]I began telling people that they should change their hearts and lives and turn back to God. I told the people to do things that show that they really changed their hearts. I told these things first to people in Damascus. Then I went to Jerusalem and to every part of Judea and told these things to the people there. I also went to the non-Jewish people. [21]This is why the Jews grabbed me and were trying to kill me at the temple.* [22]But God helped me, and he is still helping me today. With God's help I am standing here today and telling all people the things I have seen. But I am saying nothing new. I am saying the same things that Moses and the prophets* said would happen. [23]They said that the Christ* would die and be the first to rise from death. Moses and the prophets said that the Christ would bring light to the Jewish people and to the non-Jewish people."

Paul Tries to Persuade Agrippa

[24]While Paul was saying these things to defend himself, Festus shouted, "Paul, you are crazy! Too much study has made you crazy!"

[25]Paul said, "Most Excellent Festus, I am not crazy. The things I say are true. My words are not the words of a foolish man; I am serious. [26]King Agrippa* knows about these things. I can speak freely to him. I know that he has heard about all of these things. Why? Because these things

---

Pharisee The Pharisees were a Jewish religious group that claimed to follow carefully all Jewish laws and customs.

believers Literally, "holy ones," a name for people that believe in Jesus.

synagogue Synagogues were places where Jews gathered for prayer, study of the Scriptures, and other public meetings.

say bad things against Literally, "blaspheme," the same as saying they did not believe in Jesus.

Jewish language Probably Aramaic, a language like Hebrew that was spoken by the Jews in the first century.

holy A holy person is pure and belongs only to God.

Agrippa Herod Agrippa II, great-grandson of Herod the Great.

vision Something like a dream used by God to speak to people.

temple The special building in Jerusalem for Jewish worship.

prophets People who spoke for God. Their writings are part of the Old Testament.

Christ The "anointed one" (Messiah) or chosen of God.

happened where all people could see. ²⁷King Agrippa,* do you believe the things the prophets* wrote? I know you believe!"

²⁸King Agrippa said to Paul, "Do you think you can persuade me to become a Christian so easily?"

²⁹Paul said, "It is not important if it is easy or if it is hard; I pray to God that not only you but every person listening to me today could ₁be saved and₁ be like me—except for these chains I have!"

³⁰King Agrippa,* Governor Festus, Bernice,* and all the people sitting with them stood up ³¹and left the room. They were talking to each other. They said, "This man should not be killed or put in jail; he has done nothing really bad!" ³²And Agrippa said to Festus, "We could let this man go free, but he has asked to see Caesar.*"

Paul Sails for Rome

27 It was decided that we would sail for Italy. An army officer* named Julius guarded Paul and some other prisoners. Julius served in the emperor's* army. ²We got on a ship and left. The ship was from the city of Adramyttium and was ready to sail to different places in Asia.* Aristarchus went with us. He was a man from the city of Thessalonica in Macedonia. ³The next day we came to the city of Sidon. Julius was very good to Paul. He gave Paul freedom to go visit his friends. These friends took care of Paul's needs. ⁴We left the city of Sidon. We sailed close to the island of Cyprus because the wind was blowing against us. ⁵We went across the sea by Cilicia and Pamphylia. Then we came to the city of Myra in Lycia. ⁶In Myra the army officer* found a ship from the city of Alexandria. This ship was going to Italy. So he put us on it.

⁷We sailed slowly for many days. It was hard for us to reach the city of Cnidus because the wind was blowing against us. We could not go any farther that way. So we sailed by the south side of the island of Crete near Salmone. ⁸We sailed along the coast, but the sailing was hard. Then we came to a place called Safe Harbors. The city of Lasea was near there.

Agrippa   Herod Agrippa II, great-grandson of Herod the Great.

prophets   People who spoke for God. Their writings are part of the Old Testament.

Bernice   King Agrippa's sister. She was the oldest daughter of Herod Agrippa I.

Caesar   The name given to the emperor (ruler) of Rome.

army officer   A centurion, a Roman army officer who had authority over 100 soldiers.

emperor   The ruler (leader) of the Roman empire.

Asia   The western part of Asia Minor.

⁹But we had lost much time. It was now dangerous to sail, because it was already after the Jewish day of fasting.* So Paul warned them. ¹⁰"Men, I can see that there will be much trouble on this trip. The ship and the things in the ship will be lost. Our lives may even be lost!" ¹¹But the captain and the owner of the ship did not agree with Paul. So the army officer* did not believe Paul. Instead, the officer believed what the captain and owner of the ship said. ¹²And that harbor (Safe Harbors) was not a good place for the ship to stay for the winter. So most of the men decided that the ship should leave there. The men hoped we could go to Phoenix. The ship could stay there for the winter. (Phoenix was a city on the island of Crete. It had a harbor which faced southwest and northwest.)

The Storm

¹³Then a good wind began to blow from the south. The men on the ship thought, "This is the wind we wanted, and now we have it!" So they pulled up the anchor. We sailed very close to the island of Crete. ¹⁴But then a very strong wind named the "Northeaster" came from across the island. ¹⁵This wind took the ship and carried it away. The ship could not sail against the wind. So we stopped trying and let the wind blow us. ¹⁶We went below a small island named Cauda. Then* we were able to bring in the lifeboat, but it was very hard to do. ¹⁷After the men took the lifeboat in, they tied ropes around the ship to hold the ship together. The men were afraid that the ship would hit the sandbanks of Syrtis.* So they lowered the sail and let the wind carry the ship. ¹⁸The next day the storm was blowing us so hard that the men threw some things out of the ship.* ¹⁹A day later they threw out the ship's equipment. ²⁰For many days we could not see the sun or the stars. The storm was very bad. We lost all hope of staying alive—we thought we would die.

²¹The men did not eat for a long time. Then one day Paul stood up before them and said, "Men, I told you not to leave Crete. You should have listened to me. Then you would not have all this trouble and loss. ²²But now I tell you to be happy.

---

day of fasting   The day of Atonement, an important Jewish holy day in the fall of the year. This was the time of year that bad storms happened on the sea.

Then   While the island protected them from the wind.

Syrtis   Shallow area in the sea near the Libyan coast.

threw some things ... ship   The men did this to make the ship lighter so that it would not sink easily.

None of you will die! But the ship will be lost. [23]Last night an angel came to me from God. This is the God I worship. I am his. [24]God's angel said, 'Paul, don't be afraid! You must stand before Caesar.* And God has given you this ₍promise₎: He will save the lives of all those men sailing with you.' [25]So men, be happy! I trust in God. Everything will happen like his angel told me. [26]But we will crash on an island."

[27]On the 14th night we were floating around in the Adriatic Sea.* The sailors thought we were close to land. [28]They threw a rope into the water with a weight on the end of it. They found that the water was 120 feet deep. They went a little farther and threw the rope in again. It was 90 feet deep. [29]The sailors were afraid that we would hit the rocks. So they threw four anchors into the water. Then they prayed for daylight to come. [30]Some of the sailors wanted to leave the ship. They lowered the lifeboat to the water. The sailors wanted the other men to think that they were throwing more anchors from the front of the ship. [31]But Paul told the army officer* and the other soldiers, "If these men do not stay in the ship, then your lives cannot be saved!" [32]So the soldiers cut the ropes and let the lifeboat fall into the water.

[33]Just before dawn Paul began persuading all the people to eat something. He said, "For the past two weeks you have been waiting and watching. You have not eaten for 14 days. [34]Now I beg (ask) you to eat something. You need it to stay alive. None of you will lose even one hair off your heads." [35]After he said this, Paul took some bread and thanked God for it before all of them. He broke off a piece and began eating. [36]All the men felt better. They all started eating too. [37](There were 276 people on the ship.) [38]We ate all we wanted. Then we began making the ship lighter by throwing the grain into the sea.

The Ship Is Destroyed

[39]When daylight came the sailors saw land. But they did not know what land it was. They saw a bay with a beach. The sailors wanted to sail the ship to the beach if they could. [40]So they cut the ropes to the anchors and left the anchors in the sea. At the same time, they untied the ropes that were holding the rudders. Then they raised the front sail into the wind and sailed toward the beach. [41]But the ship hit a sandbank. The front of the ship stuck there. The ship could not move. Then the big waves began to break the back of the ship to pieces.

[42]The soldiers decided to kill the prisoners so that none of the prisoners could swim away and escape. [43]But the army officer* (Julius) wanted to let Paul live. So he did not allow the soldiers to kill the prisoners. Julius told the people who could swim to jump into the water and swim to land. [44]The other people used wooden boards or pieces of the ship. And this is how all the people went to land. None of the people died.

Paul on the Island of Malta

28 When we were safe on land, we learned that the island was called Malta. [2]It was raining and very cold. But the people who lived there were very good to us. They made a fire for us and welcomed all of us. [3]Paul gathered a pile of sticks for the fire. Paul was putting the sticks on the fire. A poisonous snake came out because of the heat and bit Paul on the hand. [4]The people living on the island saw the snake hanging from Paul's hand. They said, "This man must be a murderer! He did not die in the sea, but Justice* does not want him to live." [5]But Paul shook the snake off into the fire. Paul was not hurt. [6]The people thought that Paul would swell up or fall down dead. The people waited and watched Paul for a long time, but nothing bad happened to him. So the people changed their opinion of Paul. They said, "He is a god!"

[7]There were some fields around that same area. A very important man on the island owned these fields. His name was Publius. He welcomed us into his home. Publius was very good to us. We stayed in his house for three days. [8]Publius' father was very sick. He had a fever and dysentery.* But Paul went to him and prayed for him. Paul put his hands on the man and healed him. [9]After this happened, all the other sick people on the island came to Paul. Paul healed them too. [10-11]The people on the island gave us many honors. We stayed there three months. When we were ready to leave, the people gave us the things we needed.

Paul Goes to Rome

We got on a ship from the city of Alexandria. The ship had stayed on the island of Malta during

---

Caesar The name given to the emperor (ruler) of Rome.

Adriatic Sea The sea between Greece and Italy, including the central part of the Mediterranean Sea.

army officer A centurion, a Roman army officer who had authority over 100 soldiers.

Justice The people thought there was a god named Justice who would punish bad people.

dysentery A very bad sickness that causes serious diarrhea.

the winter. On the front of the ship was the sign for the twin gods.* [12]We stopped at the city of Syracuse. We stayed in Syracuse three days and then left. [13]We came to the city of Rhegium. The next day a wind began to blow from the southwest, so we were able to leave. A day later we came to the city of Puteoli. [14]We found some brothers *(believers)* there. They asked us to stay with them a week. Finally, we came to Rome. [15]The believers in Rome heard that we were there. They came out to meet us at the Market of Appius* and at the Three Inns.* When Paul saw these believers, he felt better. Paul thanked God.

Paul in Rome

[16]Then we went to Rome. In Rome Paul was allowed to live alone. But a soldier stayed with Paul to guard him.

[17]Three days later Paul sent for some of the most important Jews. When they came together, Paul said, "My Jewish brothers, I have done nothing against our people *(the Jews)*. I have done nothing against the customs of our fathers *(ancestors)*. But I was arrested in Jerusalem and given to the Romans. [18]The Romans asked me many questions. But they could not find any reason why I should be killed. So they wanted to let me go free. [19]But the Jews there did not want that. So I had to ask ⌊to come to Rome⌋ to have my trial before Caesar.* But I am not saying that my people *(the Jews)* have done anything wrong. [20]That is why I wanted to see you and talk with you. I am bound with this chain because I believe in the hope of Israel.*"

[21]The Jews answered Paul, "We have received no letters from Judea about you. None of our Jewish brothers who have traveled from there *(Judea)* brought news about you or told us anything bad about you. [22]We want to hear your ideas. We know that people everywhere are speaking against this group *(Christians)*."

[23]Paul and the Jews chose a day for a meeting. On that day many more of these Jews met with Paul at his house. Paul spoke to them all day long. Paul explained the kingdom of God to them. Paul tried to persuade them to believe the things about Jesus. He used the law of Moses and the writings of the prophets* to do this. [24]Some of the Jews believed the things Paul said, but others did not believe. [25]They had an argument. The Jews were ready to leave, but Paul said one more thing to them: "The Holy Spirit* spoke the truth to your fathers *(ancestors)* through Isaiah the prophet.* He said,

26 'Go to this people *(the Jews)* and tell them:
You will listen and you will hear,
    but you will not understand!
You will look and you will see,
    but you will not understand
        what you see!
27 Yes, the minds of these people *(the Jews)*
    are now closed.
These people have ears,
    but they don't listen.
And these people refuse to see ⌊the truth⌋.
This has happened so that they will not
    see with their eyes,
    hear with their ears, and
    understand with their minds.
This has happened so that they will not
    turn to me to heal them.'
                                        Isaiah 6:9-10

[28]"I want you Jews to know that God has sent his salvation to the non-Jewish people. They will listen!" [29]*

[30]Paul stayed two full years in his own rented house. He welcomed all people who came and visited him. [31]Paul preached about the kingdom of God. He taught about the Lord Jesus Christ. He was very bold *(brave)*, and no one tried to stop him from speaking.

---

prophet(s) People who spoke for God. Their writings are part of the Old Testament.

Holy Spirit Also called the Spirit of God, the Spirit of Christ, and the Comforter. Joined with God and Christ, he does God's work among people in the world.

Verse 29 Some late copies of Acts add verse 29: "After Paul said this, the Jews left. They were arguing very much with each other."

twin gods Statues of Castor and Pollux, Greek gods.
Market of Appius Town about 27 miles from Rome.
Three Inns Town about 30 miles from Rome.
Caesar The name given to the emperor (ruler) of Rome.
Israel The Jewish nation (people).

CHAPTER 29

THE BOOK OF ACTS HAS ONLY 28 CHAPTERS, BUT AS AN INTERESTING ENDNOTE TO **VOLUME ONE** OF **THE** *NOW* **BOOK OF ACTS**, THIS UNIQUE STORY IS GIVEN.

1 An incident occurred in the Pilot Point church during Rev. J. B. Cole's pastorate, which involved a point of doctrine that subjected Pastor Cole to criticism, and gave the incident much publicity and notoriety.

2 Pastor Cole went fishing one day with a business man who was not a Christian, and he availed himself of the opportunity to talk to the lost man about his unsaved condition, and led him to an acceptance of Christ.

3 Joe Ives, the man converted, said to Pastor Cole, "Here is water, what doth hinder me from being baptized?" Obviously Brother Cole thought of the story of Philip and the eunuch, and, taking that incident as an example, he led Mr. Ives out into the water and baptized him.

4 Rev. Cole had been a Baptist but a short time and was not up on their conception of baptism, and how and when it should be administered.

5 The news of the incident soon spread among the members, and then the show began.

6 The following Sunday Mr. Ives presented himself to the church, asking membership, and his application was rejected and he was hurt at the action of the church and turned to another church, which readily accepted his baptism.

7 The criticism of the pastor caused him to ask a committee of eminent brethren to sit in judgment upon his conduct -- Drs. A. J. Holt, J. B. Link and R. C. Buckner.

8 After reviewing the details of the incident they wrote the church advising it to drop the matter, and Pastor Cole to go his way, but not to repeat the act.

This story is copied verbatim from the book, **History of The Denton County Baptist Association**, *and the Sixty Churches Organized Within its Jurisdiction*, by James Newton Rayzor, furnished from the A. Webb Roberts Library of Southwestern Baptist Theological Seminary, Fort Worth, Texas, by Ken Parks, Circulation Librarian, November 25, 1998. It covers the history of Shiloh Baptist Association at Friendship Church near Pilot Point, October 18, 1862; and the founding of the First Baptist Church in Denton County, at Lonesome Dove, Saturday, February 21, 1846.

The account of the pastor's MISbehavior, *as judged by Baptist church doctrine,* is significant. Cole's action was in perfect harmony with the divinely approved example of Spirit-led Philip recorded in Acts chapter 8. The young pastor used this as his authority and pattern, yet he was resisted by Baptist theologians.

It is clear in each account in the *Then* Book of Acts written in the first century by the inspired historian Luke, that baptism (immersion) always followed *immediately* after hearing and believing the gospel of the Lord, that is, before the candidate rejoiced, ate a bite, drank a drop, or slept a wink! There was never any vote by the church as to whether to accept him into membership because baptism by faith immediately added that person to the body of Christ, the church family, by an act of God (cf. Acts 2:37-47; Romans 6:3-4; I Cor. 12:13; Galatians 3:26-27). Siblings do not vote on whether they will receive a newborn brother or sister into their family; it is an act of God!

Conversions conducted according to Baptist tradition and doctrine, as seen here, do not coincide with biblical cases of conversion. Therefore none are included in the *Now* Book of Acts. We have only included those which follow the same pattern of New Testament procedures, and pray that all preachers like the "Pastor" at Pilot Point will abandon traditions of men which Jesus said "nullify" God's Word (Mk 7:7-13).   - Editor